Conflict: Phases, Forums, and Solutions

Conflict: Phases, Forums, and Solutions

FOR OUR DREAMS AND BODY, ORGANIZATIONS, GOVERNMENTS, AND PLANET

• • •

Arnold Mindell PhD

First 2017 edition prepared by the World Tao Press and Amy Mindell
Front Cover Painting by Arnold Mindell
Back Cover Photograph by Kira Held

ISBN: 1540770443
ISBN 13: 9781540770448

Library of Congress Control Number: 2016921441
CreateSpace Independent Publishing Platform, North Charleston, SC

Other Books by Arnold Mindell

Dance of the Ancient One: How the Universe Solves Personal and World Problems
ProcessMind: A User's Guide to Connecting with the Mind of God
Earth Based Psychology: Path Awareness from the Teachings of Don Juan, Richard Feynman, and Lao Tse
The Quantum Mind and Healing: How to Listen and Respond to Your Body's Symptoms
The Deep Democracy of Open Forums: How to Transform Organizations into Communities
The Dreammaker's Apprentice: Using Heightened States of Consciousness to Interpret Dreams
Dreaming While Awake: Techniques for 24-Hour Lucid Dreaming
Quantum Mind: The Edge between Physics and Psychology
Sitting in the Fire: Large Group Transformation Using Conflict and Diversity
The Shaman's Body: A New Shamanism for Transforming Health, Relationship, and Community
The Leader as Martial Artist: An Introduction to Deep Democracy
The Year I: Global Process Work and Planetary Tensions
Working on Yourself Alone: Inner Dreambody Work
Coma Key to Awakening: Working with the Dreambody Near Death
City Shadows: Psychological Interventions in Psychiatry
The Dreambody in Relationships
River's Way: The Process Science of the Dreambody
Working with the Dreaming Body
Dreambody: The Body's Role in Revealing the Self

Table of Contents

Acknowledgements

• • •

THANKS TO MANY INDIVIDUALS, BUSINESSES, and to those government leaders who asked for help, initiating me into the world's large organizational and political conflicts.

Thanks to leading people at a United Nations group for their encouraging words: "The UN, as it is, would work better by noticing double signals," and "Countries need to approach their problems with these new methods."

Thanks to Albert Einstein and relativity expert Edwin Taylor for relativity theory and practice, and to quantum physicist Richard Feynman for helping to explain quantum theory.

Thanks to spiritual teachers from Africa, Australia, Europe, India, Japan, Korea, Russia, South America, the United States, and Canada who showed me many faces of the divine. I am especially grateful to Fukushima Roshi, the Rinzai Zen master and head abbot of Tofuku-ji Monastery, for his understanding and personal support. I especially love his idea that "empty mind" can be understood as "creative mind." I also feel very close to the Dalai Lama's interest in the "dreambody" concept and his fascination with quantum theory. I am indebted to South Africa's leader, Nelson Mandela, for his autobiography.[1]

I am thankful to the ancient Chinese for their divination by fire, for the *I Ching*, and for Lao Tse's *The Tao Te Ching*. Taoism helped me develop new ideas about the phases of world process.

Thanks especially to C. G. Jung and my Jungian colleagues for having supported my interest in dreams and my early studies leading to "the

Dreambody." Thanks to C. G. Jung for your synchronicity concept, and to Nobel prizewinner in physics, Wolfgang Pauli, for your support of Jung's concept.

I appreciate Michael Murphy of the Esalen Institute in Carmel, California, for hiring Amy and me to be teachers after the great Gestalt psychologists, Fritz Perls and Dick Price, died.

Thanks especially to Hellene Gronda, Susan Newton, and Margaret Ryan for their invaluable expert editing help!!

My thanks once again to amazing Susan Kocen for her labors in writing up the many lectures from which this manuscript was derived.

Thanks to you, dear reader, for trying to help yourself and the world in your own special way.

A very special thanks to Amy Mindell, my wife, best friend, and partner in all things, for learning with me, testing, practicing, and co-teaching much of this work around the world. And…thanks Amy for helping to publish this work!

List of Pictures and Diagrams

(Credits appear with pictures)

• • •

INTRODUCTION:

A New Approach to Inner and World Conflict

• • •

BETWEEN THE YEARS 1900 AND 2000, over one hundred million people died in conflict; that is over 100,000,000![2] I heard recently on the BBC that just now, there are more than 65 million refugees. That number is the highest number *ever*. Are you shocked at these numbers? I am!

So what's next? Our world needs many changes, but certainly, it needs new ways to work with conflict, new ways for all of us to relate to one another! Therefore, the goal of this book is to develop new methods that enable all of us to *feel that there is no one, and no group or organization on this earth we cannot communicate with!*

By the end of this book, I would like you, the reader to be able to work with conflict and tension in yourself, your body, your dreams, your relationships, as well as in organizations, open forums, and government situations. The work I suggest might become a kind of life style, that can be practiced to improve life for all.

At present, most of us hate conflict; we are usually in conflict with the very idea of conflict and don't want to think about it. That is one reason why developing new methods for conflict goes slowly. We are brilliant at developing electronic machines to interconnect, but less intelligent about WHAT TO DO once we connect!

Inside ourselves, we are often in opposition with our own feelings and body problems. Outside, most of us experience some degree of conflict with others, with our groups, with other nations, with people from different religions, or with different sexual orientations, colors, ages, and on and on. Either our organizations and governments try to avoid conflict or else they strive to defeat the "bad" ones who seem to be causing conflict.

To work on our human conflicts in a sustainable way, we need new ways to relate interpersonally and to resolve problems not only in our organizations and in the world but also inside ourselves. We need not only powerful leaders, but wise leaders who are also *elders.*

We need everyone to notice that conflict can lead not only to violence and war, but also to illness and air pollution. Pollution? Yes, due to filling the atmosphere with bombs, fighter planes, warships, and smoke. We need to realize and always deal with these factors:

> Personal, local, and international diversity issues lie behind all conflicts.
> Conflict is a recurring phase inside us as individuals, groups, and nations.
> Conflict is a central, and perhaps the main, world issue.

In this book, I introduce new approaches to dealing with conflict, updating my "deep democracy" concept both in theory and practice. This update includes not only

conflict's typical *levels*, but also its
characteristic *phases* and
potential *forums.*

This book's individual sections apply the new conflict work methods not only to world problems—but as I have said—to dreams and bodywork, inner meditation, and large group and organizational work. After reading this book, you may want to return to specific chapters to recall special applications to body problems, inner, or outer relationship work. To make such a "return" easy, I periodically review basic concepts, before discussing their special application to the specific topic you may be interested in.

The new deep democracy approaches integrate psychology and physics, spiritual experience and politics, inner work and organizational process. Central to this new work are dreaming processes and methods that unify all applications.

When I read what I just wrote, I thought, "*All* this sounds too amazing and optimistic." Then, I recall that I have tested this new conflict work not only with international government leaders and large organizations, but also with people who might be called "terrorists." What I have found is that this new work not only helps people who want to come together to discuss things, it is also useful in gathering people who dislike the idea of discussing anything with their opponents!

This new approach to conflict is built on my understanding of conflict's typical levels, its characteristic phases, and its potential forums. Understanding of CONFLICT's LEVELS, PHASES, FORUMS, and SOLUTIONS can help outer tensions, and as I have just indicated, can be used for inner tensions seen in dream and body experiences. You might be wondering, "Dream and bodywork? Why focus on those areas in a book on conflict work?" I promise to show how learning to dream privately and in public can help resolve issues that our everyday mind—suffering from tension—often misses. We need access to deeper, creative ways of dealing with reality, as well as factual knowledge about the issues and people involved!

This book is both theoretical and spiritual, and it is also ultimately *practical.* Here you will find concrete hands-on training exercises that have been found helpful by government and business leaders trying to resolve international issues.

If I were you and interested in studying conflict, I would wish that this book would be 25 pages long and require only 30 minutes to read. I share your hope!

I promise that with practice, the methods I suggest in this book can be applied within 5 minutes to help ease tension. The conclusion contains two 5-minute practices that will help you work on conflict and tensions rapidly whenever needed.

Explaining the background of these methods takes more pages, however, and I hope you will enjoy the examples and theory as I describe the new methods of deep democracy. Throughout this book, I present practical exercises, including real questions from students who tested these techniques and the theory behind them. I illustrate their value with examples from my private practice and world conflict experiences.

The successful application of any conflict resolution approach requires practice, and I hope you will consider making these techniques part of your lifestyle.

If I were you, my next question would be, "Why listen to this Mindell person? Who is he to act like an authority on conflict? Does he know much about inner or relationship conflict, not to mention organizational and world conflict issues?"

Let me assure you, dear reader, that in most ways, I am a total learner, just like most of us. Earlier in my life, I did not do as well with conflict as I would have liked. By now, however, after working with thousands of individuals in their private lives, with many kinds of people, businesses, and world leaders for more than 53 years, I have learned a lot. First I worked in my private practice as a Jungian analyst, later as a process-oriented psychologist. Then at the end of the 1970s, I began to apply "processwork" with large groups and open forums facing all kinds of business and global diversity issues (e.g., around gender, race, religion, sexual orientation, wealth, nationality, and general rank unconsciousness).

For around 35 years, "deep democracy"[3] has been used to help the military, government leaders, spiritual organizations, and some of the largest world commercial groups.

However, if I were you, I would think that just because Mindell has a lot of experience does not mean he has the final word on conflict! I agree with you. I am a learner, and I hope you will update the work you find in this book. As long as the earth and all the parts of our universe are changing, conflict will be an ever-changing study. Methods must always be developed to fit each given situation, specific conflict phases, and the history of the peoples involved. Conflict studies will always be an ongoing research and experimental project.

I hope this work gives you new concepts and practical techniques with which to work on the conflicts around you and within you, and that together we may create a more sustainable world filled with creative relationships.

Conflict Is Probably Our Biggest Problem

Today, many good methods work in a "calm-let's-talk-business" sort of situation. But few methods work with calmness *and* also with violent, murderous conflict. Moreover, few methods work with individuals and groups from just about every corner of the world.

As I have suggested, conflict is probably the human race's biggest problem. The daily news is a reflection of our central *individual and international inability to deal with violent disagreement.* Instead of addressing our internal tensions, we take drugs and otherwise repress conflict inside and between us. Or we buy bombs and guns to kill the "bad" ones. Yes, repressing or winning a conflict is important, but neither is a sustainable solution.

Conflict work needs to become a lifestyle that promotes new, creative solutions and relationships. We need to deal with outer facts and remember to work with our internal feelings as well. There is no way to cut off your personal feelings, your own relationship troubles, or business and group conflicts from the world situation. We also need to learn about all sorts of diversity issues between us as individuals, as businesses, and as governments. Such issues include conflicts concerning nationality, race, religion, sexual orientation, gender, and unresolved historical problems.

We need to realize that how we deal with conflict depends upon our own, and our opponent's, state of mind. This present work has been applied in just about all cultures and states of mind. *States of mind*? Yes, here I refer to so-called "normal" as well as "extreme" or unusual states of consciousness.

The basic processwork paradigm gives rise to many methods that apply to individuals and groups, at specific times and places. My colleagues and I have written other books on processwork, which you can find in the Bibliography. (See also Dr. Alan Richardson's concise overview of processwork.[4])

First and Second Trainings

Processwork's unifying approach involves two different trainings: a first and a second training.

The first training is about "deep democracy": this includes not only equal rights and powers, but also the study and recognition of all kinds of signals, projections, dreaming, and universal experiences behind democracy.[5] I explain deep democracy in the first chapter.

The second training is needed in times of tension when we can't use our first training. When individual, group process, business, and government situations become tense, using the cognitive first training skills we learned in school often becomes difficult.

The second training is devoted to the deep experiences of ourselves, to subtle sensations that even precede big dreams. The ancient Taoists might have said that the second training is about the "Tao that cannot be said." Some Buddhists have called this training *learning to use our "empty mind."*

The first and second "worldwork" conflict trainings should begin early in life, even in elementary school, and be practiced whenever there is conflict. Then, by the time youngsters become adults, they will be better equipped to deal with world conflict. I discuss educational suggestions in Chapters 27 and 28.

Einstein and the Second Training. Einstein sensed the importance of both consensus reality and the spontaneous insights that suddenly come to us in dreaming states. These insights are aspects of the second training. Einstein might have referred to such spontaneous insights as a *"mysterious tune"* in the air. He was an ardent realist, but he also sensed the need for a second training in which we all learn to sense feelings "in the air." He said,

> *Everything is determined, the beginning as well as the end, by forces over which we have no control. It is determined for the insect, as well as for the star. Human beings, vegetables, or cosmic dust, we all dance to a mysterious tune, intoned in the distance by an invisible piper.*[6]

Here Einstein is suggesting that organizing "forces over which we have no control," "mysterious tunes," and "an invisible piper" create feelings and move us through life. Over the years, I have become convinced by Einstein's statement that "we all dance to a mysterious tune." Learning to sense that "tune" is part of the second training. The Taoist spiritual leader Lao Tse might have called that "tune," the "Tao that can't be said."

Dear reader, please don't worry. I promise that the main focus of this book is neither physics nor spirituality! Just about everything I mention, including "space–time fields," connects you to everyday experience. So let me give you an example of what Einstein may have meant when he said that everything is moved by "mysterious tunes."

An Example of "The Mysterious Tune" in a Conflict on London's Regent's Canal

An example comes to mind of how the second training (or hearing Einstein's "mysterious tune") helped Amy and me in a serious street fight. My conflict story has a lighthearted conclusion and will, I hope, encourage the reader to continue on with this book. (I promise to explain and demonstrate more advanced methods with more aggressive conflict situations later.)

The Story: Conflict on the Canal. After conflict work in London a few years ago,[7] Amy and I packed up to leave for work in Moscow. However, before catching our plane to our next training event in Russia, I had the feeling that we needed to go for a run to get some exercise before all that plane travel. We love running!

We decided to run near our hotel in London, on the Regent's Canal near Camden Lock. (See the picture—which Amy had taken a couple of days earlier, not knowing that this would be the place of a big fight that we would soon run into!)

Running on the Lock early in the morning, there were few or no people, and no boats around. As we ran over the bridge and down to the canal (see the arrow -➔-➔ in the picture), we suddenly encountered an active conflict. As we entered that secluded spot under the bridge on the canal, we heard two people yelling and fighting violently!

***1.* Conflict in Camden, London.**

A younger man was screeching as he was trying to rob an older man who was shaking with fear. The young man pushed the older one up against the wall into a corner and was trying to force the older man to give him money.

Amy and I thought that first we should protect both people and call the police to stop the fight. Then we remembered our second training work! The conflict was in one of the most dramatic (conflict) phases. We remembered we were part of the atmosphere or "field" on the canal, part of the situation and events occurring.

For a moment we "felt into" the violent atmosphere. The extreme tension in the air made the older man shake, but it also made us shake as well!

As we allowed this screaming "field" to shake us, we began to experience a kind of "dance and song." (Remember Einstein's mysterious tune!) As if moved by some tune, we expressed the tune and situation in sounds and, after a minute or two, in words.

We heard the young thief screaming, *"Give me your MONEY!!,"* and we tried to join the "field." In other words, we began to explore sounds and sing whatever came to mind. The same words and energy emerged from both Amy and me in the midst of this potentially violent situation.

Amy and I began to sing together . . .

♪ *"I want money, give me more MONEY!! I*
want money, money, money!
♪ *Money is all there is, give me money*
now or I'll give you a kiss . . . ♪

These words sound weird and paradoxical now, but they poured out of us spontaneously in a kind of dramatic form on the Lock. Amy sings well, but my singing is not worth talking about. Yet, in spite of the inner and outer difficulties, to our great surprise, the more vehemently we sang, *the more the thief began to sing as well!* In fact, to our great shock, he joined us, and the *three of us* sang, "MONEY, MONEY, MONEY . . . "

Was he on drugs? We weren't. Without knowing anything about the situation or understanding what was going on, we saw the young man back away slowly, no longer pressing the older man up against the wall. The young man seemed to forget the older man from whom he was threatening to steal. The young man moved away from the older one and to our even greater surprise, the older man took out his wallet and gave the "thief" some money!?

In contrast to the violent atmosphere that dominated during the fight, now they both looked amazed and almost happy as they parted from one another. We left too and continued to jog further down the Lock in order to catch our airplane at Heathrow airport to fly to Moscow.

After working in Moscow, we shared this story when Amy and I were working at the United Nations University in Tokyo, at their Institute for Advanced Studies. One of the government officials said that this story could be used by his country to resolve its problems!

What had happened in that unexpected encounter with violence? From our viewpoint, I would say that we noticed, entered, and shared the tense conflict-phase "field" and found a bit of Einstein's "hidden magic" or tune in the air. Instead of conflicting energies, there was at least a momentary sharing or unity in conflict.

We did what we had been teaching. We used our second training to find our own "centers" and let those centers create the next steps in the midst of that conflict. Then the next phase occurred, a phase characterized by role switching. We felt deeply into the "thief" and became him, followed by a phase of detachment in and around us as we also screamed, "Money! Money! Money!" We were happy that neither of the conflicting partners were hurt, both somehow felt addressed and the conflict relaxed—at least for the moment.

Obviously this was just a moment in conflict work. Much *more work* was needed for sustainable solutions. If we had had more time, we would have tried to help not only these two people, but also help work on the economic diversity issues of the canal area of London as well.

Individual conflicts are always related to the surrounding world. All cities need help in working on economic diversity issues. Everywhere, people are unaware of how unconscious privilege and rank upset those with less privilege and rank.

This bigger context was evident when, two months after our encounter, the London newspapers announced a "class war" as seen in the *Camden Street News.*[8] That conflict we worked with on the Lock was symbolic of a larger conflict in the area.

2. Class War in Camden near the Lock.

A next step in the conflict around poverty would have been to work on the rich–poor diversity problem in an open street forum as well as on TV and the Internet. However, we needed to leave London for Moscow.

I could tell many important but less dramatic tales about international conflict between governments, between groups belonging to the same government parties, about organizations, and businesses. But this story arose just now. Why? Perhaps because it's less terrifying and a bit more fun (at least for us) than other more threatening stories I must tell in this book.

Sensing and expressing Einstein's "tune" helped relieve the momentary situation so that next steps could happen. Singing our tune apparently related to the potential songs inside the "thief."

Recall Einstein's idea: "We all dance to a mysterious tune, intoned in the distance by an invisible piper." If Einstein were here now, I would suggest to him that our next steps in physics and psychology, in politics and worldwork, are to become aware of that "piper" in order to communicate best with others in the same "conflict field."

Follow up steps in this process might have also included an open street forum to help government leaders on different sides of the issues, to address both the rich and the poor, those with greater social rank and privilege, and those with less felt social power. Once people feel addressed, next steps can lead to a greater community feeling for all.

This example was simple, and the intervention was fun—at least in part. Although the deeper social issue of economic diversity is more complex, like many of the other problems we examine later in this book, my point is that relating to all parties in a conflict requires inner work, creativity, as well as factual knowledge of the surrounding consensus reality.

Leadership

According to studies of the future conducted by some of the larger nations around the world, the biggest problem facing our planet in the next 25 years will be finding *good leaders*. I won't go into detail about these studies here (see Chapter 10), but want to stress that climate change, water problems, diversity issues, and international conflict depend in part upon our *future government leaders and their ability to relate.*

We need new methods and leaders that work *with facts and with relationship issues.* Dear Reader, we need you to *try to become such a leader—for yourself and for the world around you.*

In this book, you will find the following sections devoted to creating such leaders.

I. THE PHASES OF PEOPLE AND ORGANIZATIONS
II. YOUR BODY PHASES
III. MEDITATION PHASES
IV. YOUR DEEPEST ART AND BEST SCIENCE FOR OUR WORLD
V. PREPARING FOR GROUP WORK
VI. FROM 360 TO 721 FEEDBACK
VII. BRING YOUR DREAMS AND DREAMBODY TO LIFE
VIII. COMMUNING FOR CONFLICT AND PEACE
IX. EDUCATION FOR NEW GOVERNMENT
CONCLUSION: 5-MINUTE SOLUTIONS TO WORLD TENSION

PART I

The Phases of People and Organizations

• • •

THIS FIRST PART OF THE book introduces my new ideas about the phases of process. Understanding process phases can support powerful facilitation practices to transform conflict into sustainable relationships and creative community. I describe the connection between process phases and the levels of deep democracy.

I introduce the phases by focusing on large group contexts like organizations and nations because of my deep feeling about war and our need to address violence. In the following sections of the book, we turn back to the individual and look at how working on our own body symptoms and dreams using phase understanding is vital for solving the world problems that we face.

I begin by describing the first training in understanding phases—how to recognize the signs and signals of different process phases particularly in groups and organizations. Then I start to illustrate the phases with examples of different techniques that work with particular phases. The phase concept allows us to understand why these techniques are effective.

CHAPTER 1

The Phases of Deep Democracy

• • •

In this chapter, you will find new ideas about democracy and deep democracy, particularly focusing on its levels and phases. These levels and phases create an overview of the typical situations and processes that all individuals, groups, and nations go through over time.

This chapter introduces four phases that can be observed in the processes that are experienced by individuals, relationships, groups, and nations. I describe how you can identify these phases and how phase awareness can help you work more effectively with yourself, with individuals, with relationships, and in groups. The subsequent chapters explore the practical application of the four phases in detail, as well as many new techniques.

Here, I summarize the framework of deep democracy and then show how an awareness of phases can expand our understanding of deep democracy, giving us new ways to facilitate conflict resolution and deal more effectively with difficulties.

My work and research over the last 35 years have revealed that to work effectively and sustainably with individuals and groups, it is helpful to experience the first and second trainings. In this chapter, I present a first training in phase awareness as a foundation for understanding phases within the second training.

First Basic Trainings. As I mentioned in the introductory chapter, helping people and our planet requires first training in psychology and organizational work. Such training involves, at the very minimum, developing the ability to notice your own and others' momentary and ongoing signals. Such first training develops the capacity to notice and work with:

- *Verbal messages*: Listen for the content and the intention.
- *Body signals*: Notice hand and facial gestures, sounds, movements, etc. Do these movements go along with the content of the verbal messages? Are the people congruent? Yes, if their body signals and the content of the verbal messages are the same. No, if a background feeling and movements are present that have not yet been spoken. Bring out the background.
- *Atmosphere:* What does the space between us feel like? Does it seem heavy, light, imperceptible?
- *Diversity:* Notice and appreciate different groups, nationalities, ages, races, genders, religions, financial situations, etc. Notice who has more or less rank and social power in the given context.
- *Dreams:* What do people dream, what is their vision, what is the meaning of the body signals with which they do *not* identify?
- *Phases:* Phases? Everything has phases. Just think about how the seasons change and our earth and moon go through changing phases over the course of one month or a year. Our timing is phase-oriented. There is morning, afternoon, evening, and nighttime. Summer turns into fall, then to winter, then spring etc. See the phases of the moon over the course of one month. (Thanks to NASA.[9])

In my earlier work, I have focused on signals and messages,[10] and I continue to study these elements of communication. However, in this book, I emphasize my new concept of process *phases*.

Our everyday mind is usually more fixed and less process or phase-oriented. Therefore, realizing that our psychology and world events are also phase-oriented can be surprising for some of us.

Remember in your own personal life, there are sometimes periods of doubt and enlightenment, confusion and understanding, inwardness and outgoing behavior. Recognizing phase changes can give us a little detachment when working on our own problems as well as those of organizations and the world.

It is helpful to notice some of the common phases of inner, relationship, and organizational processes. Once we understand these phases, we will know which *psychological, political, and conflict resolution methods would work best* and why. Phase awareness belongs to our "first training."

- *Phases.* A person or group can be in many phases, though often one predominates at any given time. The background idea of "phase" is that *everything changes.* For example, in dealing with a momentary or past conflict, the following simple phase descriptions can be helpful. Use these descriptions to help you identify in which phase you or the relationship or group find yourselves.

  Phase 1. Let's enjoy! Here personal or relationship atmospheres are characterized by "let's be happy" and not ask ourselves to deal with any tensions.

  Phase 2. Tension or conflict. We can't avoid noticing bad moods, tension, and conflict. Let's run or fight!

  Phase 3. Role switching. Sometimes it is possible to "role switch" and dream into the "other side" of an issue or relationship, the side that is bothering us. In this phase, as in dreams, we can imagine and sometimes even feel into the people or things that are bothering us.

  Phase 4. Detachment, sensing how the universe moves you. Inevitably, through relaxation, some detachment often occurs. At such times, our minds open up and we become more accepting of life. Phase 4 is a *phase*, however, which means that it too will change, and we move to another phase, often phase 1, hoping to avoid problems—which then eventually evolves once again into the tension of phase 2 and/or other phases.

There are many ways to describe potential phases and sub-phases, depending upon an individual's or group's culture. However, these four phases and their descriptors cover *many situations,* and have been useful cross-culturally around the world.

Recognizing phases helps us realize that many excellent psychological and conflict resolution methods work best in one of the phases. If conflict resolution workers are not aware of phases, they may not understand why such methods do not always work, or they may assume that something is wrong with the people involved—or the entire human race.

For example, many methods work in phases 1, 3, or 4 when people are ready to sit down and talk. But those methods do not work when people are strongly polarized and involved in phase 2, fighting, fearful, and struggling with something inside or outside. Without a phase orientation, we often think something is wrong with people who are not responding to our interventions, instead of realizing that *we* need greater diversity and phase awareness.

As a result of state-oriented thinking, instead of phase or process thinking, we assume that people are either always bad or good. We come to fixed conclusions and forget the idea that human beings, like the rest of nature, change over time. That is also why we are occasionally shocked when people whom we thought were "evil" occasionally change! Fixed beliefs are not phase-oriented. Learning to flow with the phases of relationship and conflict processes is a key to creating and maintaining relationships and moving beyond the momentary tensions.

The universe's phases. The term *universe* contains the idea of phases or turning. *Universe*—which means the container of everything that exists—comes from the Latin *uni = one,* and *versus = turned.* So we live in a huge space–time phase-oriented "turning" body, organization, and world.

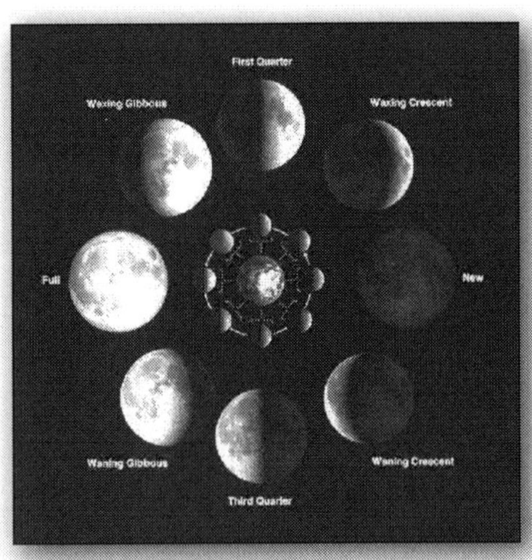

***3.* Phases of the Moon.** Thanks, NASA.

In *Dance of the Ancient One*, I spoke about practical applications of a particular movement meditation. There I showed how letting yourself be moved in a spontaneous and relaxed way can bring you ideas that you may need to resolve things in a given moment. I suggested in that book that you feel best, if you allow yourself, every now and then, to experience being moved by the universe—whatever that means to you. Notice how change is trying to happen all the time!

Our spontaneous movement dance seems to have been projected onto divine dancing figures such as the *Dancing Shiva* sculpture of Nataraja. This dancing Hindu god of the universe[11] was thought to rotate through cycles.

4. *Dancing Shiva* in CERN, Switzerland. Thanks Wikipedia.

Such phase-oriented gods may perhaps be one answer to Einstein's famous statement, "I want to know the mind of god, the rest are details."[12] Nataraja or Dancing Shiva is at least in part a projection or an experience of *how our mind works.* The god's dance movements represent phases we go through, such as rest, dreaming, annihilation, and creation. Dancing Shiva's circular dance symbolizes the destructive and creative phases of our psychology and our world.

This phase-oriented god also symbolizes a common link between physics, spirituality, and psychology. From Wikipedia we read, "In 2004, a 2-meter statue of the dancing Shiva was unveiled at CERN (the European Center for Research in Particle Physics in Geneva, Switzerland)."[13] The statue, symbolizing Shiva's cosmic dance of creation and destruction, "was given to CERN by the Indian government to celebrate the research center's long association with India." [14] Today, I would add, the symbolism of this god unifies mythology, religious art, physics, as well as *psychology and conflict resolution*—as I am indicating in this present book.

Please notice that this god has one foot on or in reality, and one foot in another "*phase*" of the dance, while its hands touch upon other phases of the universe. Like Shiva, you and I can be realistic *and also* be in touch with other phases, such as dreaming and spiritual experiences, at the same time.

It is natural for most people to forget about phases and identify as being only one kind of person in one phase or another! However, this "normal" consensus reality that consists of identifying *only* as a particular kind of individual over long periods of time, though important, often leads to depression. Becoming aware of how we all fixate our own identities in limiting ways, thinking "I'm THIS and *NOT THAT*," is crucial in raising diversity consciousness.

Rigid identification and pride are VERY important qualities to notice. To avoid marginalization, most minority peoples need to allow themselves to stand for their own identification more than the mainstream people in a given area. My point is that *our identities are a phase.* At night in dreams, other phases occur in which we are sometimes the "other." Thus, we need our identification in raising diversity consciousness, but must also sense that we are sometimes the "other" if we are to create better relationships and sustainable resolutions with the "other." *It is important to take a firm stand, and believing* "I am me and NOT the other" is *not* a sustainable solution over time.

The Phases of Deep Democracy

Before going further, let's consider the idea of democracy, or deep democracy, and expand the idea by showing how it is connected with phases. I said in my book *Deep Democracy of Open Forums* that the term *democracy* comes from the Greek *demo = citizen* and *kratie* or *power.* The idea of democracy, of sharing power among all peoples, is a fantastic and important idea! However, democracy often does not work well. Why? Democracy's biggest problem is that it is based mainly on *kratie* or *power* and not on awareness. Sharing power does not mean better relationships!!

Democracy based upon power is a conflict creator. Without awareness of power and rank, we marginalize others and create permanent states of conflict. Democracy's *demo-kratie* or equal citizen power does not work as well as it could. That is why I suggested the concept of *deep democracy.*[15]

Deep democracy is comprised of our "consensus" reality awareness of power as well as deeper levels of experience with it. Deep democracy awareness notices what people are saying in consensus reality, and what their marginalized signals are conveying as well (these often go unnoticed during interactions). Bringing these marginalized signals into awareness—signals such as irritation, boredom, relaxation, etc.—can deepen relationships and help resolve tensions. I call such signals *double signals.* We repress and rarely notice our own double signals during the daytime but can find them in dreams at night.

I found that deep democracy requires awareness of three levels, which are summarized in the following section. (See my *Deep Democracy of Open Forums* for more.) The first level is "consensus reality" where I am me and you are you. In the second level of deep democracy, in "dreamland," you find marginalized signals, visions, and big dreams. At the third and deepest level of deep democracy, the "essence" level, we sense a pre-dream experience, the realm of deep awareness from which dreams and spontaneous insights arise. (Remember the song that came to mind during the robbery mentioned in the introductory chapter.)

Levels of DEEP DEMOCRACY

Consensus Reality. The surface of deep democracy consists of the facts of everyday reality and the problems of all those concerned. At the surface is the more or less agreed-upon common notion of reality for which there is "consensus." Consensus reality depends upon given, often rigid identities. Democracy in consensus reality basically says, "You are you and I am me." Consensus reality (CR for short) represses dreams and subtle communication signals.

Dreamland. Here you find dreams and marginalized or double signals (unconscious communication sounds and gestures). In individuals and organizations, deep goals and basic visions can be found here.

Essence Level. Deep democracy's essence level is a realm of subtle experience and feelings that cannot, at first, be expressed in words. Taoism's Lao Tse would have called this level of deep democracy the "Tao that cannot be said." It is a feeling of some magnetic-like power or spirit in the air.

In brief, deep democracy is composed of CR (consensus reality), dreamland, and the essence level. Like democracy, deep democracy is about citizen power and equality, but it also stresses, rather than excludes, the *dreamlike nature of projections and feelings* needed for relating to ourselves and others.

The concept of process phases allows us to extend and deepen my theory of deep democracy.

Each level of deep democracy (consensus reality, dreamland, and essence) is associated with one or more process phases.

Consensus Reality Contains Phases 1 and 2

Phase 1 is when we and the groups we form don't want to focus on problems. *Just enjoy*! When we think mainly about ourselves and try to forget everything else, we are in phase 1. Self-absorption is a common element of everyday consensus reality. In the first phase people feel that they are cruising. This phase shares similar characteristics with a very young child in the "me-me-me!" stage of development. In this phase, there seems to be nothing else but you or "u" (as I often write)! In phase 1, individuals or groups are cruising along, focusing solely on themselves, asking for attention and fun, hoping to be parented as they simply enjoy themselves.

5. Phase 1. Enjoy
www.iclipart.com

This can be a holiday-like phase for groups. "Here we are! We just discovered that we should be together, so we have good reason to be here! We don't want to think about all the problems yet! NO, we don't want to think about problems. In this phase of our personal and organizational life, let us simply feel well. Let us forget any possible problems!"

Groups need this phase; it is not a good or bad phase. As a facilitator you might not agree with this phase, but if you can accept it, you can even use it to *very briefly* consider problems. There are many ways of processing this phase.

Phase 1, by nature, marginalizes a troublesome inner mood or outer trouble. This troublesome mood, figure, or group characterized by an "X" energy or figure is something we try to "divorce" from ourselves. That's why I call it an "X." So just as it takes a toddler a while to realize that she or he must consider the other kids or parents, in phase 1 we simply feel, "I want what I want!"

Phase 2 occurs inside when we feel tense because of something or when we and our group are angry or fear the "X" power of an internal or external situation. In phase 2, the "X" tension is linked to diversity issues and to how much or how little psychological rank and power we feel relative to the "other."

***6.* Phase 2. Tension + Conflict.** www. iclipart.com

In relationships or groups, phase 2 happens when we just don't like something in ourselves or others and/or feel tense, afraid, or angry about something. In this phase, we are upset in part because we feel that the things or people bothering us are wrong or are unconscious of their power and rank, of their social and cultural power differences.

Often at the root of phase 2 problems are issues of power and social rank; that is, feeling that you or your group or organization has less power relative to a given problem or society or culture. In phase 2, you say, "Oh! The "X" thing we were avoiding, the thing we hate, is coming up!"

If you say to someone in phase 2, "Maybe we can relate better to that "X" that is against us," you will hear the vigorous response, "No! They are *NOT* us, they bother us," or "We don't like them, we want to avoid them, cross them out, fight them!"

Our daily news is filled with the "X's" of phase 2: "The other people are bad—let's avoid or kill them!"

As long as I am a facilitator and am not in phase 2 against people, I have no value judgment against this aggressive phase. Phase 2 is just a part of nature, like a volcano. But if you or I are *in* phase 2 as facilitators, we may dislike and unconsciously struggle with the groups or individuals we are trying to help. I often hear facilitators saying, "I don't like that group or that person I am helping."

As I have already said, it is important in phase 2 to take a stand against the "bad" people" or the "bad" situation. Taking a strong stand can be a matter of life and death. Phase 2 is significant because here, nature is demonstrating her diversity. There is a "u" (an "us" energy) and then there is a divorced "X" energy that is *not* us! "We need medicine, or guns, or war to fight that 'X!'"

Phase 2 is crucial in awakening ourselves and others to social issues. In phase 2, we create tension and "fight" to make social change. However, over time, we need to remember that holding to one phase only creates diversity issues by marginalizing people in other phases. Awareness of and supporting change via the flow of phases is finally a key to creating sustainable cultures, both inside and outside ourselves.

After we struggle long enough, this tense phase or battle eventually exhausts us, and we may become distressed or depressed . . . we may fear losing money, failing, or dying. Then we are ready to leave phase 2 for phase 3 or phase 4.

Dreamland is phase 3. Here, we are more open and able to notice our own dreamlike nonverbal communications signals, dreams, and double signals. In phase 3, we can relax and dream about solutions. We begin to open up to the other side.

7. Phase 3. Open to the other.

Phase 3 is dreamlike in that signals and behavior we don't identify in everyday reality appear in dreams. In phase 3 of individual and organizational processwork, we deal not only with roles but also with "ghost roles"—that is, places, historical issues, or people mentioned but not present, as well as double signals, etc. In phase 3, playing out these "ghost roles" as if they are present often brings new solutions.

In organizations and in the life of individuals, phases 1 and 2 create walls and differentiations. However, in phase 3 (dreamland) experiences, we are able to consider fantasies and dreams, and the walls between us become more pliable. In phase 3 we can sometimes switch roles with the other—and sense that we are the other. Phase 3 is an aspect of your own, and a group's, often unrecognized life that may appear in relationship and organizational meetings of all kinds. Switching roles can reduce the tensions of the conflict in phase 2.

Essence level is phase 4. Here we feel more relaxed and detached, quiet, or effortlessly moved by some subtle sense that at first cannot be easily expressed verbally. Therefore we often don't pay attention to this subtle phase 4. However, it is an important phase because at this level, you or a group can feel detached and moved by something infinite—at least temporarily, everything is a phase! In my previous book, *Dance of the Ancient One*, I describe in detail how movements that occur spontaneously as if you were moved by the universe create this detached and creative phase 4. This present book gives you many practical exercises for accessing and using phase 4 to help facilitate the resolution of tensions in the other phases.

8. Phase 4. The universe or essence level. www.iclipart.com

Phase 4, "the Tao that cannot be said" is the ineffable atmosphere, the deep sense of the universe that can be felt but not easily expressed. Phase 4 is an experience of your deepest self, or what I have called the "processmind."[16] This essence level "mind" might appear in dreamland dream images, in the first visions of an organization, and is often behind the guiding myth or pattern for individuals and groups. Here in phase 4, you and others might sense a connection with something timeless, powerful, and infinite. It is the psychological experience behind most religions.

INTERVENTIONS IN INDIVIDUAL AND GROUP WORK

I describe many interventions that work for each phase over the course of this book. Let me emphasize one important point. Peaceful or well-organized communication methods often work in phases 1 or 3 or 4. But such "good methods" often do not work in the heavy tensions of phase 2. There we need other methods, as we shall see in following chapters.

For now, I want to provide an introduction to the way that phase understanding can guide you in choosing or creating effective interventions for particular situations.

After enough tension, with or without results, organizations and individuals get weary of long-lasting conflicts and begin to consider the possibility of submitting or negotiating. Aspects of this negotiation can be hinted at in the conflict of phase 2, but slowly, as phase 3 emerges, the thought begins to occur, *"How do we relate better to that 'X,' to one another?"*

On rare occasions, individuals and nations may even briefly consider the question, "Are we too one-sided or even have a little of the other side?" With that thought, we suddenly get closer to that which has NOT been us, closer to "dreamland."

The sun goes up, sun goes down, things cycle, everything changes, we are who we are, and we also sometimes change and realize that we are like the other. When we are solidly in phase 3, we can relax, and *role switching* becomes possible. We might even think, "Maybe we are a bit like that 'X'." This is the moment that open forum dialogues relax, and understanding becomes possible (at least temporarily).

Whereas open forums in phase 2 are characterized by intense conflict, in phase 3, open forum dialogue and actually listening to the other side becomes possible.

You can try to encourage people to move from phase 2 into phase 3 to negotiate, but this does not usually work. Focusing on anger and power in phase 2 and exploring historical abuse issues are needed before considering how we are "like" the other. In phase 2, non-mainstream people and roles often *need* to take a stand—there is no shortcut for expressing *all* parts.

If phase 2 is wearing out, and role switching and dreaming in phase 3 are difficult, depression, drug addiction, alcoholism, or suicidal thoughts often occur. Severe depression becomes a major medical problem, and the risk of striking out against the other side becomes greater, just as the risk of suicide increases. Behind depression and "killing the self" is often an unconscious drive to go straight to phase 4.

People who are very hurt, poor, depressed, or afraid of failing in one way or another sometimes become violent and suicidal—not just to die physically, but to "die out of" their earlier identities and phases to find not just "death," but a more detached, less painful and conflicted, level of reality. I give terrorist examples of this point later.

In phase 4, the idea of the infinite arises. Here, there is a sense that there something in the universe that detaches us, and is as important as or more so than earthly matters. Each individual and each group have their own sense of something infinite and of their own description of centeredness and detachment in action.

I sketched the four phases in the following picture. *Note that I have placed phase 4 in the center of the phases, and also as distinct phase in the cycle.* I explain more about this over the course of the book.

Phase 1 is quiet, phase 2 is tense, phase 3 shows we can throw the ball around as in "role switching," and phase 4 is a relaxed and detached overview of how all phases change.

***Figure 9.* Phases.**
1, just being;
2, tension + conflict;
3, rolling between sides;
& phase 4, detach.
(self-made +www.iclipart.com)

Some people might say, "I don't believe in that detached stuff, to hell with it! That is for people who are New Age, dying, or religious—that is not me!" That attitude is fine, it belongs to phase 2, and feeling stronger and fighting needs to happen. There is no need to press for phase 4 detachment, that is openness to the flow of all phases. When people are ready, they will get there themselves.

Everyone, even the most rational person and far out "gurus," go through all these phases. How do I know? I have worked with many types of people, in just about all states of consciousness.

Everyone experiences phase 4 at least in a pre-dream state or in the midst of the night. We have the sense that something moves us that has not yet appeared as an image, idea, or movement.

From a phase 4 view, happiness, fear-anger, dreaminess, and detachment all belong to process cycles. From a phase 4 viewpoint, no one and *no particular phase is better or worse than the others.* Having a phase 4 detached position makes you (temporarily) generous and open. When you are in phase 4, you are detached *and* you do not look down on others who are not detached. You realize that everything belongs, everything changes.

***10.* Phase 3**

However, when you begin to look down on others, you are leaving phase 4 and are heading for phase 1 (*me, me, me*) and/or phase 2. Why? You are in the conflict cycle again, "I am better than everyone else!" Many religions and psychologies that make too much of detachment and look down on others as not being detached are really in phase 2!—in conflict with the world . . . for better or worse.

***11.* Phase 4**

Phase 4 is a phase and it changes. It does not last forever in everyday life—as some spiritual traditions may possibly suggest. Real people seem to "reincarnate." Even the most highly spiritual people that I have ever met (and I have met a number of them)—move around the phases—though they often try to hide their phase 1 and phase 2 moments. You can tell that they are in phase 2 when they "fight" by implying that "detached people are better than others who are not that evolved yet." This statement reflects a phase 2 fighting attitude.

Facilitator Skills and Metaskills Associated with the Phases. In her book *Metaskills: The Spiritual Art of Therapy*, Amy (my wife, Dr. Amy Mindell) defined *metaskills* as feeling skills. Now, before the training exercise in this chapter, let's consider how your facilitator skills and metaskills are influenced by phases.

Phase 4 is an important metaskill for a facilitator. You can be in conflict with an individual's or organization's process, but to facilitate, occasionally remember phase 4 to see the value of *everyone*'s views and all the phases concerned. From this viewpoint, people are not only sick and horrible, they are—we all are—parts of nature. If you occasionally have this phase 4 attitude, you can (temporarily) model eldership.

Phase 4 gives you a relaxed, detached experience. Here you can support the group in phase 1 when it wants to ignore problems. If you accept this "egotistical" phase, later the group will be able to work on conflicts more readily (in phase 2). Ask about participants' backgrounds, their vision. What are their hopes? What are their diversity issues? Bring out their vision and discuss how it can help them deal with tensions.

When possible, use that vision to support diversity consciousness and differences of opinion. Explore their most troublesome "X" energies. Consider financial and social problems, sexism, racism, homophobia, ageism, dislike of certain religions. Explore national and international tension. Recall that in phase 2, people often feel abused by history *and* the present. Help groups express their one-sidedness, encourage gossip to come out in public, listen to anger, help people talk, and note the beginnings of phase 3 dialogue.

Recall that everyone, even those who have been hurt and victimized, can also be unconscious of and abuse their rank. *Victim rank* often becomes a kind of spiritual rank. If you have been downed enough, hurt, beaten, and spit on, it can be a matter of life and death to rise up in rage as if the gods are with you. Supporting this power is important. Rage is needed . . . but not as a final solution.

In phase 2, all of us become unconscious of "victim rank and power." I have learned this from working with many different people in many different countries. You can develop so much victim and spiritual rank that you want to kill the other side and you do not care what will happen to you. "I will kill them for revenge and to make my life meaningful. If I die, so what!"

Remember, the phase 2 "fight until death" process can be an attempt to leave phase 2 for phase 4.

It is important to remember that groups and individuals who have been hurt and downed are not only victims. The victim identity is only part of their story. There is a possible spiritual power that may grow in such people who have been badly hurt.

In phase 3, open forums become more relaxed as people relate more fluidly. In phase 3, you can ask, "Can you see how some of the things you are doing may be aspects of what you hate in the other?"

In phase 4, thinking globally and "nonlocally" becomes possible. Nothing that is bothering any individual or group is not bothering other people and regions of the whole world. In phase 4, you realize that problems here belong not only to one group or nation, but need to be worked on around the world. In phase 4, you notice that whatever appears to occur in one group or country is part of you and me and all people, everywhere. So if and when possible, remind yourself and the group that we are working for ourselves and also for the world. In phase 4, we work locally, sensing the nonlocal global field!

Your Inner Work on Relationship Phases

Now dear reader, please explore putting some of these ideas about phases into practice. Explore the following phase-oriented inner work exercise to understand phases better. It is best to take notes for yourself during these exercises. In this way, you can remember your experiences in this and other exercises throughout the book.

1. Choose a *relationship* or *outer world problem* on which to focus. (Later, I explain how to realize your insights in face-to-face situations.) What is your normal identity and energy? Make a motion to describe your "normal self" and energy. Let's call that the "u" energy. Make an energy sketch of this "u" energy on paper and name it (e.g., "u" is ~~~~~~ wavey).
2. Now, think of a recent difficult family, business, or relationship situation. Choose one person on whom to focus. (It could be a close partner, friend, enemy, a person in an organization that you have worked with, etc.) Imagine that person and the particular behaviour that bothers you. Ask yourself, "What is the most difficult energy of that behavior that bothers me?" Make a motion to describe their energy. Let's call that energy "X." Act out this "X" with your hands and then sketch the energy or motion of this "X" on your paper and give "X" a name (e.g., the sketch of "X" might be called "abrupt energy").
3. Now, notice which process phase you are experiencing with this situation or person. In phase 1, you are happy. In phase 2, you are irritated/troubled with the other's "X" energy. In phase 3, you are moving between the u + X, and in phase 4, you are detached and flowing.
4. Imagine that you are in phase 2, and in your imagination discuss, fight, or interact with the other person. While doing this, notice/imagine any double signals (i.e., being quiet or unusually loud, etc.) in you or the other person.
5. Now explore phase 3. That is, see the "u" and "X" energies as nonlocal (this means, belonging to everyone). Imagine there is a discussion or forum and you can switch roles between "u" and "X": That is, you can go back and forth and speak deeply for *both* sides. If possible, notice and bring in awareness of their and your social rank (e.g., race, color, gender, sexual orientation, nationality, experience, ability) or rank the degree of unconsciousness, if possible.

Role switch, act out the "u" and the "X" energies in both of you, and try to flow between them. Notice if and when insights or changes happen.

6. When you begin to relax, leave phase 3 and explore phase 4. Relax your neck and your whole body, and begin to imagine and feel how the universe's space around you begins to move you. If possible, stand while doing this, and *carefully* be moved about a bit unpredictably. Wait until repeated motions occur. Notice if the u + X energies are now parts of your dance motions. As you move, notice and catch any insights that arise spontaneously about resolving the conflict between those two energies/parts. Make a note of this insight.
7. Finally, expect that phase 1 (me, me, me) and phase 2 will naturally recur! Also consider that eventually going back to phases 1 and 2 may help you to remember and become more conscious of diversity issues and solutions.

At your leisure, consider bringing your inner work out in face-to-face relationship work. Having done your inner work in this exercise will probably help all sides.

Things to Remember from Chapter 1

1. Notice and appreciate deep democracy's *levels and phases* in yourself as well as in relationships and groups.
2. Recall that phase 1 is about trying to avoid trouble and enjoy things.
3. Phase 1 and phase 2's tension are consensus reality phases.
4. Deep democracy's dreamland is phase 3—that is, moving between sides, roles, and positions.
5. Deep democracy's essence level is phase 4, a detachment experience. From the viewpoint of phase 4, all phases are like the seasons, natural and cyclical.

CHAPTER 2

Enlightenment in Group Work? Notice Phases!

• • •

THIS CHAPTER APPLIES *PHASE UNDERSTANDING* to the facilitation of organizational and world-scale conflicts, including company mergers, street violence, war, and tense social issues involving police violence, terrorism, gender politics, and the like.

In Chapter 1, I pointed out that phase 4 represents a detached experience, detached even from itself. Phase 4 is a *phase* and, paradoxically, also the center of all phases. Being centered is always possible, even if it is in the background of awareness at a given moment. Awareness of that center, however, comes and goes from our everyday awareness. Instead, we may feel exhausted, ill, or "down." Many of the techniques and ideas in this book are intended to help you access phase 4 experience in the midst of tension (this is what we call the *second training*).

I introduce the idea of the "black box" as a metaphor for accessing phase 4, and share an inner-focused exercise so you can experiment with this practice for yourself.

In the first training, we learn to deal with phases 1, 2, and 3. In the second training, we learn to feel the universe moving us; we learn to drop the outer events momentarily and get closer to our dreaming self to sense the "black box" of nonlocal connections. The Buddhists might call this black box "empty mind." The Rinzai Zen master, Fukushima Roshi, called *empty mind* "creative mind" (in personal communications with us).

Facilitating with the Phases

Let me explain. In phase 4, you notice and move with whatever is happening in phases 1, 2, 3, and 4, whether you experience these phases in yourself, in relationships, or in groups. Remember that some of the methods you learned for individual, community, business, or group work often apply *only* to one or two of the phases. Recall also that if what you learned worked well in the quiet of phases 1, 3, or 4, it's natural to have difficulties in phase 2.

If people are happy and talkative in phase 1, first appreciate them before suggesting conflict work. If they are peaceful or in phase 4, ask them about the spirit moving them and how to use it best.

For example, I recall a phase 1 scene that occurred in a group of about 400 people working on World War II issues in Europe. A German subgroup came to the center to work on its issues. Even though the group consisted of people from Germany, they did not know each other. They were supposed to work on historical issues of their country, and so they began talking. I watched as facilitators tried to apply all sorts of methods. "Let's talk about historical issues of your country," each facilitator would say, trying to rein in the social chatter.

But the small subgroup was in phase 1, and the participants were not yet ready to speak about trouble, even though they were "supposed" to do just that. At first they wanted to learn the names of one another; they were meeting each other for the first time. The facilitators did not realize the phase the subgroup was in but tried instead to get them to play out some of the dreadful and also wonderful historical roles. The facilitators' approach did not work. Why? People needed time in phase 1 to get to know each other first.

They were using phase 1 to discover and form an identity, a "we." They needed time to feel like a group or community. When they were given the chance to stay in phase 1 and feel like a group, they were happy and *then* eventually went further.

The learning from this example is that if you can identify the phase that a group is in, your interventions may be more effective.

Try interventions you have learned a few times, but if they don't work, recognize that the individual, couple, or group may be in a process phase you have not noticed. Phases are neither good nor bad. Activist-oriented facilitators in phase 2 want to rush people out of phase 1, which ignores social problems. But acknowledging the phase people are in first usually allows them to move into other phases and more difficult situations more quickly.

Hitler and Phase 4. At another point in that large group process mentioned above, the group focused on unsettled World War II problems, and someone was playing the role of Hitler. At a given moment in that very large group, the person playing the figure of Adolf Hitler became enraged. He was in phase 2 and wanted to "kill" everyone. To help the person in that role go further, after checking with the group that this was allowable, we joined him, speaking as Hitler (in his phase 2), "I don't care anymore. I just want to kill! I don't care about life and will even commit suicide if I have to!"

Other viewpoints came up, such as, "Fight and stop that person," but Hitler said, "NO! I want to be the greatest and destroy all that I think are bad, even if it costs me my life!"

The reference to dying pointed to "letting go" or a phase 4 experience. So instead of trying to change "Hitler" at that point, we suggested that perhaps his fate was to die and let go. At that moment the person playing Hitler was relieved and immediately quieted down. Then the whole large group of hundreds moved to new phases and helpful insights and feelings about the war. Everyone's sense of "Where is my home?" and "Where can I live safely?" became the discussion.

Please note that if you want to facilitate, adapt your work to the moment and the process phase, not just your learned "map" to get to where you want to go most quickly. Many things you have learned don't work well some of the time, not only because the techniques were developed for a particular phase, but also for specific cultures. For example, if you want to work with guys in a street fight, you need different movements and language than you would need with two government officials arguing with one another.

Remember: Phases change, and some aspects of conflicts or problems recur. People say, "Why do I have the same problems as 40 years ago? Why are they returning!?" One answer, from a phase 2 viewpoint, says, "Yes, you are an idiot! You should have worked that out by now!" But a phase 4 viewpoint is more open. For example, a person who resolves her problems at one point, then later experiences them recurring, may need to learn more about her own internal diversity conflicts, phases, and overall process. Likewise with organizations; problems recur in part to allow individuals to become more conscious of group problems, processes, and phases. With greater process and phase awareness, the problems become easier to deal with over time.

Organizational Mergers

For example, when two business groups come together or merge, conflict is common. One organization I advised bought another organization. The people who were "bought" were expected to adapt to the new situation. As you can imagine, this expectation created conflict between the old and new groups. The entire group needed a facilitator to help. The bosses asked me, "What does enlightenment mean during a group merger?"

I laughed. From the phase 4 viewpoint, realize and use the phases the groups are in. The original group was in phase 1, proud of themselves. But the people who were "bought" and were expected to adapt to the new circumstances were in phase 2, conflict. The total organization, now composed of everyone, entered into phase 2; everyone needed to talk and re-create a new identity. "Who are we now?"

As a whole, the group was in phase 2. So the first step was to address the conflict. I said, some want peace (as in phase 1) and some need debate as in phase 2. Let's explore the roles of the newcomers and of the original group. Perhaps, if possible, we can reach phase 3 and switch roles. This may lead to either affirming or adding to the old organizational vision. Let's affirm and be open to re-creating the same or a slightly new vision for the organization! That approach worked well.

Groups that merge need to ask if the old visions are still acceptable or if everyone should take part in updating those visions so that all members feel included. To begin a merger, a phase 1 question needs to be asked first. The main group must ask, "Will you work for and with us in our vision?" Asking such a question makes everyone feel included and enables mergers to occur with less tension.

Facilitators do best if they recall that in times of conflict, in phase 2, acknowledging and emphasizing the amazing diversity situation between groups is crucial. Say, "I see two groups within an organization that are irritated with one another. They have different viewpoints, so let's listen to and discuss these viewpoints."

The needed feeling skill or "metaskill" (to use Amy's term)[17] is, "Be proud of our diversity!" Strengthen each group and each viewpoint as much as possible, and participants will have an easier time coming together.

Conflict with "Downsizing"

Think of another organization that is reducing the size of its staff. Conflict arises because some people are losing their jobs and feel ignored, whereas others are saying, "We don't need you—goodbye!"

In phase 2 there may be a discussion: What else can we do besides just downsizing? Try to involve as many people as possible in phase 2 discussions and possible solutions so that the organization feels more intelligent and more sustainable as a whole.

Some groups that have faced this issue created new kinds of jobs without firing their older workers. Other groups simply needed to downsize and to help everyone with the next steps in life. The point is that addressing the phase 2 situation that downsizing creates can save everyone time and feeling. If you facilitate this process with awareness, you might be able to reduce the depression and the anger that come from it.

Nonviolent Communication[18] and Open Space[19]

Nonviolent communication and *open space* are two brilliant methods for working with groups to transform phase 2 into the more creative phase 3 or 4 activities. For example, in the "open space" method, people come together and talk, bring up topics, then divide into small groups to talk about those topics. They all come together afterwards to share and develop new concepts. This is a great intervention when the conflict situation in phase 2 is mild, or phase 3 is present. However, if phase 2 conflict is severe, these brilliant methods may not work as well as possible.

Open Forums

Open forums flow best if some participants can experience phase 3. If some group members can switch roles and see the "other" in themselves—if they can be the "other" in inner work and outer open forums—then relationships improve. When a group is in phase 3, the facilitator can model dialoguing and switching roles in an open forum situation. Show people how to dialogue by acting out the parts yourself and then encourage others to do so. Use your knowledge of double signals and ghost roles to help the process deepen and flow here.

Remember to work with double signals. They occur when a person says one thing, and her or his body is doing something very different! The idea of *tracking* such signals and ghost roles (i.e., the absent other in our conversation) is *always* a good idea, but *following* them works best in phase 3.

Remember that there is a connection between double signals and ghost roles. For example, if someone in conflict says, "I like you," but her or his signals imply, "I'm angry at you," she or he may be representing an angry person or group that is *not present.* Double signals mirror ghost roles. If the person is smiling and, at the same time, clenching a fist behind her or his back, that person may actually be speaking for someone who is not present and who is very angry—that someone is a "ghost role."

Phase 3's "open-door policy." When one party can open up to the other party, it is as if the border between their residences opens up and phase 3 becomes possible. As I have already indicated, this can happen after having first affirmed the presence of phase 2 tension. A good facilitator can then model the "open door" by modeling *role switching*—that is, by showing how to open up to the other side. Such moments are keys to conflict resolution. In phase 3, the facilitator can model how to "feel into" the other party's world. Sometimes you might be a bit mediumistic by guessing into the double signals of all parties. When people feel understood, they are often ready to "understand" the other side.

Phase 4 Is a Mysterious Black Box

What happens in this detached phase 4 often occurs at a non-cognitive level. Phase 4 reminds us of being moved by our dreams. The idea of a subtle intelligence behind dreams appears in science's concept of the "black box." The darkness of *black* refers to the inability of the normal observer to track or see into the black box—to understand what's going on in there with the input that might explain the output. The black box is like a phase 4 method. You cannot track how problems stimulate or create responses in phase 4. The interconnections are often irrational, sometimes nonlocal, and connect to the idea of a "group mind."

The input into the black box in organizational work consists of the facts, problems, and the people in a given situation. The output is often some kind of product.

Your facilitator's mind. In psychological terms the *black box* refers to an *altered state*, to the facilitator's *nonlocal* mind that belongs to her and—at the same time—to the system of which she is currently a part. She receives ideas and impressions, but what happens between the input and the output is organized by "the field." That field is the processmind or the "Tao"—the nonlocal quantum world, the essence level, so to speak.

That idea of the black box came from one of my professors at MIT, the cybernetics creator Norbert Wiener.[20] Outputs happen, but no one can track exactly how things move through the black box. Organizational system minds are, in principle, black boxes. In phase 4, you go into an altered state and create interventions and often results occur. The black box or system mind of an individual, organization, or group has nonlocal characteristics connected to everything in that system.

If you go deeply enough into yourself and connect with phase 4, with the universe's "black box," it becomes activated and something useful almost always comes out. Phase 4 operates like a black box. It is a gift of relaxation, detachment, and creativity.

To reiterate, in the first training, you learn to deal with phases 1, 2, and 3. In second training, you learn how to feel the universe moving you, how to drop the outer events momentarily and get closer to your dreaming self in order to sense the "black box's" nonlocal connections.

***12.* Black Box.** Thanks Wikipedia.

The black box is *nonlocal* in quantum terms. In quantum physics, the smallest particles can be described as discrete elementary particles and also as waves. They are both particles and waves, and they can be nonlocal—that is, they can connect with one another in mysterious or what Einstein called "spooky" ways.

The black box *couples or links* personal and organizational systems. That means that if we are in the same physical or emotional system, your process is coupled with mine, and with everyone else's in our "system." All the changes you make affect me because of our shared system or process-mind, which is a black box whose behavior can't be explained in causal terms such as "*a* causes *b*."

Just as with cloud formation, all clouds seem to work together in cloud formations, so also on earth, processes such as the earth's movements, rainfall, temperature changes, and human activity may be interconnected in ways we cannot exactly track. The black box is a kind of "mind" behind a system's process. From a limited viewpoint, each person is crucial, and from a broader viewpoint, we are all interconnected.

It is hard to specify exactly how any one thing causes another. Similar complex coupled system processes determine the global financial markets, climate change, etc. Working on one process by itself is never enough to explain system-wide events. The black box is, in principle, connected with the entire universe.

Wikipedia points out that the human brain[21] *can be considered a black box.* This sounds similar to Zen Buddhism's *mushin* or "empty mind" concept, which is what Roshi Keido Fukushima called "creative mind." These terms are shortened from *mushin no shin* (無心の心), a Zen expression meaning *mind without mind*, also referred to as the state of "no-mindness."[22]

The opposite of a black box is a system in which the inner components or logic are available for inspection. This opposite kind of box is sometimes known as a clear box, a glass box, or a white box.[23]

In any case, the black box or processmind organizes our dreams and couples them with our body, creating a dreambody and creating what Jung called *synchronicities* in the world. Jung defined *synchronicity* as an *acausal connecting principle.*

In practice, I use phase 4's black box experience but am careful to also relate to the consensual phase 1 and phase 2 of reality if people are there. If people are shy about spontaneous creativity, I try to adapt to their belief system. Then I might still use phase 4, but silently meditating for myself, go inside in a way that others can hardly notice. I try to respect the group I am with, if I am in front of them.

Inner Work with the Black Box

I want to demonstrate and use the black box with inner work on an organizational problem. This will help you prepare to facilitate group work. Think about, and then let's work on, an organization you are part of or would like to join. You can also use a job situation, family, or city problem. You will soon consider the most difficult (for you) person or subgroup in that organization. We are going to try to use "black box" dreaming and all the phases to work with this difficulty.

After we do the needed inner work, we will use your inner work to facilitate an organizational issue, with other imagined people acting as if they are part of that organization. In this exercise, we will be using your most detached phase 4 awareness to move between the different sides of the conflict. Your "black box" will show you how to flow between positions to create more community.

Inner Work: Process Flow Awareness in Family/ Group/ Organizational Processes

1. Choose a *difficult or interesting group, family, or organization* that you are part of. What phase is it in? Phase 1: Developing or re-developing its identity. Phase 2: In overt or covert conflict. Phase 3: Flowing between sides. Phase 4: Detached, spontaneous, and creative. Make a note.
2. What role are you ("u") in, in that group? What is your usual "u" nature and energy in that group? Make a motion to describe your normal "u" energy, and then sketch and name it on your paper.
3. Think of a most difficult person or role "X" in that group for you. What is that energy like? Make a motion to describe that energy, then sketch and name that "X" energy on your paper.
4. Now imagine being in the tension of phase 2, trying to relate or discuss difficult things with "X." When things get stuck, or you want to go deeper, move to phase 3. Try to see and feel that *difficult person*, "X," *as part of you*. That is, act out that person and try to feel into her or him deeply. Make a note. And now stand, if you can, and imagine role-playing u + X, as in a forum, where you go back and forth between u + X, acting them out and "*communi-flowing,*" *that is,* going deeply into each side as you communicate. Move with u + X energies, noticing rank awareness, if possible.
5. Whether you have a solution or not at this point, let's move to phase 4. Relax, and let yourself use the black box. That is, relax into the spaces around you, and as you do, let the system mind of the black

box begin to move you about spontaneously. As you move, notice if the u + X energies are in your movement somewhere. Continue being moved and let the black box system mind give you a spontaneous insight about the u + X relationship. Make a note.

6. Finally, create a story about this process. Here is an example: *"Once upon a time there was a person, "u," trying to relate to another person, "X," in a certain organization. This and that happened and new discoveries suddenly arose, and the relationship, group, or organization changed. . . .*
7. Makes notes about the story and how things changed. Then think of how to actualize this change.

The following interesting questions and comments came from participants who tried this exercise.

Q: The police I work with would say, for example, "I know how bad it has been for these people disobeying the law. That is why I know how dangerous they are, and that is why I have to shoot them before they shoot me."

Arny: The first thing I would say is about phase 2. "Yes, protect yourself if needed," but if possible, dear police person, "read into the other side's feelings. Take at least a minute and remember phase 3. Switch roles and speak for the brutality and trouble the people disobeying the law may have experienced."

Q: OK, yes, I could help the police say to the bad guys, "I know where you're coming from, I know what your life is like. We come from the same place. I know your life, we came from the same place."

T: On that topic, I work on the street in the midst of racial conflicts. I find that if you start off having human contact, it changes the whole experience. I know by working like that saves a whole lot of stress on both sides.

Arny: Yes, "human contact." That makes me almost cry. Thank you for your work on the streets. "Human contact" involves all phases: chatting, fighting, reading into the heart of the other, and letting go.

Exercise: Small Group Flow

The following exercise is something to try with friends, family, or colleagues in a small group. It is a guided practice to help you use your inner work while in the midst of a small group of people.

I. All together (15 minutes)

Introduce yourselves and each briefly mention a group, family, or organizational issue that interests you. Mention the u + X in that situation for you ("u" = the side you identify with; "X" = the most difficult person or role in that issue).

Spin a pen to choose someone's issue as the focus of your present group process. (The person the pen chooses will use her or his issue and also read and guide everyone through the exercise.) Chosen person, please speak a few more minutes about your group issue.

II. Inner work led by the chosen person, the guide (15 minutes)

Think about the guide's issue and ask yourself what role might you ("u") play in that group if you were part of it (this could be the same or different than the chosen person's "u.") Make a motion to describe your energy in that role and sketch and name this "u" energy on paper.

What's the most difficult figure/energy "X" for you in that issue? (This could be the same or different than the chosen person's "X.") Express this "X" energy with a motion and sketch and name it on your paper. How does "u" differ from "X"?

What phase do you think the group is in around the issue? Is it (1) discovering or rediscovering itself, (2) in conflict or tension, (3) flowing between all sides, or (4) detached? Make a note.

Try phase 3; that is, see the "X" role/figure as a part of you in some way. To do that, feel that "X" role and its energy. Feel into it deeply and act it out. Then in your imagination "communi-flow," that is, act out and flow between u + X as fluidly as possible.

Now, relax and open up to your black box system mind experience, as it moves you about in phase 4. Relax and let the space around you begin to move you spontaneously; notice if the u + X energies are present somehow in your dance. Continue being moved and let the black box system mind give you a spontaneous insight about the "u" and "X" energies and how to actualize this learning in you group. Make a note.

Finally, still each focusing on inner work, create a story: *"Once upon a time, there was a group with a problem. When "u" related to "X," the group discovered* . . . . " Make notes.

Turn to a neighbor and each share your story for 2 minutes.

III. All Together (30 minutes): (Note: Read all of this first.)
Guide will be the person whose issue was chosen. Guide, make spots for the u + X energies you mentioned in the beginning, and ask a couple of people to speak for these roles for a few minutes.

Then, everyone joins in this diversity issue by expressing the u + X roles, and switching roles. Remember to notice and bring in double signals, ghost roles, and rank awareness. Try to *communi-flow—that is, try to feel deeply into all sides*! At hot spots, stop and go deeper. (If needed, use black box dreaming and let insights pop up.)

Each participant makes notes about her or his learning and then come together to discuss your impressions insights as a group. Could you sense your phase 4 flow and insights?

Things to Remember from Chapter 2

1. Bring out and explore the hidden diversity in group tensions. Diversity is part of the group's life energy. During the merger of individuals, organizations, groups, or nations, bring out the diversity that is present and make it conscious for all to use.
2. Use your phase 4 "black box" processmind experience for guidance. It will connect to the situation you are in.
3. Know the people in a group or organization in phase 1. Then notice the diversity issues and tensions in phase 2 and feel into both sides

in phase 3. In phase 4, meditate or "dance" (when possible) during meetings to access your own and the community's black box.

4. Enlightenment in group and conflict work means noticing and flowing with phases 1, 2, 3, and 4 . . . and 1, 2, ...

CHAPTER 3

The One to Infinity Inner and Outer World Theatre

• • •

PEOPLE OFTEN ASK, "WHAT IS processwork's approach to world conflict situations?" I call this approach *worldwork*! In this chapter, I go further into deep democracy, phase awareness, and the second training to prepare you for tackling difficult conflict and world issues. I describe the factors that typically escalate conflict into war or warlike behaviors, and show how an understanding of the four phases can be amplified by powerful worldwork techniques to de-escalate and transform conflicts toward deeper, and more sustainable, relationships. I share two practical exercises for preparing for worldwork, and illustrate the approach with an example of an open forum that occurred in one of our seminars, focused on men's issues and the intersection with race.

The goal of worldwork depends upon the people involved, the facilitators, and the momentary themes and phase. Typical goals, depending upon the individuals and cultures, may be to become better known, make more money, resolve diversity tensions, help mergers occur, advise governments on their next steps, resolve conflicts in open forums, deal with terrorism, etc.

In general, worldwork is a method that processes relationship and organizational problems. It is an awareness-raising method that helps the world discover and appreciate itself, its diversity, its communities, its mysteries, and people's real goals.[24]

Finding solutions can be an urgent matter of life and death. Solutions are crucial, but they are often unsustainable without everyone learning to *relate better to one another and to the issues involved.* Relating is an art, a psychology, as well as a hard science (e.g., quantum nonlocality, which I discuss later).

Worldwork teaches this art and science. It is about following the phases and *recycling* problems and energies we don't like. Don't throw out garbage; also don't throw out double signals or ghost roles—recycle them. All signals, roles, and projections need recycling and consciousness. This is not just about me changing you, or you changing me, *but also about us learning to relate together.* (An enjoyable and good introduction to worldwork can be found in Amy Mindell's *Worldwork: A Lighthearted Approach* on our website.[25])

The Second Training in Worldwork

In the first training, you learn relationship and community-making skills, and use the methods you already know—whatever they are called. For example, you learn to follow signals and to notice roles and the levels of deep democracy. The first training prepares you to use your own or other methods of dealing with groups and organizations.

The second training is about finding phase 4 in yourself and others and using it whenever you can. After you have learned the skills and knowledge in your first training, then you can recall and use phase 4's "black box" (see Chapter 2) to help you bring forth creative and unexpected solutions. This means, let the universe "elder" the situation.

The second training is not just about using your learned "science," but about "eldering." The elder is the wise one in everyone, in a part of us that knows that phase 4 black box feeling inside. Normally people say, "I want a solution and I want it today! Our organization or country has been working on something for years, we have been arguing all the time. Damn it! I don't want an elder, I want somebody to solve my problem!"

Eldering affirms this need and uses first training knowledge. This knowledge includes asking about the phase that group is in. If it is in phase 2, I would say, "Great! I want to elder and try and solve that problem right away!" Eldering embraces a fluid approach to all possible phases based upon the sense of being open and moved by the field or the universe around us. Using the first and second trainings together is, in a way, going from "One to Infinity," the title of this chapter.

Example: Violence in an organization. I remember an example of eldering that occurred when I was working with a large organization that had called for help. They never told me exactly what the problem was. In short, I arrived at their offices and opened the door to an organizational meeting that had already begun without me. As the door opened, someone in the front of the room started to yell at me immediately, "Get the F--k out of here!!"

Inside I shuddered, but because I have been in a lot of street fights, the scene appeared almost normal to me. I realized we were in phase 2. I opened the door and I said, "If I am scared of you—and I am—I will bet you some other people in this room might also be afraid."

Suddenly the other people in the room started clapping and laughing and began to fight "the monster" person! The "big monster" was part of this group that had a social rule of being good-hearted. So they did not know how to deal with people acting powerfully.

In any case, I walked into the midst of a phase 2 scene. Things went well then as they joined together to learn how to fight, and they even moved on to phase 3, switching roles and taking the monster's side.

The point here is that whatever you are feeling as a facilitator is probably *not only* yours, it is often nonlocal. If you are scared or excited, chances are your feelings also function as a role in the group. Noticing and affirming this sense of a shared experience is Amy's "metaskill," a feeling skill. Sensing my own feeling of terror was shared was behind my phase 4 detached mood and enabled me to say, "Perhaps I am not the only one who is afraid here."

A normal phase 2 reaction might have been to shut the door and run away to protect myself. Protecting ourselves is important. But with awareness, as a facilitator you can say, "Who else wants to run away?" Remember that *your feelings may be nonlocal.* Stay in touch with your "black box" when possible. Remember, phase 4 is a *phase and the center of all phases.* It can make facilitation a little easier.

Conflict and War

Let's explore conflict and war. Can we reduce the number of wars on our planet? I know each of us has ideas about how to reduce violent conflict. To reduce war, let's first study how it is created.

If you are a "rebel" group and want to go out and kill more powerful people and nations than your own, *how did you get to that point*? There are a million reasons, but basic to all of them is

- *the sense of being marginalized,*
- *not feeling seen or appreciated, empowered, supported financially or emotionally or otherwise by your world,* and
- *being rejected for who you are and the group you are a part of.*

Marginalization and lack of recognition are main causes of inner and outer conflict. Learning to recognize and appreciate *everyone* early on in schools and communities can help. Everyone and every group has many amazing and wonderful qualities! Yet, we all inadvertently co-create violence and war by *having little or no diversity appreciation or phase awareness.*

Remember, at the very least, the social and economic *rank differences* between people and be careful about racial, sexual, gender, national, international, intellectual, and health differences.

If you want to contribute to war, just forget diversity and rank differences. There is nothing as good as rank unconsciousness to create violence. Everyone becomes upset or violent if they are consistently ignored, marginalized, and left feeling hopeless.

Just hoping, believing, or expecting everybody to be equal can make you unconscious of diversity and may inadvertently create tensions. One of the best ways to anger people is to try and force everyone to be the same! Rank unconsciousness marginalizes all sorts of differences.

The second best way I know for leaders to create a long and bloody war is to say, "The other is not me, and I refuse that phase 3 role switching concept!" It's normal in phase 2 to say, "The other is not me." But if you are in a position of power, to constantly say the other is not me sustains violent conflict. Any institution, religion, or psychology that ignores rank consciousness or consistently refuses to consider how the other "is me" contributes to war.

Being mainly heroic can also contribute to great tragedies. We need heroes. But remember that consistently heroic people who stand and inspire others are *sometimes* suicidal. They may feel, "I will go to battle to succeed and help." So far, so good. But be careful if they say or imply, "I'll go to battle even if it costs me my life—I don't care! I will go to battle. I don't have anything else in my life that is as worthwhile."

Some of our great leaders, activists, and also police and military people actually need help because they too can be unconsciously suicidal. Heroism is extremely important for a while, but too much does not help us resolve problems or relate to one another.

It can be meaningful to sacrifice your life for "important " goals, and it is crucial to feel, "I am doing something important with my life!" But it's dangerous for the individual to say, "I don't care about my life anymore." If we get locked into phase 2 situations, dying is but one way of relaxing and getting relief. In many ways, ongoing phase 2 conflict is an attempt to get to phase 4, to a big dream. But the same lack of interest in personal life in favor of social and world effects can also often be achieved without sacrificing a hero's life and by more consciously fostering a detached phase 4 awareness.

We need to be careful about possible background issues such as, "I don't care about life; I am only 18 or 20, or 90 and I don't really care about anything. I will never succeed as much as I could by sacrificing my life." These thoughts are often found behind many of the military people I have worked with as well as those in terrorist groups.

A seminar participant asked,

> *When your call from the inside comes to try and make some change, from lived experience of oppression, it is not a choice. How do you hang on to your own human life when consistently the change is so little?*

This is a great question. One answer is to bring as much awareness to this situation as possible; let the great spirit in phase 4 move you to the next step and recall phase 3—that is, role switching in your community work.

Finding the Essence of Belief Systems

Another way to help a group, a leader, a large organization, or a country that is about to go to war is to find more universal meaning and significance in their belief system, their motto, emblem, slogan, or goals. For example, Greece has an incredible flag and one of their mottos is, "Freedom or Death!" That motto is important for that amazing country in part because letting go, or relaxing into "death" or nothingness, is itself a form of freedom. I would suggest exploring a more universal meaning to their motto, such as, "Freedom or detached interaction!" Each of us will have our own creative insights into updating our mottos.

The motto of the United States is *E Pluribus Unum*—Out of Many, One. That is the motto on the "Great Seal" of the United States, and it is also on passports and the $1 bill. It could imply a quest to find the oneness, the process in the background of "the many." Find the phase 4 center, which is a phase and center, a "1" of all phases. Find the deepest feeling, "out of many, the one." Again, each person will have their own creative way of understanding that.

My point is to encourage you to take the belief system of the group, appreciate it, and explore its meaning and phases to reduce conflicts and improve life for all.

Exploring the belief system of a large organization can help you better communicate with the leaders. Let the momentary discomfort and the conflict illuminate the diversity. Recall that you can get rid of so-called "bad" people, you can even kill them, but that won't be enough. Recall the importance of diversity. *You can kill the person but you can't kill the role.* Bring that role out in group processes when possible and try to make it useful. You might be wondering, like one of our seminar participants,

> *What about countries like Israel and Palestine where Hamas is not allowed to participate in any dialogue. You can't connect with them. How do you use deep democracy when there is a collective consciousness that says keep "evil" people out?*

This action of keeping others out means that "X" or "bad guys" don't belong. There are moments when that stance can be meaningful, but ignoring people or the roles they play means that the *"u" will become the "X,"*—that is, the so called "good guys" will eventually become exactly what they hate—regardless of the country or issue. Recall phase 3 and explore one-sidedness to show how it eventually can be relieved temporarily by role switching and flow!

To reduce war, educate people about phases. Phase 3, for example, can be taught in kindergarten if teachers modeled working with conflict on the playground. Create role-play games between shy kids and bullies. Educational systems could greatly increase our phase awareness. I focus on this important topic in Part IX: Education for New Governments.

Remember what I said above: Unconsciousness around social rank creates monsters. For example, Hitler did not arise all by himself. After the Treaty of Versailles ended World War I and humiliated Germany, the German people felt oppressed, and that oppression contributed to Hitler's easy entrenchment as their *Führer*, which simply means leader or guide in German. We the world create the monsters; they do not simply arise under their own steam. The following example illustrates how you might use phase awareness in facilitating the dialogue process in Israel. It is not easy, but the underlying principle is to relate to where people are.

G: Let's say I am talking to somebody from the Israeli government, and I say to them, "Why, instead of just waiting for the next bombing and rockets with Hamas, why not open a dialogue and invite the bad guys in? It could be helpful." And let's say the other side responds, "We don't talk to terrorists, we won't talk to terrorists." How could you change that closed-mindedness?"

Arny: I would say, "I like your closed phase 2 attitude to take a stand against terrorism." What would he say then?

G: "Yes! We won't talk to terrorists, that is absolutely right!"

Arny: "I am right on your side. If you talk too much to terrorists, who knows, you could be killed soon!"

G: "Yes, they are people who are cruel, they have no humanity, they want to kill us, and we will not talk to them. We only want to find a way to slowly destroy them."

Arny: "I totally understand your reaction. I am like you at least half the time."

G: "Really?"

Arny: You are smiling . . . you see. If, to begin with, you relate to people where people are at—if, for example, they are in phase 2, then stay in phase 2. Have a phase 4 view that all phases are natural, and don't fight against them, you and they will begin to smile. Gain confidence by "eldering," by following the moment and the phase, not your map of the future. Then change happens more easily.

In this example, I waited for a smile from those government people. Then I would say, "Let's have lunch, let's get to know one another." Let's relate . . . one drop at a time.

A key metaskill is knowing that you are, or have been at one time or another, just like the attitude or behavior that you are against. I have done a lot of harsh stuff too against others. Many of us have been there. Eldering all sides is helpful when you are ready. This means, recalling your deepest phase 4 experience, your center, to help everyone, activists and all sides.

Push your phase 2 reactions, then let go and let nature show you the way with the other side. I can say all this, but I cannot do it all the time. Only your body and its connection to the infinite can teach that. Therefore, check in with your "teacher," your own inner work about helping a group or organization with its tasks.

Exercise: Phase Awareness Inner Work

To prepare for facilitating a group, use this inner work to check your observations and ability to flow with the phases.

Make notes, if you can, after each question. Think of a group you belong to or another group with which you sometimes have problems.

Phase 1: How do you feel you are doing in supporting a group's identity and vision in phase 1? Can you support people to find their basic identity, the me-me-me?

Phase 2: Are you able to notice, support, and appreciate the diversity in the group while you and they are in tension? Which tensions would you like to learn more about? Can you support the dialogue between the parts and help people communicate?

Phase 3: How are you doing in phase 3? Are you noticing and following your own and others' double signals? Roles and ghost roles? Can you express roles publically? Are you able to notice rank and help yourself and others become conscious of it? Can you model and bring out each role? How are you doing with flowing back and forth, deepening each role and modeling that? Can you switch roles with the bad guys?

Phase 4: Do you notice when you get tired or down or even depressed, perhaps not even wanting to live? Do you notice the need for detachment? Do you notice when you want to drop out and then actually go to another level to get information? Go deeper now to let the universe move you. What does the universe tell you about your current learning or what you still need to learn? Make a note about your next steps in learning and the time and space in which to do more of that.

Demonstration: Large Group Open Forum

The following example illustrates the possibilities of this work in the context of a large group forum in one of our seminars.

The participants from many countries and regions of the world brought forward a list of topics that they wanted to work on, and then, to save time in the seminar, we spun a pen to choose which topic to focus on. Large group process generally takes more time in the beginning to listen to the different issues and asking participants where they want to go. However, for our teaching purposes, we used the "black box" method to choose the topic. The following topics came from the people at the seminar:

- Mining oil and ruining the environment.
- Police violence against unarmed black men in the U.S.
- Race relations and the dominant power structures.
- "Men's Issues."
- Thousands of people have no water in Flint, Michigan!
- Materialistic medical attitudes towards the suppression of symptoms.
- Conflict in the Ukraine.
- Looks-ism: The concept of beauty and how it impacts men and women.

We spun a pen and it chose "Men's Issues." I'll call the person who led the group, the "Facilitator." He began by sharing his thoughts on the topic.

Facilitator: OK, I would like to focus on the men issues. This topic is also about healing the earth in that somebody else mentioned a hyper-rationalism that often comes with masculinity, and that hyper-rationalism often overlooks the harm it does to the earth.

Arny: Some men are hyper-rational, and neglect others and the earth!

Facilitator: It is complex. I am standing up here, a man, and I have all those parts in myself and I am nervous.

Arny: That sounds realistic because there are female voices and racial diversity issues out there that can be irritated with you, with us males, and we will have to bring them out and try to communicate with them and with other issues as well, if possible.

Before the group began the open forum, we guided participants through the following inner work to help them prepare to focus on the theme of masculinity. Then we used the second part of the exercise to guide the group process. You may want to use these instructions in a group to work on a social issue that is important to you.

Facilitator-Led World Theatre

I. Infinity World Theatre
Discuss the world problem and the worst "X" figure/energy and the "u" energy.

II. Inner work for everyone in the World Theatre (led by the facilitator)

1. Who are you? What is your "u" in relation to this world problem? Make a note.
2. What is the most difficult figure "X" for you in this world problem? Make a note.
3. Imagine talking with "X." Dialogue and see if you notice your own rank.
4. Try to see "X" as part of "u." That is, feel "X's" energy and deepen your experience of it. Then begin to role-play and flow between u + X as if in an open forum.
5. Now, relax and let the universe move you spontaneously and find the u + X energies in your dance. Catch insights about dealing with the "X" energy/figure. Make a note. Then tell yourself a little story: For example, *"Once there was a u + X conflict. The people in conflict found the universe's black box solution and this is what happened. . . ."* Make notes about your story, and then we can begin group work.

III. Group Work (led by the facilitator). Call everyone together in the open forum and introduce the chosen topic and the u + X roles.

1. Have someone speak for the "u" energy and another person speak for the "X" energy (3 minutes each).
2. Facilitator, now communi-flow: that is, support the u + X, follow the double signals, roles, ghost roles, role switching, hot spots, etc. (Try to follow and see others nonlocally as yourself.) Notice if phase 4 arises and use your experience of the black box.
3. If time, Facilitator, make a summary/review.

Amy: First, perhaps you want to set up a couple of roles and ask people to dialogue.
Facilitator: Men, white men especially from Western cultures are split between violent power and flowing in communication with others.
Arny: Don't forget that a ghost role for a white men's group is often race and color unconsciousness.

The forum evolved from this beginning, bringing forward marginalized positions speaking up vehemently for protection against mainstream white male rank unconsciousness. The African American community asked for less marginalization. Near the end, after anger and agony, people in the center went deeper and said, "Minorities need protection and oppressors need more consciousness." Others came in and hugged one another, feeling the need to watch out and care for one another.

This forum went to a deep level. White men, all whites, need to change and wake up to their social rank, perhaps even before they work on their own internal issues. We learned that speaking only about one gender without mentioning race inadvertently marginalizes other gender orientations and races. We should remember a woman who spoke at the end saying, "All people have equal human value, but some have less mainstream rank. They need protection against mainstream and police unconsciousness."

Seminar participants shared the following comments and questions after the open forum.

L: Waking up to social rank means being an ally of those who have less mainstream rank. You are in a grocery store and you notice that the checker does not see the black person, may be looking right through that person. Say, "Hey! That black person was here first!" This is a white person's problem and we all need to fix it!

T: Thanks for bringing us back to phase 2, taking a stand, being an ally. But as an African American, I can say that this is not only a white problem, it is a human problem. We have got to start seeing black folk as "hope." We are humans, no matter of position, gender, or color.

Arny: T. is bringing a needed phase 4 view to us of detachment that sees everyone as part of this process. Thanks, T., you modeled that detached phase 4 metaskill. We need phase 4 eldership and phase 2 diversity awareness and consciousness. Thanks to all in the middle who brought diversity consciousness into the foreground.

And don't forget at the end when W. gave us all a clear phase 2 comment: "Minorities need protection." Remember to step in and protect those with less rank. Recall in phase 3 the potential dialogue between the u + X, and phase 4's potential for new and unpredicted solutions for all people.

Arny: Dear Facilitator in training, how are you doing? What are you learning?

Facilitator: I am learning a lot. Thank you for bringing rank awareness in here; I need more diversity awareness. I should chat more with activists, and when I am in my country, I will try to honor the indigenous people and all others in that country.

Arny: Wonderful. A facilitator who wants to be a learner is a great facilitator, even if the momentary process did not appear with the ideal of peace for all that occurs in phase 4.

We began this forum focusing on white men's groups, heard about marginalized groups, about women, the Asian community, homophobia, and African American community issues. Remember, you *cannot work on one subject such as men's issues* without *mentioning all the other related subjects such as sexual orientation, race, culture, etc.* Neglecting related topics inadvertently creates phase 2 tensions. Showing awareness of marginalized topics, even suggesting more time for them in the future, can lead to less conflict and more community.

Things to Remember from Chapter 3

1. Reduce conflict and war through awareness of diversity, marginalization, and rank.
2. Notice suicidal tendencies in potential heroes or leaders, and help them to reach their goals more safely.
3. Facilitate and be a learner at the same time. Your learning is always nonlocal—that is, it belongs to everyone (or at least to many people).
4. Every forum is a chance for great learning. For spontaneous, creative solutions, recall your own phase 4 "black box."

PART II

Your Body Phases

• • •

Now we turn our attention from outer conflict in groups and relationships to our bodies. I show how phase awareness can assist you in working with difficult body symptoms, and how working with our bodily experience is an essential second training preparation for working with outer conflict.

CHAPTER 4

Process Phases in Body Work

• • •

Your ability to do worldwork with small or large organizations depends partly on your state of mind and your awareness of your own body feelings and relationship skills. Your outer work depends partly on your own inner awareness and fluidity. That is why in this section of the book, I focus on conflicts within yourself. We shall be using your own body awareness, meditation, and relationship awareness to further prepare for worldwork. We return to worldwork again in Part IV when we focus on finding and using your "deepest art" to facilitate world challenges.

In the following three chapters, I introduce the application of phase understanding to working with our own troubling body experiences. I explain how bodywork can and should be seen as an aspect of worldwork. I offer a process-oriented model that views body problems as part of a broader personal and world challenge to embrace the diversity within and between us.

This approach can be seen as a challenge to conventional ideas of the body as a mechanical object; it is, indeed, an invitation to include all levels of our embodied experience, not just that of consensus reality. We often forget that our bodies are processes, with phases. I share practical techniques to help you engage with body symptoms in each of the four phases. This inner work is essential preparation for any outer work in the world, particularly the facilitation of conflicts.

My basic theme here is that problems cannot be solved sustainably only in the outside world. Why? Conflict work depends, in great part, upon everyone's ability to resolve conflict within themselves, at least temporarily.

Otherwise, we eventually act out our inner tensions with others in the world. For example, you can give everyone equal voting rights, but without worldwork, ongoing deep democracy open forums, and inner work, conflicts about "equal rights" will arise again and again.

Until now in this book, we have been using body awareness in the form of following your relaxed movement awareness for the benefit of group and worldwork. Body experience can give us the sense of "a field" around us, which sometimes can be used for phase 4 detachment and insight into outer circumstances.

The inner work and body work I suggest here are forms of inner "group processes" between your different parts; between the "u," or your everyday normal energy, and the "X," the symptom that bothers you.

In many ways, body work is an internalized form of worldwork.

In many ways the troubling energy of a body symptom represents a hurtful "X" energy and is an internal form of a diversity issue asking for greater consciousness. With recognition, that irritating symptom often becomes a more conscious aspect of your own internal diversity issues. Knowing this often relieves the symptom itself!

To work best with symptoms, recall process phases. As we have been exploring in the first three chapters, life is an ongoing process with different phases. I have been calling them phase 1, phase 2, phase 3, and phase 4 (or infinity). This approach may seem obvious, but it is not obvious to those consensual attitudes most of us use to deal with our bodies. We often think of our bodies as Newtonian objects. If the body does not function correctly on a given day, give it a push, pull, or fix and repair it! We often forget that our bodies, like the whole of us, are *processes* with many different feelings and different states of flowing consciousness.

The success of medical and bodywork methods depends on the phase we are in. If we view ourselves as Newtonian objects—as psychiatric or medical patients—then the symptom determines the medicine. This approach may be helpful, but the person or personality and her or his phases are often neglected.

Let us look at how the phases can be identified in the doctor–client relationship.

> *Clients in phase 1.* For example, if you are a doctor or therapist in phase 2, you see body symptoms as something you must fight. "Let's heal them." However, the patient or client may be in phase 1 and is just hoping to be listened to. To help that patient or client the most, listen and learn about her or his phase 1 "me, me, me!" Then it may be easier to switch phases.

> *Clients in phase 2.* If, on the other hand, you are in a detached phase 4, and your client is in phase 2, asking you to "fight it and heal it," then your detachment may be good for you, but not for the client. The client wants to be "healed." Understand and address the client's *current* phase as best you can.

If somebody fears they are in an emergency, even if you know it is *not* an emergency, respect the client's phase 2 fears and be concerned about helping. Otherwise, that client must go to another doctor or therapist to feel heard!

Example of stomach trouble. This reminds me of a particular client who had a stomach ulcer and had just eaten something that was too spicy for that ulcer. He was in a terrible condition and went to his doctor, who is a very nice person. The doctor may have been in phase 4 and was very detached. He simply smiled, gave the man some medicine, and said, "This will solve the problem." But the person felt the doctor did not listen to him. Yes, the medicine worked in about 7 days, but those 7 days were full of hatred towards the doctor. That doctor did not empathize with the patient's fear. Address the fear, the phase, the other is in.

The important point is to relate to the person in the phase she or he is in; then more communication and "healing" can occur. Follow the client's signals *and phases.*

Phases and Body Experience

Let's now apply phases to body experience and bodywork. I describe in more detail some of the characteristic signals of each phase and how to work with them, and also explore how the phases relate and flow into each other.

Just to clarify, when I talk about body symptoms, I am also referring to emotional symptoms. Phobias, anxieties, depression, and extreme states of all sorts and other problems are often considered by mainstream medicine as mainly biological. For example, depression and the feeling "I want to die" are essentially phase 2 signals, and people are given medicine to get out of that phase. But, wanting to die may be an inadvertent attempt to "let go" and be moved as in phase 4.

Phase 1: Me, Me, Me

If people are in phase 1, they enjoy expressing themselves. Better not talk about phase 2 troubles yet!

Phase 1 can look like picture #5 on page 20.

You can imagine lots of noise too . . . "Waaaah!" "Grrrrr!" Imagine a mother saying, "Be nice to your grandmother!" And the kid says, "Waaaahhh!!!" Implying, "I am basically a mouth and eyes, and I won't relate!"

A person in phase 1 is not necessarily a young child, but *anyone* in phase 1 needs to be heard and cannot relate well to others in that phase. Phase 1, as I have said before, is "me, me, me!" Most kids are in phase 1 until the age of 3.

Adults in phase 1 give you the impression that they hope you are simply a pair of ears interested in what they have to say. Of course, you can try to say, "I would like to put in a word, can I say something too?" But their signals are often, "No, just let me talk!"

In phase 1, the child or adult is not relating to you or anything else except her or his own experience. Here the "u" prefers, if possible, to marginalize any and all "X" symptoms and problems.

Phase 2: Fighting and Healing

Then in phase 2, the "u" of children and adults is aware of a disturbing "X" energy. In phase 2, "X" appears painful or troubling. An adult may say, "Oh, I have a problem, I can't stand it." A child might say, "Oh! I hate my sister or brother!" or "I am so tired or in pain."

Years ago I mentioned in a lecture that my daughter, who at that time was 3½ going on 4, announced happily and firmly one day, "I am me, I am not Robin!" (her brother). She was growing out of phase 1 and entering phase 2, where she was discovering diversity. In phase 2, I am me and not him! He was sometimes an "X" for her.

Bodywork in phase 2 appears in this tone: "What is that discomfort in my tummy? In my head! Oh my god, this 'X' does not belong to me and should not be there! It is an *'X'* energy—bad!!!" Most people wanting help with body problems are in phase 2: "I don't want this 'X'—get rid of it! I am the point, *ME*! Not 'X'! HEAL me and get rid of IT!!"

Phase 2 involves an internal diversity issue: "I want to be me and I *don't* want to integrate any damn physiological or psychological stuff! I want a doctor who can help me fight that damn 'X.'" In phase 2 we hope to get rid of everything that bothers us. As a therapist for a client in phase 2, you had better join the person in that battle, that fight, that expression, and help the person realize eventually—not too quickly—that she or he is suffering from a diversity issue that is being called a symptom.

The diversity problem is due to "u" marginalizing an "X." In phase 2, "X" appears in a symptom, and the "u" hates it. In phase 2, people imply, "Kill that symptom—that 'X' does not belong in my world! I don't like 'X' or people who remind me of that pain!!"

Healing is for phase 2. Say, you have a symptom. You might want to try this new vibration, take this pill, use a supplement, take regular or alternative medicine to fight the symptom, the "X." If I have the flu, I might take an antibiotic in the hopes of killing that "X" experienced as the flu.

Medicines and drugs can help a lot—at least, temporarily—by relieving phase 2 and helping you get back to phase 4, to a no u + X conflict experience. Bodywork and all psychological and medical methods and medicine work best when they relate to the person's particular phase. But don't forget that "X" part of the symptom; it may be a part of the person, perhaps a dream figure, that may want to be integrated into her or his daily life.

Someone asked,

> *What about body symptoms such as an ugly rash that lives on the face but has no feeling or energy movement. The person wants to hide it but can't. Would you approach this symptom as containing something hidden and something that wants to be seen?*

This example describes a *visual experience of "X" in* phase 2. "X" is that *"UGLY RASH!" Visual* means that from one viewpoint, that rash *"looks"* bad! To work on that, explore how the "X" rash can make a face red and get into the emotions behind the face. In phase 2, one part of you is judging the rash as "ugly." The "u" HATES IT—hide it with makeup! Yet, within that "X" could be a lot of power, such as red hot force!

Phase 3: Dreambody Awareness

In phase 3 body experiences, a more fluid and dreamlike role play becomes possible, and with that possibility, the dreambody can appear. In phase 3 worldwork, you will recall that there is the possibility of an open forum and switching roles. In body awareness work, you realize that you want your "X" energy to speak, so you have a chance of rolling between the "X" and "u" sides to express all sides. Then you might be able to see how that "X" appears in dreams.

Dreambody awareness is a phase 3 consciousness. It is the experience that the body symptom's "X" energy can be seen as an aspect of your dreams and relationship problems. This dreambody is an *evidence-based idea.* If you have a symptom, you can always see it in the energy of a dream image or in the projection onto someone in an outer situation. If it is a chronic symptom, it can almost always be seen in an early childhood dream. So dreambody thinking understands the "X" as a dream image and as a body energy that needs to be experienced and integrated into life as a whole. Dreambody work is mainly phase 3.

We are all in phase 2 sometimes: "What is this thing bothering me? That is *not me*; *I don't want that 'X.'* Heal it!!" But in phase 3, the dreaming body experience can arise by asking if that troublesome "X" energy is part of you, if it is a body experience that you may need! Is there a nighttime dream that reflects that body "X" experience? Perhaps you can talk to that "X." Perhaps you can use and act out that "X" energy.

Phase 4: Compassion and Flow

Phase 4 often occurs spontaneously after you have picked up the phase 3 dreaming part of your symptom. Phase 4 is characterized by flowing or being moved. This phase 4 experience opens up your "empty Zen mind," your creative mind, or your processmind. There are many names for this open state; it is the Tao that can't be said, a spirit or a goddess, a field power, your love, and so on.

In phase 4, the universe moves you, and you begin to flow with the energies inside and outside that were bothering you. You flow seamlessly between all energies without even trying. You are, for the time being, able to see how all the various energies relate and are even needed.

One of our participants commented that she understood phase 4 as "detachment from being angry and sick of things. This phase includes going into essence level, or else you get fatigued by conflict!" In phase 4, you are no longer sick of anything—you just flow with it and everything else. Phase 4 is detached-healing-flowing well-being.

Another participant observed, "Phase 1 can be such an exhausting experience for the doctor! Some people go on and on and on and on about nothing. You want to help them but they talk so much!" Understanding the phases means that you notice that the person will complain, but then never ask for help because she or he just wants to be heard—whereas you are in phase 2 and want to battle with the symptom!

So you have to say, "I am in phase 2 with your symptoms. I would love to help you by trying this and this against that 'X.'" But if the feedback is, "I want to keep talking!" follow the person if possible. Perhaps you are wondering how long can someone stay in phase 1? That depends upon both of you. Sometimes 10 years. If you can't stand the person, perhaps another therapist can help.

Processwork appreciates people who have never had a chance to feel heard. Listening in phase 1 can be absolutely healing in its own way. We have all been there at one time or another, and we come back to it again and again—not just to phase 1, but to all process phases.

Privileged classes are often in phase 1 in public situations. White people in the United States are often unconscious of their rank and unaware of being in phase 1, not wanting to hear about others' problems. In a way, the whites when rank unconscious are unaware of their privileges. Then others must say, "Woof!" to create conflict and momentary diversity awakening. I say a *momentary* awakening because, that *woof* usually has to happen again and again before people realize there are "u's" and "X's" that need an open forum and inner work!!

Hand-holding in phase 1. All this reminds me of a woman I worked with many years ago. We had worked together for four or five years, and she was really happy about that work. I thought I had done a most brilliant job, working mainly as a Jungian at that time. I helped her work out many problems. She even had some enlightenment-like experiences, and now she was going back to the city of her childhood.

I naturally asked her if she had a going-away dream. She said, "Yes, in my dream you were holding my hand." I said, "Is that all??" And she said, "I like you," and "that hand-holding was the most important and the only thing I needed. You listened to me and befriended me."

I had been in phase 2 with her, trying to figure everything out, and thought she would have praised my ability at dreamwork. But no, she was closer to phase 4 and phase 1, just wanting friendship. So she taught me about the importance of phase 1. She needed to be listened to and cared for. She was nice to me, we had a great connection, but the important thing for her was *hand-holding.* I am touched when I think about her now.

As normal beginning therapists, we often follow the methods and maps we learned. Most of our teachers did not follow phases, so today, we need to learn to follow process and notice what phase everyone is in.

Phase 4 is an empty-mind experience often preceded by fears about death. People close to death often go through phase 4. In everyday life, fearing death can be a problem from the phase 2 viewpoint, but from a phase 4 perspective, it can be "lucky" in at least one way. If you get nervous about health issues or impending death, "die right away," so to speak; that is phase 4. Don't waste the death idea until you are old and dying. When experiencing phase 4, always be aware of dangers and be careful when you are moving, not to hurt yourself.

As some of you know, when Amy and I were coming to the U.S. together on an airplane about 27 years ago, I realized I was going to be 50 years old! OH! I was getting old!! I said, "Oh dear, one day I am going to die." Fifty was a big age for me. Then, I remember "dying" in the sense of just relaxing. So beginning in a way, in 1990, I *retired*. Of course, that is not quite true, as it is now 2017. I do not succeed at phase 4 and the idea of letting go and retiring all the time, but at least some of the time, I find phase 4.

When working with people who are struggling with aging, it can be important to clarify if they are troubled by specific symptoms of aging—for example, arthritis—or if they are disturbed by aging and death in this moment. If it is the symptom experience and they are in phase 2 or 3, you might work with the aging "X" energy experience of arthritis. If aging and dying are emphasized, consider going into phase 4 movement.

In phase 4, life and death may not exist! This phase, like the others, is a fluid process. The concepts of life and death belong to phase 2. So if you fear death, take your vitamins, stay alive, but in phase 4, you were not born or may not simply die; here a change occurs so that you can identify with your ongoing process, whatever that will be. (In image 13 you see a "warrior" or shaman transforming into a Jaguar.)

From the realistic viewpoint of phase 2, this phase 4 attitude seems like a spiritual thing, and so it is normal to doubt it. Phase 2 is important

***13.* Nagual (or shaman) transforming into a jaguar.** Wikipedia

too. Yet in phase 4, people who are actually dying often dream of doing new things. Perhaps this process-oriented, non-death idea also appears in the customs of many cultures to name children after their grandparents?

Phase 4 makes me consider that perhaps something goes on after "death." People have always sensed some weird "process" that does not die. My point is to affirm all the phases and their processes.

Phase 4 is also compassionate with all the other phases. From this phase 4 viewpoint, everything is a temporary phase. It is normal to be in phase 1, and it's OK now in the phase 2 stance, "Let's fight that symptom." In phase 3, how about being the symptom? Then in phase 4, let's explore infinity and just be moved. Phase 4 accepts the return to other phases, and does not criticize you for going back to your original diversity issues all over again.

In phase 3 and phase 4, your "u" opens up to "X," and in that opening moment, shamanism becomes possible. Why? When you start to move freely in the world, you are on the verge of shamanizing. Like Don Juan and Castaneda said, "A warrior can no longer make the world chronological, there is no yesterday or tomorrow."[26] Instead there is a timeless letting go of identity.

In phase 4, you enter into a shamanistic, timeless, quantum-like world where the possibility of doing shamanistic things occurs, perhaps even changing genetic predispositions. I have never seen statistical proof of this particular ability, but have experienced "healings" that indicate such a possibility.

SUMMARY

Now let's briefly review the phases in bodywork, before I illustrate with an example of doing bodywork with phase awareness.

Phase 1 is amazing. You can tell a young child she might die, and she shrugs her shoulders. There is only the now, and rolling along in it. No problems!

Phase 2 is about diversity issues, about the "X" disturbance that is *not* "u." Internal diversity issues often manifest as symptoms. Remember, working on outer diversity issues is an internal as well as an external process.

Phase 3 is about dreaming and role playing. Dreambody work in phase 3 may initially involve showing clients how *you* might pick up *their* "X" energy. Do it for them first, and even if you do it incorrectly, that's OK because *they* will correct you. Their acting out the "X" energy and doing the role play is the point.

Phase 4 occurs when you are moved by something infinite. When you are moved in this way, you can notice the u + X energies in your spontaneous movements and your parts begin to flow. In phase 4 the experience of "X" and "u" occurs as part of a fluid process that is no longer broken up into individual u + X parts. *As with worldwork, phase 4 in bodywork can help to resolve the u + X conflict by revealing the diversity involved as well as the potential unity of u + X.*

Now I illustrate this phase-oriented bodywork with an example from one of my classes, working with someone on her chronic experience of shoulder pain.

Demonstration: Work in the Middle with Shoulder Pain

H: My symptom is an old one, a shoulder tension that becomes a headache when it is really bad. It does not become a headache so much anymore, but most recently it became a cold, and that is very alien to me. I don't like it and I want to get rid of it.

Arny: Yes! Let's get rid of it. Conflict with that "X," with coldness in phase 2!

H: Yes, it is hard and solid and cold in there.

Arny: Can you show me? (H demonstrates by pressing "hard" on Arny's body.) *That feels good to me. I can feel your energy and strength. So this coldness thing becomes a headache?*

H: Yes, it can become a headache, it goes up to my head (demonstrates).

Arny: Let me check on the consensus reality of body things. Do you sometimes exercise?

H: Swimming, but it does not help, it just stays. I had it worked on by a Chinese herbalist, and putting heat into it helped, but it comes back again.

Arny: Have you done pushups? Do they help? No? Just checking out phase 2 approaches. Any other cramps in your legs or your tummy?

H: No, but I have another symptom in my foot that is not related. It's a pinched nerve, it is similar to this (makes a pinching movement).

Arny: OK, so what phase would you say you were in these days—phase 1, being like a creative baby; phase 2, nervous about your body and fighting it; phase 3, picking up its energy; or phase 4, more in a spiritual and blissed out mood?

H: Phase 2, fighting it, worrying about it!!

Arny: So let's go to phase 2. Let's start with that strong "X" grip you gave me—go ahead and use that grip on me again.

H: (Grabs Arny's back.)

Arny: I have to feel your symptom to help you with it. Can you put that "X" energy on me even more?

H: (clenching fists and making a twisted face) *It's horrible! I want to be relaxed . . . friendly, loving.*

Arny: Can you make a diagram, an energy sketch, of that relaxed, friendly "u"?

H: (Draws a wavy spiral ~~~~~.)

Arny: And now would you make an energy sketch of the "X"?

H: (Draws a tight zigzag. \/\/\/\/\ )

Arny: Now, before we go further, can you just tell me your first memory or childhood dream that comes up now?

H: It is my first memory. When I was three years old. I was in Athens. In my dream, I was in the central public square, and there was a machine there that creates paintings by squirting out colorful paint. If you go to that square, you can pay money so the machine squirts out colors, like red and green. As a child, my family bought one of these paintings and took it home and had it for years. The machine was square and grey and wow, suddenly out comes this color. (H makes strong zigzag movement outwards with her hands.)

Arny: I saw some of your "X" energy in that (imitating her movement, showing her strong zigzag movements).

H: (Giggles.)

Arny: Good, your giggling is a kind of positive feedback. Why do you giggle?

H: Because I see the machine pulling in and the painting coming out, yet . . . I am never going to be that wild in my life, for sure! No, phase 2 is dangerous . . . it is just so "out there" and bold! (smiles).

Arny: It is out there and bold in the public square, squirting color! OK, it is not your normal "u" identity, but that is OK, your "X" creates a diversity issue.

H: Yes, I would like to be more open to that.

Arny: OK. Would you do that powerful movement again and see what that "X" really wants? Let's pretend that "X" energy has a deep desire, we don't know about what.

H: (Makes the "X" movements again with fists squeezing inward.)

Arny: OK, let's explore phase 3 where the "u" can switch roles and be the "X" to see what the "X" wants.

H: "X" is crushing, squeezing . . . getting to the bottom of things, getting into the (squeezing fists more tightly) *. . . getting right to the bottom of things, to the essence of things. Oh! I like that! It relaxes me.*

Arny: OK, phase 2 squeezing got us to phase 3, so now let's explore phase 4, the essence. Try to relax your neck, your hips . . . and be moved.

H: (Goes into a movement, a flowing dance, into space–time dreaming.)

Arny: While you are moving, do you notice a bit of your "X" energy in there?

H: Yes, I can feel that force in my spine . . . and feet (laughs).

Arny: It makes you happy, good, so . . . let's create a story: Once upon a time there was a little girl, and the story goes that she was in the central square, and let's see what happens with the story now as you are moving around.

H: (moving more) *Aha! The little girl SHOWS the picture! "Look at this picture!" I didn't do it, "It" did it! Look what the power in me can do! See what "It" can do!*

Arny: And the people in the square looked around (group applauds) *and a little boy came along and said, "What can you do?"*

H: We can all be bright out there! Look what we can do!

Arny: And the people of Greece said, "Wow, we need somebody like you to lead the country! We need the center of the square filled with a woman like that!"

H: Yes, I am working on coming out, on developing things in the world. It is like I am . . . Wow! Out there! Wow! Thanks, Arny!

Arny: Thank you! We are all so lucky you have this "central square" power.

Chronic symptoms can be amazing because they are trying to bring out a "mythic power" from your childhood dream pattern so it can evolve and organize your life. Other participants who practiced this exercise brought out many insights and stories, including,

> *"I became less of a victim."*
> *"I started looking for a community instead of being all alone."*

To try this approach for yourself and practice phase awareness, use the following inner work exercise to explore the connection between a troubling symptom and your childhood dream.

Exercise: Process Phase Awareness + Your Childhood Dream

1. How do "u" identify yourself today and what "X" symptom energy did or does concern you? Feel and sketch u and X's main energies.
2. Feel and note your process phase (phase 1, enjoying life; phase 2, fear and/or need to heal "X"; phase 3, flowing between u and X; phase 4, infinity—just being danced by universe + flowing).
3. Explore phase 2. Is there simple medical help for "X"? If yes, try it. But now, see-imagine-feel the energy of that symptom "X" and express it with "its" sound, movement, and feeling, involving your entire body (toes, head, muscles, face). What does this energy express?
4. Explore phase 3. Now go back and forth between "u" and "X." Insights? Make notes.
5. Recall a first memory or childhood dream. Is the symptom energy "X" there? Now dance phase 4 and, when ready, create a *NEW* dream/memory/story (e.g., "*Once there was a 'u' who dreamed about u + X. This 'u' changed and discovered how u + X can flow, and sometimes 'u' detached and flowed with u + X. . .and did not-doing*"). Make notes.

Things to Remember from Chapter 4

1. Groups of people as well as individuals go through phases.
2. Knowing phases is as important in (dream)bodywork as it is in group work.
3. Typical body phases are phase 1, enjoy life, no problems; phase 2, conflicts between the everyday "u" energy and an "X" body symptom energy; phase 3, dreaming into the "X" and "u"; phase 4, shamanism—creating and re-creating dreams and stories through movement and imagination to possibly reveal next steps in life.
4. Remember, life itself is a process that goes through phases. A phase 4 view of life sees phase 2 conflict as a natural tendency.
5. Phase 2 problems often return in part because, from a phase 4 view, we need more awareness of our inner u + X diversity as well as how u + X appear in the world.

CHAPTER 5

How Symptoms Can Help Relationships

• • •

Body work and relationship work overlap because you cannot *just have a body problem or be upset about an "X" inside your body without also being upset with a real person with that "X" energy in your outer relationships.* In a way, your body is not just yours!

This chapter goes further into phases 3 and 4 and their connection to quantum nonlocality, shamanism, and "not-doing." We explore how your bodily experience is a nonlocal phenomenon that can lead you into altered states of consciousness that bring new insights for relationships and your life. In this chapter's demonstration, we follow a woman as she unfolds her symptoms of vertigo into a fluid, spontaneous dance that challenges ageism and connects her to her deepest self.

Interconnectedness (or nonlocality) is basic to shamanism, and I bring that perspective into symptom work as well. Altered states of consciousness can give you insights not only into your body but also beyond your body and might help you with life as a whole.

> Arny comes into class and hears music on someone's cell phone speaker, then addresses the class,
>
> *"You have to be careful because what you thought was secret, isn't any more. If that phone is on, aspects of your private or inner life are public."*

Whatever you feel as a body symptom is *also connected nonlocally to the people and the system or community* of which you are a part. People worry about catching a cold; similarly, the energies and dreaming in symptoms can also be "caught" in the sense of shared diversity issues.

My message is: Process your so-called "own experiences" to help yourself and others. Diversity issues as well as healing can be "contagious." You needn't talk about all your symptoms, but when possible, talking about your u + X symptoms may be a nonlocal occurrence . . . like the music that was coming from someone's iPhone.

About thirty years ago, Amy and I discovered a shaman-based community near Mombasa, Kenya. The members taught us about nonlocal shared altered healing states. They worked with us, and after that teaching was complete several minutes later, those wonderful shamans turned to work with about ten or fifteen other people who were standing around the ceremony that we thought was focused only on us! They continued singing, drawing things out of everyone's body, and throwing that stuff away into the universe, etc.

At first I thought, how can they focus on "my" or Amy's problem(s) and then immediately use their altered state to work with others? It would be like having surgery, then inviting in all your friends to get surgery as well! Initially, I thought, *huh*? Now I understand their ancient practice a little better and I love it. Their work was about "not-doing."

Not-doing awareness tells me to notice that I am *doing* this lecture, but . . . I can also *not-do* it. If I close my eyes and go inside, I can feel this *not-doing* immediately. Both doing and not-doing are fine, but not-doing is easier on your body. "Do" things, and then when you start getting tired or strained, realize that phase 2 is present and you are struggling against time or something else. That means it's time to get to the essence of all phases, phase 4, the processmind. Perhaps it can do more effortlessly what you are trying to do with effort.

In the last chapter I talked about how important it is to notice body phases. Recall phase 1, *me, me me*: People need to be listened to in this phase. The guidance for this phase is, "Listen first and try to empathize." Such empathy is what people are looking for when they go to "support groups" with other people suffering from the same illness/problem/issue. They need connection—phase 1—and hope to be related to and supported.

Phase 2 arrives with the feeling, "I've got a problem, and I want to resolve it!" Now it's time to apply the symptom work you have learned. Fight it, repress it, meditate on it, give medicine or alternative medicine for it, etc. Fight the "X" energy. As a therapist, if you know what to do, good. If you know about medicine, good. Or send the client to someone who knows more than you about fighting the symptom; the client will trust you more for it.

For example, a woman came to see me years ago with lupus. She said to me, "Nobody can help me with this difficult autoimmune disease. What are you going to do?" I answered, "Shall we find out the meaning of it?" She said, "No!" I responded, "But that is what I am here for." And she replied, "I will have to leave." Then I awakened and said, "OK, I will tell you what to do!" and got a big smile from her. I said, "Try not going in the sun for two months, stay out of the sunshine, don't go outdoors unless you must." After two months she got better. From working with people in the Alps, I knew that sunshine can trigger lupus. However, I cannot say for sure if what I said and did "healed" that problem or simply collaborated with her need for definitiveness in phase 2. My point is simply that people feel best if you address the phase they are in then and there.

In phase 3, you often hear, "I have tried everything, but this problem still comes and goes!" In the third phase, it may be time for supporting the everyday "u" *and* the "X" energy of the problem that comes and goes. As I have said, phase 3 is dreambody work, a way of integrating that "X" energy. Get into the energy of the symptom, let people express it with their hands, feet, and face, etc. Be sure to encourage the client to bring that energy into a facial expression, because doing so helps her or him become conscious of the "X" energy. Then let the "u" interact with that "X" experience.

Phase 4 is about mindful detachment. Although phase 4 is indeed a "phase," remember that it is also the center of all the phases. This deep, imageless movement and dreaming experience seems to come from the personal mind as well as the system mind or processmind, which organizes phases and the world around us.

METASKILLS AND PROCESS PHASES

With a process-oriented view of life, you become more fluid and have more empathy with what is happening. Let me show you what I mean.

> *Arny: Amy, how are you? What symptoms do you have?*
> *Amy: I have a problem—I often can't fall asleep.*
> *Arny: Oh no, oh no* (tone changes), *I know what that problem is like.*
> *Amy: You do? Oh!*

I can't explain empathy in words very well; it is like joining where she is at, *feeling with* her. Empathy is a metaskill; it opens up the phase and the space between people. One of our class participants shared the following example of using phase awareness to join with a client.

> *A: I have a client who has spent a lot of time in a session with me in phase 1, and before this class I was subtly fighting against that phase. But once I was able to really relate to where she was at, she did not need as much time in phase 1! I think really being with the person accelerated the moving on.*

Accepting a phase means that you are empathizing with the person and allowing the phase to roll along. In a way, people don't get stuck; rather you, as the helper, might get stuck in the way you are trying to help or push them.

In phase 2, objectivity and an orientation toward consensus reality (CR for short) are helpful. If someone says, "I've got a problem," or "I've got an addiction," or "I can't stop eating sugar," or "I have a pain in my stomach," you can be empathetic but in phase 2 you might also be "objective." Too much sugar is not good! Advise the person, "Put your foot down and say *stop*!" You might stamp your foot to show the energy that belongs in phase 2. Say, "If you have an addiction, the first step is try and stop it!" This is not yet the place for spirituality. No, means no. *Stop.*

The best metaskills in phase 2 involve objectivity and concreteness. Watch the feedback. If the client is not in phase 2 when you act like that, objectivity won't work.

Remember also that phase 2 does not last forever. If a client is eating or drinking something that is not good for her, and she has tried many different methods, including forcefully stopping, the moment for meaning and phase 3 may have arrived. Dreambody work in phase 3 becomes crucial; that is, finding the meaning of that "X," of the alcohol or other addictive substance. Access that state without the substance! You might help the client by playing out the "X" energy or helping her to do that—and don't forget to express "X" with your face! This is the time to explore the dreaming part of body problems. Also, in phase 3, tai chi can be helpful, as can Freud's "free association" method or Jung's "active imagination" or Fritz Perls' acting out technique. If none of these approaches help, return to phase 2 and say *STOP*! And go on!

Phase 4 is implied when people get tired, dizzy, or depressed, for then "letting go" may be trying to happen. After the age of about 10 to 15 years old, we are all afraid sometimes of being annihilated by a body problem. How many of you have felt that some symptom might be really bad news? Such a fear is really common. When someone fears he may die or get very sick, try to be reasonable, look for its meaning, but after all that, remember phase 4.

Say, "Let's let go; drop your everyday self and go deeper." This "spiritual" or detached dimension can bring great relief. It is behind many near-death fears and experiences as well as the spiritual ecstasy implied in many addictions. More connection with the universe is very helpful.

Shamanism is based mainly on phase 4. Here you sense that *life is not only your business.* The idea that your life is moved by something that you cannot describe, can be "big medicine." Here is where mindfulness, emptiness, quietness, space, silence, and movement are important. Here is where *not-doing, or what Don Juan called controlled abandon,* can happen. Some get here through tiredness or overwork, or more pleasantly, through *dreaming while awake.*

Quantum Nonlocality

Phases 3 and 4 are linked to what quantum physics calls *nonlocality.* My big point is that your body's double signals are found in your dreams, and often in your symptoms. So, these signals and symptoms are *yours,* and at the same time, they are characteristic of the system you are in.

To repeat an important point: You can't just have a body problem or be upset about an "X" inside your body without also being upset with a real person with that "X" energy outside in relationships. You will be upset with "X" as it turns up not only in others, but in your own double signals as well. Here is where body work and relationship work overlap.

Try this simple exercise to explore the connection between a troublesome body experience and your relationship challenges.

> Think of one of the energies in your body that bothers you right now. Raise your hand and let your hand make a motion expressing that "X" energy that bothers you. Now amplify that motion, making it twice as strongly . . . even more intensely . . . and now express that energy in your face!
>
> Are you shy about bringing this "X" energy into relationship? Expressing that "X" in relationship may be one of your personal contact edges and may also be an edge for those close to you. Your "X" energy is not just dreamlike, but perhaps a shared dream in the field around you.

Quantum Theory is weird. Remember, in quantum physics, weird things happen without classic analogies. We say that electrons "spin," but we can't see them spinning. We can only "feel" the spin in the field or world around us. Likewise, there is no exact definition of a particle in space and time; an elementary particle cannot be defined exactly as something only here and now. As soon as you look at it, the way you look at it changes it; you cannot hold onto it. This is a physical aspect of what we know in processwork, in psychology, and in shamanism. Just focusing on something without doing anything can change it.

You cannot be exactly defined for more than a moment. We are not only partly Newtonian "objects" with local receivers called *brains*. Our minds also seem to be nonlocal.

In 2000, when I wrote *Quantum Mind*, some physicists said, "How do you know for sure about some of these things, such as the quantum mind? That mind seems like a logical conclusion from your work, but it is weird!" Now times have changed a bit. One of the leading relativity experts in the world is exploring processwork with me. He wants me to edit his work on black holes and dark matter. Mainstream science changes slowly, in time.

I am interested in applying quantum thinking to our experiences of symptoms.

Remember that particles can be represented as little dots being moved about. The dust in your living room is full of particles of dust. Elementary particles can appear as small localized objects that have physical properties like volume and mass. But they also appear as wave-like vibrations!

The quantum waves of quantum physics are like phase 3. Tiny particles may seem localized when you look at them, but they can be described by a wave function and remain as vibrations or energies in the field at the same time. Particles have both wave-like and particle-like characteristics, depending on how we look at them.

We human beings seem like parts or particles that can be pushed around in phase 2, but in phase 3, we are not only parts (i.e., individual people) but also *waves*. Quantum physics tell us we have local and nonlocal interconnections with all the people and things we feel connected to, people we work with, people we know and like or dislike. If you are aware of this wave-like nonlocal field in and around you, you can switch between being "u" or being "X" to being the process relating them to each other. Thus, you can be in phase 3 and/or in phase 4.

When you fear annihilation, you may be near what Feynman called the annihilation point of an elementary particle in a field. You might notice phase 4 thoughts such as, "I don't know if I can live through this—I will die from this!" Here in principle, and in your feelings, you can drop out, *let go*, and go *backwards in time or forwards* in time, reemerging as you move and feel in new ways. Here we are in the world of quantum physics, shamanism, and psychology.

A class participant commented,

> *I had this huge conflict with a roommate, and it brought out a part of me I was not in touch with, saying, "Grrrr!, don't do that . . . over my dead body!" My primary process thought that I was going to die, because it was not open to that Grrr, the "X" in me. I really felt like I was going to die. Now I have more of a union between the "u" and "X!"*

In phase 4, instead of being annihilated, you might be moved to swing between your ordinary self and the annihilating energy. You can be nice *and* fierce.

Someone else asked,

> *"Are you saying that, when we are born and become a "u," "X" becomes split off and all these weird things begin? So "X" is like antimatter?"*

That is exactly what I mean: "X" is like the "anti-you," the part of yourself that you fear will annihilate you. "X" is the psychological analogy to antimatter in Feynman's sense; again, it is a part of you that can annihilate you.

My point is to show how nonlocality in physics can be experienced in psychology and medicine. If the discoverer of the wave equation, Erwin Schrödinger, lived today, I am almost certain he would say that all matter, including human beings, is both particles and waves. I guess he would say that the "wave-like" nature of the quantum world appears in the "hum" or the "buzz" we can feel around people, a buzz that is not located only with the individual, but can be felt at a distance as well. We are nonlocal beings, like all matter; we are "buzzes" and can sense this "buzz" in and around us. Sensing that buzz is like sensing the dreamlike nature of yourself or others, a "buzz" we sometimes experience or "project" upon ourselves and other people. In Chapter 7, I talk about how the dreamlike hum of yourself or another can give you a key to the process phase in which you or the other is in.

Your childhood dream or first memory hints at the timeless pattern or buzz moving you between "u" and "X." In your childhood dream or first memory, you usually identify with one part and reject (or are rejected by) the others. But in phase 3, you can switch roles with your "X." Changes in "u" will change "X." We are weird, space–time dreamers with quantum minds, processminds.

Nonlocality—having invisible waves or buzz-like characteristics—is a central aspect of phase 3. Nonlocality is a core idea in this book, and is key in studying the "communing" core of empathy, or what I call, "commune-ication" with others. I introduce the concept and the practice I call "commune-ication" in Chapter 18, and then use it extensively in Part VIII, Communing for Conflict and Peace.

We should all remember that life is not entirely predictable. For example, how did we get here, how did I get to Portland? I cannot figure it out. How did I get to Zurich? My undergraduate school professor thought I should go to Zurich, thought it would be good for me to study physics at the E.T.H. Why did he think that? In any case, the first time I went Zurich, I arrived the day Jung died, June 6, 1961. At that time, I had never even heard of Jung. C. G. Jung? Who is he? What I am trying to say is that our lives are moved about by nonlocal fields.

Normally, you move along identifying as only you, not in touch with your deeper, fluid, more quantum-like self. Then suddenly you think, "Something is going to get me, and I'm exhausted, some 'X' might kill me." You realize you are in phase 2, being attacked. Your process is trying to go from phase 2 to phase 3 and/or phase 4 to move you along. If you let go and flow, your path changes according to the fields, and you are moved by the universe.

Phase 4 Benefits for Health and Relationship

If Einstein were here, he might speak about phases 3 and 4 as *spooky because of their nonlocal characteristics.* How can there be nonlocal connections in these phases? Spooky action at a distance! In the world of physics, the word *spooky* means *weird*, since we cannot empirically track how nonlocal connections occur.

Spooky connections belong to shamanism. As a helper, healer, or whatever you call yourself, you need to be a "little spooky" or mystical now and then. Otherwise, you can't open the door for others to enter phase 4. As a helper, you can model letting go. Loosen up your neck, your hips, and model the freedom of phase 4. This can have a good effect on others, helping them to find phase 4 as well.

Everybody, even the firmest rationalist, goes through phases 3 and 4. Aspects of shamanism are everyone's fate now and then. Why? Because we go to sleep and dream. Even the most rational person becomes a bit dreamy sooner or later.

Health and illness are phase 2 concepts. In phase 4, we are neither healthy nor ill. Remember, you are either living or dead in phase 2. *In phase 4 you are a process.* Phase 2 is important. So if you are nervous about death, get your life in order. But in phase 4, you can move beyond the everyday classical physics categories, beyond everyday life to be the field itself in which we all live.

I worked with someone today whose parent had died recently. I asked, "What happened to your parent, what was the last thing your parent said?" "It was weird," the person answered. "The last thing my parent said was, 'So, did you get the tickets?'" In Phase 2 you think of beginnings and endings. But in Phase 4, you realize you are a fluid process, a "trip." So get your tickets and travel!

In phase 4, remember *controlled abandon.* Relax. This can be very relieving and impart a sense of wellness. As Don Juan said, "Practice controlled abandon." Here, *controlled* means let go of phases 1 and 2 and abandon yourself into the dreaming of phases 3 and 4—and be careful not to hurt yourself.

Control requires that you care for yourself, and *abandon* means letting go to discover something in this dreaming state. Then use *control* again to catch and write it down. Remember, be careful in altered states; some people need to hold a chair while "being moved."

Now, to illustrate nonlocal phase 3 and phase 4 bodywork, enjoy the following example and then try the practical exercise that follows to experience this for yourself.

Demonstration: Dreambody Work with Nonlocal States of Consciousness

In this example, I work with someone on the altered state within her troubling body symptom and in the process, she discovers how to transform ageism and live her deepest nature.

L: I love working as a massage therapist. I am so glad to have transitioned from my earlier work on newspapers.

Arny: Wonderful. How are you doing physically? How is your body doing?

L: I have had a strong symptom, vertigo. It is beyond dizzy and lightheaded. It's called BPPD—benign paroxysmal positional vertigo. The room spins, it is not just lightheaded. I feel like the whole house is spinning around me. It's due to something in the inner ear. It's positional.

Arny: If this happens mainly in the morning when getting up, sometimes doing rolling movement exercises can help the calcium crystal deposits, which sometimes get stuck, creating vertigo.

L: Yes, normally, but those exercises made it worse.

Arny: Let me try one more phase 2 idea. How is your stomach?

L: It gets nauseous.

Arny: Any acid stomach?

L: No.

Arny: Do you take any aspirin?

L: No.

Arny: Great. Now I am ready to leave phase 2 and play.

L: Your smile takes me into the easy state.

Arny: Please sketch your normal energy, the normal "u" without the symptom?

L: (Moves a bit and draws a wavy line.)

Arny: I hate to talk about vertigo, and I don't want you to have to feel much of it, but can you remember it a little bit, enough to feel it—or I can do it for you.

L: I hardly can, but maybe with my hands and arms I can show it . . . it's almost like a tornado that picks me up and whips me around.

Arny: Can you sketch that?

L: (Draws a spinning tornado.) *Ohoooo, it took me to that dizzy state for a millisecond.*

Arny: OK, we have the "u" (the wavy line) and the "X" (the tornado). Now, let's explore phase 4. I want to be protective of you so at any time, sit, if you need to. But now I want to ask you to act out that "X" a little bit, and sometimes be "u"—I will do it for you to begin with. I am doing the "X" with my hands and not the whole body. Can you try that, just the hands?

L: (Moves her hand as the "X.") *Buzzzzzzzz! There are bees buzzing around. Oh! I just got a little insight: The brain overworks—it's buzzing around! I don't know if it is a good thing, but something in me goes after things all the time.*

Arny: Good, so now, let's go further with that "X."

L: As "X" I say, "Study, study, take action, don't take action, do this, do that!"

Arny: As "u," I must say, "I'm getting older—give me a break."

L: (as X) *There is not much time left, and there is so much to do* (laughs).

Arny: That laughter is fun and good feedback. Why are you laughing so much? Sounds a bit like loosening up. So, let's try phase 3, going back and forth a bit between "u" and "X." Can you go back and forth between "take it easy" and "let's get going, there is much to do!"

L: (Models the two sides, back and forth, in sound and movement, and dances between the two.)

Arny: Now be careful with yourself. Relax while standing, loosen your knees a little bit, and let yourself wobble in phase 4.

L: (Goes into movement and buzzes around.)

Arny: When you're loose enough and feel OK, I will ask you some questions.

L: I'm OK (moving more gently now).

Arny: While you are in that relaxed phase 4 state, let's explore if this state can give us any tips about your body, about anything.

L: I catch a subtle movement, a little thing, a little movement, and it feels so powerful! (Explores that movement more.) *I am just so myself* (laughs, with tears).

Arny: You are laughing and crying at the same time; you are just yourself, swinging.

L: Yes, and now I see a little girl. My earliest childhood dream comes back to me. I'm a little girl around 7 going down the street looking at the cracks in the street. My head is down and all of a sudden I realize, "L is naked! You naked little girl, put some clothes on!" and I look up and people are looking at me! I don't want to put clothes on. I stamp my foot, "Don't say those things to me and tell me what to do!"

Arny: (as the little girl) *"Don't tell me to put clothes on! I want to be naked!" I think the little girl is trying to come out! She may be your medicine. A little bit of that little girl is there in spite of ageism.*

L: I am so old . . . and . . . I am not *so old!*

Arny: Yes, you are the everyday critic and *the spontaneous child. Your spontaneous movement was like an adult who became a little girl. That is controlled abandon. Total abandon is everything coming off; controlled abandon is being naked carefully so your basic flowing nature appears. In your movement was both control and abandon—creative mind, open mind, little girl just beginning her life. So you are getting older . . . and not!!*

L: Ohhh, that movement with both parts of me is such GOOD medicine! Ageism was bothering me!!

Arny: You are good medicine! Not just for yourself but all of us! It was good to play with you. (About an hour after this work, L said that all of her symptoms had disappeared.)

Arny: (going around the room talking to the students) *I'm wondering about the nonlocal nature of this work. How old are you?*

B: Forty-six! It's too much!

Arny: (Asking someone else) *How old are you?*

C: I'm already 51!

Arny: And how old are you really?

C: 5!

Arny: Beautiful. We are all 100 years old and not. Consensus reality thinking and ageism can contribute to making you feel sick. It is a nonlocal problem affecting everyone over the age of 21 around the world. Remember to work on your symptom experiences, and when possible, bring them out in public. It might be healing for everyone!

A week later,

Arny: (in a conversation with L. about her work in class the last week) *I was very touched last week by you. You went into the processmind state and while in there, I asked what you thought about your vertigo symptoms and energies, and you found the adult and that little girl, and you looked like you felt better.*

L: Yes, I did, I definitely did feel better and have felt better since then. The slight remnants of the dizziness and headaches have gone away!

Arny: Yes, in the vertigo was the altered state of realizing you are an aging adult, yet also a little girl with lots of zooming energies. Ageism is a tough critic; you think you are 73. But that is a consensus reality view of the body, which takes you away from your ageless process pattern.

Try the following symptom exercise to explore how your altered states can help with your physical symptom problems and your relationships. Work with a helper so that you can dialogue about the process.

Exercise: Dreambody in Relationship

1. Feel and act out your normal "u" and your *worst* body symptoms and energies—your "X"—and sketch them. Can you find "X" in a relationship or an organizational or world issue? Do you notice it in some of your own double signals? Can you find that "X" in any of your childhood dream figures?
2. Now feel into your u + X energies *one after another* and try to support and value both u + X.
3. Amplify and "burn" the "X" with your whole body till the final state produces a clear message. (*Burning* means to go further than you would normally do in expressing that "X" energy, so that it may give you something brand new.) Now explore phase 3 by role-playing and switching between u + X. Any insights?
4. Relax and be moved by the universe. Can you find u + X in that dance?

While the "client" is dancing, the helper can ask her or him how that dance might provide a tip about symptoms and some relationship situation. The person working might want to talk about the symptom or relationship or both—or something totally different.

"Client," if you can, speak shamanistically; *go into a bit of an altered state* and advise yourself and your partner as if *your "X"* was present for both of you. *(For example, speak to the other person as if she or he was you.)*

Partner, if you know your own u + X problems, was the advice your "client" gave to her or himself useful to you in any way? Could you feel the effects of nonlocality?

Things to Remember from Chapter 5

1. If voice and music come from someone's cell phone, music is in the "air." Likewise, the "X" with which you dialogue may be in the air as well.
2. Phases 3 and 4 are nonlocal; they are parts of you and parts of the field around you. So, your problem and its solutions may be good not only for you but others as well.
3. Shamanistic phase 4 experiences may create good health, in part because they are free from the tensions of everyday life and are detached from the polarities of health and illness, life and death.
4. Whatever you feel as a body symptom is obviously yours, but it may also be connected nonlocally to the world(s) in which you are living. This means that everything and everyone around you may know "your u" and "your X" energy in themselves. Hence, not only you but all of us are involved in resolving what looks like *your* symptom.

CHAPTER 6

Reincarnation? You Are a Timeless Process Pattern

• • •

THE IDEA OF PHASES IS simple. Things change and go through cycles in the world and in you. For example, conflict and trouble repeat. Inside you, in your relationship, in your community, and in our world, the "X" goes through cycles. Psychology, which was built on "integrating" different parts of ourselves into a whole self is important, but such integration and "dis-integration" also cycles over time. Overall, working on ourselves gets easier, but things still cycle.

In this chapter, we find that from the viewpoint of phase 4 experiences, chronic symptoms are timeless process patterns, not just recurring problems. We witness as a woman works with her chronic asthma symptom to find the timeless process pattern that gives joy and meaning to her life today, and perhaps also to her past and future lives.

The techniques I am sharing in this book can make the cycling easier, particularly *feeling into* the other side. If you feel deeply, you "commune" with those you cannot stand. I talk about communing in greater detail in Chapter 18 (and in Part VIII, Communing for Conflict and Peace). In any case, communing is not a permanent fix, but part of the cyclical nature of process phases. Learning about phases and relating to others as a process is more sustainable than aiming for a fixed state of resolution.

But you might be wondering, if I am always changing, then who am I? Did you get born by accident? When were you born and when will you die? Many people around the world believe in the idea of reincarnation, the idea that after death the soul or spirit or whatever you call it gets reborn and begins life again in another body.

The question about reincarnating often arises when working with individuals: "What will happen to me in the future—is there a next life? Where was I—if anywhere—before this lifetime? Or did I just get created only for this time around? Is a past lifetime the cause of my troubles in this lifetime?"

If you say "Yes, I got created only for this time around," I accept that. If you sense you have some sort of field or wave-like existence at other times, I accept that as well. If you say, "These questions are a lot of woo-woo, foolish mystical stuff," I will accept that too. Each individual will have her or his own answer to these questions.

Phase ideas may help us gain an overview of life. The psychologist and physicist parts of me want to explore our experience of existence, because we are bodies in time and space and often seem like field-like powers that are not just located in one spot (as in quantum theory's nonlocality). In many ways, we are like the rest of the matter in our universe.

Before I further explore phases and particularly the timelessness of phase 4, let me give an example from some work I was doing recently.

I was busy helping people with problems in Africa—there was an all-African meeting that I can't describe in detail. People were trying to get together to make a decision about the future of Africa in terms of food and ecology and things like that.

So, you would think that people who want to get together and help Africa would create an easy and helpful meeting. But the group was having a lot of trouble. Why? Take a guess. Old problems came up again to recycle. Past unresolved historical ghosts intervened!

People were very angry at each other. But then after arguing, they seemed tired, so I said it's OK to begin with phase 2 fighting, but if they'd had enough of the tension, perhaps their tiredness indicated we needed time to briefly relax (as in phase 1) or detach (as in phase 4). Everyone relaxed and even detached temporarily, so we could go to the next big steps.

Phase 4 detaching helped everyone into a re-visioning effort. In a relaxed state of mind, the participants realized that they could not yet work on the topic of ecology, because they needed to address unresolved historical issues such as women's rights in Africa. Phase 4 gave us the detachment to work on unresolved historical issues (phase 2). After phase 4, we returned with renewed interest and could discuss gender issues, and then ecology as well.

In phase 4, we are all ready for philosophy, religion, theology, the love of nature, emptiness, shamanism, and work of any kind. Here we can, "listen to the universe" and ask, "What does the wind say to you?" Remember, however, if a client or group is not in phase 4, I would not stress the phase 4 view, even though it is part of the overall process.

There is a lot of music about this phase 4 experience of "being moved." For example, you might know this song:

How many seas must a white dove sail
before she sleeps in the sand,
The answer my friend is blowing in the wind,
the answer is blowing in the wind . . .

***14.* The answer is blowing in the wind.**

That's Bob Dylan[27] describing phase 4.

So, listen to the "wind's" messages, the field, to phase 4's view of you and others as part of nature, where you appear as a *timeless process pattern*, not just as a solid object. In phase 4, you are also a wave, not only a particle.

Phase 4 is the experience of a timeless process pattern. It seems to me, after working with perhaps thousands of people and their dreams from all over the world, that the first childhood dream pattern or memory does not seem to change too much in a lifetime. It predicts the changes you will go through, and if you make that dream pattern conscious, you seem to flow well with life. From the general phase 4 viewpoint, nothing can happen to you that is not part of your timeless pattern.

From a phase 2 viewpoint, relationships can be created and destroyed. But from phase 4's view, *you can't get out of a relationship*; there is no getting out of a relationship completely. You can hate someone, you can divorce them a thousand times, you can create settlements, but you will still dream of them. From the essence viewpoint of phase 4, relationships are timeless as well.

A question came from a class participant about how to apply this idea in helping people who are very sick and are placed into palliative care.

> *I want to translate this idea into helping patients who are very sick. They have been working with their doctor to cut out or kill the cancer, and now the doctor says, "There is nothing more that I can do, so we are going to make the shift to palliative care." Doctors sometimes say, "Let the hospice care people tell the patients about all this!" Instead of the doctor trying to cut out or kill the disease, now they say, "We are going to focus on comfort, we are going to focus on controlling the pain and maximizing your quality of life."*

I like the doctor's phase 2 view of fighting the pain of "X," but I would prefer to say, "As usual, we will be dancing with your experiences into the future."

In such a situation, I might say to the person, "The doctor is OK but limited. She, he, or they are saying they have done as much as they know about in phase 2, and they don't really know your future. They only have their phase 2, consensus reality statistics, about whether people have a longer or shorter time in their present form. But I would say, 'I am interested in that view, but am more interested in bringing you out now to discover and be yourself as much as possible—regardless of what that means—whether fighting more, or going deeper and letting go, or both!'" In phases 3 and 4, the process pattern implies that *whatever happens* will be (vaguely) already known because we all have some sense of a repetitive dream pattern occurring.

This idea has many roots in human philosophies and worldviews. One of my class participants shared its similarity with the ideas of Chinese medicine.

> *Classical Chinese medicine aligns with what you are saying about the process patterns. For example, it may look now like it's night and then later daytime—it's yin and yang—and the five patterns, the five elements, the five forces, all in movement.*

Chinese medicine is based upon the idea that the human body is a miniature of the universe and that health is a matter of swinging between and balancing yin and yang energies. Here you find the idea of phases and turning as aspects of theory and of health.

In Western medicine, diseases are names describing measurable physical facts. So diseases are "local," in your body and in phase 2. But from the broader view of phase 4, a disease is a bit like a weather pattern. How you align yourself with the pattern is in part up to you. Your myth, seen in your first childhood dreams, is a structure that organizes how you might swing between polarities, and this myth seems to travel with you from the time you were born.

A class participant summed up a basic difference between process-oriented thinking and a state-oriented approach,

> *"In processwork, you are not trying to change your pattern, you are trying to use it differently."*

This is my point about recognizing your timeless process pattern: Can you flow with your amazing gift? Can you know and use your pattern more *consciously*? Why? Such processes feel best. It is different from saying there is something deadly wrong with you, as in phase 2: "I am sick." Phase 2 is OK, but in phase 4, we view life from our *center* as part of the universe.

My point is that we are material bodies, and we are also wave-like patterns, looking like people. How you become aware of and use that pattern is up to you, to some extent. Your childhood dreams shows some of the parts, figures, and energies between which you can and do swing.

Now, returning to my theme about reincarnation and the question, "Do we die from the viewpoint of phase 4?" I will leave the final answer up to everybody's own way of thinking and feeling. I have pointed out many times that at the end of life, people seem to go further in life, though it is obvious they are dying. In situations where I knew their childhood dreams, it seemed as if their childhood dream figures often appeared to organize near-death experiences.[28]

I recall Jung's first dream as he related it in his book *Memories, Dreams, Reflections.* In his childhood dream, he is looking down and sees what he calls a dark Christ figure that looks potentially violent. Jung was viewing it from above.

Then some 86 years later, when he was dying, this wonderful man dreamed something similar. He told his last dream before dying to Marie-Louse von Franz, hoping she might understand it. She generously told it to me before she died, hoping I would understand it. In his final dream, he is looking down from above and sees warring armies in conflict. While above, he is not only looking down but also looking in his mirror, self-reflecting, as he moves forward and above the war below.

My point is that your first and "last" dream patterns often look similar, and that is why I am suggesting that we are process patterns. In his mirror in that dream, we see Jung's interest in his personal development—that is, in his self-reflection—and also in his view of the conflict problems of our violent world below. I am so very thankful to him for telling von Franz, and to her for telling me. His final experiences and his childhood dream of the "dark Christ figure below" have similarities.

Reincarnation

Let me ask an almost unanswerable question: Do you think our early dream patterns were present before we came to this earth? Are those patterns around after our present form changes? Religions from around the world, but especially in Asia, have included reincarnation as a central belief: for example, Hinduism, Buddhism, Jainism, and Sikhism.

In the Western world, historic Greek pillars of philosophy, such as Pythagoras, Plato, and Socrates, also expressed a belief in rebirth.

This idea of phases—of birth, death, and rebirth/reincarnation—sounds something like, "We are timeless patterns that may be around in the universe and are looking for personal forms." I realize that there are various viewpoints, such as we should not come around again, or we won't reincarnate again if we are enlightened.

In my experience, if you are in touch with your basic patterns, you have more of an overview of your life and seem to feel well. That is why I want to explore the river and waves that you are!

Remain open to the possibility that you are here on this planet to enable your basic pattern to realize itself. Also, as I have recounted before, many people have asked me near the end of their lives, "Did I do the right thing?" as if they sensed that there was a reason for their being here. "Was I the right person? Is my life going on the right track?" These questions imply that they suspected their life had some meaning. I've noticed that we all feel best knowing our life's potential pattern and meaning.

Whether your rational mind believes this or not, simply explore your basic childhood dream pattern to fantasize about your past and future.

Now, I illustrate these ideas with a demonstration in which I worked with someone's chronic body symptom of asthma to find the timeless process pattern. Afterward, I present the exercise so you can try it yourself.

Demonstration: Working with the Experience of Asthma

Arny: The pen spun and chose you to work in the center today. Hi, and what do you do?

S: I have been practicing Aikido for 24 years, and also teach. I love it because it connects me with people in a way that feels resonant. It does not need a lot of words.

Arny: How do you normally identify yourself? You are a person who . . . ?

S: I have ups and downs, but usually I'm fairly calm, unless I'm upset.

Arny: Can you sketch that calmness?

*S: (*Makes a gentle wiggle sketch.)

Arny: What is your most feared symptom?

S: Asthma. I have had it since birth and the fear I have that comes with it is that I cannot get air in. (Clears throat.) *The lungs feel tight and full, like there is not a lot of extra space.*

Arny: They feel tight and full? I hear the words, but to explore that trouble more, can you help me feel it even more somehow?

S: (Puts pressure on the front and back of Arny's chest.)

Arny: I kind of liked it.

S: Yes, but when it stops your breathing, it is more radical!

Arny: Can you try to stop me from breathing and be more radical?

S: (Squeezes Arny tighter towards neck.)

Arny: Aha! You are coming to my neck, so I can feel it now. If you allowed yourself not to be your normal shy self, if you allowed yourself to be a little more radical, what would you look like doing this to me?

S: (Her two hands come together in a tight squeeze in the air, eyes closed.) *Something about a distillation process—getting to the essence of something and hanging onto it. Reducing it down to the core, the essential, basic stuff.*

Arny: How beautiful! It's horrible to have asthma, but that's a beautiful thought—the essence of it is a distillation process, getting to the core of things. How are you not at the essence?

S: When I escape or I don't pay attention to the whole of me, or if I am focusing on one aspect of something and not seeing the whole system that it fits within. The large pattern appears in my artwork. It is about working with patterns. When working with people, sometimes my large pattern comes in usefully, especially in Aikido and in Processwork, and also that "distilling" comes in when I work as an editor. I love looking for patterns, for the essence of things.

Arny: Yes, you must grab people by the neck and seek out their patterns.

S: (Chuckles.)

Arny: I did not expect a chuckle! Imagine using that "trouble energy" in the world. How could you squeeze the people you work with to get the best out of them? You are smiling.

S: There is the sense of squeezing in the things I already do. When I teach, I can squeeze a little!

Arny: Let's go into phase 2 for a moment, perhaps you can't or can. Does your asthma get worse at particular times of the year?

S: Yes, these fall months. Any time of day, though later in the day tends to be a little harder when I am getting tired.

Arny: Did your mother smoke?

S: Yes, and my father smoked, yes.

Arny: My experience with people who have had asthma is that their mothers smoked. This is just the consensus reality part of all of this; the mother and father both smoked, so part of the asthma may be connected with history. Who knows? Do any particular foods turn it on or off?

S: No.

Arny: Alcohol does not bother it?

S: Beer makes me congested, so I am not fond of beer.

Arny: It is good to know about the consensus reality part of this also. If it gets bad, is there some medicine that helps to keep it in check?

S: I have been working with it using Chinese medicine, herbs, and acupuncture for the last 30+ years, and that is working well. And if those remedies do not work, I have Predonine, a steroid, that I can take if I need to. I use it rarely, once every year or once every two years.

Arny: I am asking you not just because I want to know but because I want other people to think about the consensus reality, phase 2 reality of asthma. But now, let's move on to phases 3 and 4. Relax a little more and let yourself be moved. Let yourself be wobbled and moved around a little bit spontaneously.

S: (Moves gently in small movements; with eyes closed, her upper body leans and her knees bend slightly.)

Arny: As you are dancing, do you notice a calm movement and also this powerful, distilling process? I can almost see them from the outside. Do you feel them inside too?

S: Yes.

Arny: Now, while you are moving, tell me a little story. Something like, "Once upon a time, the world may have needed somebody to put that calmness and that tight distilling energy together." Why would somebody put those energies together? What kinds of tasks does she need to be doing in this life? As you dance, let your fantasy come up if you can.

S: Honor nature, recognize essential energies and patterns, and in some way give expression to them.

Arny: And if she lived earlier, what do you think she was doing in her earlier life before she came around as yourself? Who was she then?

S: Maybe a landscape painter in Asia somewhere, showing those patterns in nature.

Arny: Ahhh, an Asian landscape painter. Yes, and if she could live a hundred years from now, we don't know for sure—but if she did, what do you think she might be doing?

S: Looking for patterns, essences, and sharing them with others. Honor nature and honor beauty—making a thing of beauty as an expression of nature.

Arny: Ah, you can do that in this lifetime too, making a thing of beauty that expresses nature. Anything else it wants to tell us?

S: In this space I am now, my lungs are open! And they had not been earlier today. *I did not expect it, and it is welcome!*

Arny: Oh, perhaps that crunching and confining process relaxed when its nature was appreciated. Our world needs visionaries, painters who show us the essence of things, teachers who make things that express the essence of nature. Thank you. That was amazing.

EXERCISE ON REINCARNATION

Try this exercise alone or with a partner to help you.

Phase 1. Alone, how do you most often identify yourself? Note and feel your primary everyday identity and express *and show this ME energy.*

Phase 2. Is the energy of your most feared real or imaginary symptom different than the normal "u"? What sort of TROUBLE energy has been bothering you most over the past months?

Phase 3. Burn-amplify that TROUBLE; that means, get into it until you get its message. Burning the TROUBLE energy means *feeling it and using your entire body to express it,* from your face down to your toes. Consider how you might use this TROUBLE energy and message in world.

Phase 4. Now let the universe field move you, go into "space–time dreaming," and note when, where, and how your ME and TROUBLE energies and ideas appear in the dance.

While you are dancing, catch your fantasies and let a story arise. Let those fantasies create your timeless story, your myth. For example, "*Once upon a time, the world needed a person to help bring ME and TROUBLE energies together, and you were born.*" Note while you are dancing that there is no ME or TROUBLE, there is just the dance—and the dance may integrate the ME and TROUBLE in a fluid movement. Keep an open mind and ponder the possibility that the universe gave birth to you perhaps to help bring those energies together.

While dancing, perhaps your spontaneous movement can give birth to a fantasy of your "universal tasks" (define these as you like).

Now if possible, take a guess *who or what you were 100 years before birth and who you might be 200 years from now?* Just play with any fantasy that arises while you are spontaneously danced by the universe. Record your experiences afterwards.

Seminar participants who tried this exercise shared the following learnings.

R: From this exercise there was no need for a new pattern because it was functional 200 years ago and will be functional in 200 years' time. So, no need!

A: This exercise helped me revise and update my pattern. Part of me is shy and part very sharp. I often judge this shyness as "shyness," but now I realized this shyness is a very important time for me to have visions. I am a visionary leader, but to have a vision I have to go shyly inside!

Arny: Shyness is needed in a visionary leader. You are the leader we need!

Remember what you discover and write it all down in your dream book to understand your dreams better.

Things to Remember from Chapter 6

1. From the viewpoint of phase 4 experiences, chronic symptoms are timeless process patterns, not just parts or particles that get born and disappear.
2. To feel best, identify with your timeless process pattern.

PART III

Meditation Phases

• • •

IN THE FIRST PART OF this book, we explored the process phases of deep democracy particularly as they apply to large group work. In the last three chapters, we explored the phases of body symptom work, including the nonlocal connection between body trouble and our relationships, the value of altered states of consciousness, and the idea of a timeless process pattern guiding our lives. Now in the next three chapters, before going back to worldwork, I want to focus on *using phases and worldwork ideas in process-oriented meditation.*

CHAPTER 7

Process-Oriented Meditation Awareness for Everyone

• • •

MEDITATION IS NEEDED FOR WORLDWORK because inner work is a big part of relationships and of large group work. You can resolve outer problems sustainably only if they are resolved internally as well.

By meditation, I do not mean achieving a certain state of consciousness, but rather *awareness of your changing states.* Watch change happen! Awareness means *noticing* what you are experiencing. What is happening? What is going on in your inner house? In your inner apartment? Usually we wonder what to *do* or how to *be.* That is OK. Meditation focuses instead on what *is happening.* It notices what you experience and follows that experience to help you make decisions.

Meditation is a form of consciousness. It is about following your *awareness of awareness.*

Earlier, in my book *Working on Yourself Alone,* I introduced "channels" into meditation methods and explained some similarities and differences between process-oriented meditation and some Eastern meditation procedures.[29] In that book, I focused mainly upon the meditation experience as it appears in your sensory-grounded channels. For example, notice events in the sensory-grounded proprioceptive channel—what are you feeling? Notice movements. What movements are you making? In the auditory channel, what sounds do you notice? Visually, what is catching your eye?

What are you dreaming? *Channel awareness is important. Now I want to extend the process with phase awareness.*

Process-oriented meditation is not devoted to discovering and holding on to one particular state, or to only achieving detachment, but to knowing and flowing with yourself and others in *all* of your and our diversity. Detachment, as we know from phase 4, is part of inner work and meditation. Process-oriented meditation focuses on:

What you experience and notice.
The *channel and phase* you are in.
Following and unfolding those channel and phase experiences.

Phases as Sounds

Making sounds and focusing on them with a meditative awareness is a less usual but very powerful way to gain more awareness of who you are and what you are doing. Sound is a particularly good way to bring attention to our more subtle moods and to recognize the phase we are actually in. Sound allows you to "hear" the phases of the Tao.

Moods and phases are easier to work with if we identify these sometimes vague experiences with sounds. If you know your moods and can make a sound expressing them, your dreams will be easier to understand, you will feel better, and you will be more fluid and related in working with yourself and others in the world.

In one of my classes, I invited participants to make a sound as I went near them, to express how they felt in the moment. As they answered me with their sounds, we could experience the energy and the phase of their process.

Arny: How were you before you went to bed last night? Can you make a sound to express that?
C: Crrrcccccccklklklllllll
Arny: Wow! Those sounds are what we will be working with.

L: Ah!! Ah!! Ahhhh!!
Arny: Now, what does that sound express in your mind, in words?
L: Both excitement and nervousness—
Arny: I would not have seen excitement and nervousness in you, but I certainly heard it! That sounded like a phase 2 experience, as if you are nervous about some "X." Wow.

As always, when you work with yourself and others, the key is to hear, and of course, to see and feel signals. You can discover a lot just noticing how people walk in the door to greet you. Just listen and watch their process, notice their signals and double signals. Listen to their voices.

Most people like being in phase 1. It sounds happy, and for me, a song comes to mind. Phase 1 is like an old song that I know, that goes something like "aba daba daba honey moon." It's an old song, so not everyone will know it. Just think of a simple or silly, happy song—that is phase 1.

Phase 2 may be a dramatic or depressed sound. No one likes to think about phase 2, so it is often repressed, and that is why we are often moody or can't sleep at night.

Phase 3 is creative and gives you the idea of fluidity; this phase integrates high and low sounds.

Phase 4 is a steadier, quieter, detached sound.

Compassion: Perceiving the Sounds of the World

Before I give a class, I always watch my dreams to update myself about the "field's" viewpoint. Before teaching about process-oriented meditation, I dreamed I was at one of my favorites spots, the Sensoji Temple in Tokyo. It is the oldest temple of that type in Tokyo, and it is a mixture of Buddhist, Hindu, and aboriginal Japanese beliefs and religions. *Guanyin*, an East Asian spiritual figure of mercy and a bodhisattva associated with compassion, as venerated by Mahayana Buddhists, is central to this temple.[30] Apparently a statue was found in the Sumida River near the temple, and the people recognized it as the goddess of compassion, Guanyin. The name Guanyin is short for *Guanshiyin*, which means "Perceiving the Sounds (or Cries) of the World."[31]

In any case, my dream told me that while I am thinking of meditation, I am dreaming about the spirit of self-compassion, a very ancient, phase 4 idea, a spirit of "perceiving sounds."

Notice yourself in phase 4, have compassion, and "appreciate yourself" in all phases. Sometimes compassion, like Guanyin, goes underwater—especially when you are too much in consensus reality—but you can find it again by appreciating yourself in meditation and getting closer to phase 4, the center of the phases. If you can appreciate yourself some of the time, good work! You can disagree with yourself too, that is just as natural.

Often, when you start to work with a person or a group, you say, "How are you doing?" Sometimes the answer is, "No change," or, "We are in the same situation!" or, "We hate that bad person or group" or, "Some are good, some people are difficult," etc. Likewise, the world news often says or implies, "There are bad people out there who are never going to change!" That is phase 2 in meditation. But the larger phase 4 viewpoint is that nature goes through phases, and at some point all the energies of things you like and don't like will be needed. To resolve problems, phase 4 is needed.

For example, I just worked with somebody who said she had recently almost died. She was still in pain. She said, "I was giving up, it was so awful, how could I go through this any longer, it was not possible!" She wanted to kill herself. I said, "I know, I don't blame you for wanting to kill yourself. No blame, that is natural. Night is natural."

"What?" she said, surprised and happily.

I said, "If you did kill yourself in your imagination, what would happen next?" She said, "Oh, my body shivered. I don't know why." I asked her, "Is it possible to stand?" She stood up, and I said, "What happens now with that shivering movement?" As she stood up, she noticed to her surprise that there was a little hop. "I hopped!" she exclaimed. "It wants to move!"

I said, "I thought you were dying?" She replied, "Yes, I was, but not now!" And she started to move around as if she was a little kid. In her most recent dream there were children and only after her movement work did we know where the children had come from. The children had come from that part of her wanting to "die" out of her old "dying" identity to get into her dreaming body. So in phase 4, she came into life as a child!

Process! With awareness, she noticed that her process moved from a bad mood in phase 2 directly to phase 4 and onwards, using shivering, and then that detached children's dance. I can report that she proceeded to fully recuperate in contrast to her own and to her doctor's prognosis.

Lao Tse said that the Tao that can be said is not the eternal Tao. In process terms, we could say there is a Tao that can be said in terms of signals and phases 1, 2, and 3. The Tao that cannot be said is an essence-level experience. It cannot be formulated at first in words or images; it is a detached sense that something is happening, but you don't yet know what. In meditation, follow what can be said and seen and don't forget to also feel and follow phase 4, the field that cannot be clearly expressed. Remember the "mmm," which is the pre-feelings and pre-sounds that cannot yet be said, felt, or spoken.

You can celebrate your birthday, but also celebrate change itself, the mystery behind life. When it's your birthday say, "OK, I am growing a year older." That is the Tao that can be said, but also celebrate change itself. That is the power moving all of us, the Tao that cannot quite be said.

Deep Democracy Meditation Phases

In the first chapters I spoke about levels of awareness in deep democracy. Remember that in consensus reality, you connect with your normal self in phase 1, and you also connect with troubles in phase 2. "Oh, I have got this and that to do." Or, "Oh, my body/ my relationship partner is a pain!" Or you might feel, "I am depressed by something—my critic is after me, the 'X' that is after my 'u' in everyday reality."

Then in phase 3, dreamland, you are sometimes able to be like that "X." In phase 3, there is "u" and there is an "X" that *switch back and forth.*

Psychology has long been based upon the phase 3 idea that your thoughts and dreams are parts of you trying to become conscious.

But experiencing phase 3 is unusual in daily life. Very few people think they are the good *and* bad guys in the news. Very few political leaders that I know say they are like the "X" in the world. They can't do that publicly because they will lose their jobs. If a leader says today, "I am a little bit like the bad guys we want to fight," they fear that no one will vote for them again—and they are probably right.

Yet this dreamland phase 3 experience of being the other, politically incorrect as it is, is probably the most powerful way of working with world conflict.

At the essence level of deep democracy, we find phase 4, and can experience the deepest movements and feelings that can't easily be said. This is where sounds can help express things. Sound and movement are important ways to express the essence level.

Recall, that feeling centered is a phase 4 experience as well as the center of the other phases. *Phase 4, which I have also called your "processmind," is the best facilitator!* Why? Just as two groups in conflict seek a neutral facilitator, so also when we are in internal conflict, we seek some form of solution or relaxation. Some take drugs. Others try to sleep. Others meditate to be detached.

Perhaps the easiest way to work on yourself is to sense your own processmind experience in phase 4. It can often give you tips about the next steps. Remember that though you can be centered and resolve things temporarily, don't be surprised if you come out of it and are back in everyday reality fighting something all over again!

In phase 2 you feel distressed, and so you go around in cycles. If you remain in phase 2, then tapping into phase 4 experience can give you more compassion, more "Guanyin," to support yourself in all phases instead of criticizing yourself for having inner or meditation problems.

As we have studied in earlier chapters, phase 1 is "just me." "I don't want to think about anything troublesome—don't talk to me about any problems today." Phase 2 is about fighting and avoiding. In group work, people can become more fearful or ambitious in phase 2, trying to beat another group. Governments are similar: "We are the best government, we are going to knock over that old terrible dictatorship/regime." However, soon that "best government" becomes like the other group without realizing it.

There is no government on earth that does not reverse itself in small or larger ways. Think of the USA. We overcame the "king" a long time ago, but aspects of the United States still act like a "king." Like most nations and large groups, we become rank unconscious.

Remember, phase 2 is a struggle and can be accompanied by many possible sounds. If phase 1 is, "de-de-de-de-de-de-de," phase 2 might sound like, "boom boom, " or " dum-da-da-dum–daaaa! " The "X" often "spooks" you with its sounds; you feel nervous and want to run away from the dread in this phase! Phase 2 is what makes the news and gives politics, gun makers, soldiers, doctors, and therapists lots of work! Defend yourself and fight in phase 2. Try to resolve the conflict as best possible, and don't forget to express all sides.

In phase 3, you remember that you can use that "X" energy. If the problem "X" person or symptom is a cramp, use the cramp's power to do things. In phase 4, a more detached, compassionate, shamanistic experience is possible.

For example, let's say I am bothered by an "X" energy, WOOF! My normal "u" energy is more dah-de-dah. Now, I stand up, comfortable and relaxed, to see how my spontaneous *phase 4 movements will put those "X" and "u" energies together.* I let myself be moved. In my spontaneous body movements, I find both the quiet "u" and the "X" WOOF energies. The dah-de dah and WOOF are both present. As I relax, I notice unpredictable, apparently random or stochastic movements. In this spontaneous phase 4 movement, I can see a little bit of both the u + X energies. For example, there is a relaxed movement of my body going down, and then a sudden sharp upward arm movement.

Each of us has her or his own (changing) phase songs. Those of you who love music, look for music that expresses the phases you are in. Music is popular in part because it expresses different phases. This is where our interest in music comes from; we need music to express our phases . . . so we feel deeply, so tears flow, or so screaming begins.

My point is to use your meditative awareness to discover your phases and try to process them. If you get stuck, go to the center of your process, to phase 4, and be danced. Your meditation goals are created by your needs. The most general goal is following nature, knowing where you are in your own "house." Are you in room 1, 2, 3, or 4? Find out and then just be in your house. Use your *awareness of your awareness.*

Remember, we are all aware of phases, but we are not usually *aware of that awareness.* That is why I *don't* use the term *unconscious*, because we are aware of things *but we are not aware of our awareness.* Such awareness can be cultivated.

Consciousness is being aware of what you are aware of. Usually because we are not aware of our awareness, often consciousness is forced to awaken by the conflict in phase 2. Some inner or outer diversity issue disturbs, scares, or depresses us and tries to awaken us. So eventually use awareness meditation, consciousness, and phase 4 to help when needed.

Many wonderful spiritual traditions ignore phases 1, 2, and 3 and set phase 4 as their goal: "Be detached from your normal 'u' and all those problems, 'X,' for enlightenment." Enlightenment for me, however, includes even being detached from this traditional "enlightenment" and instead, being open to all phases.

Phase 4, your creative mind, is often amazing and will appear in you spontaneously.

As an example of how your phase 4 meditative experience can help you in worldwork, I have to share a story I have written about previously. We were in Ireland years ago working on the conflicts there, just prior to the "peace accord" (dubbed the "Good Friday Agreement," reached after nearly two years of talks and 30 years of conflict). Just before the agreement, people were yelling at each other, everybody was screaming at the same time at each other in our seminar of several hundred people!

I lost all my normal awareness. There was so much noise with everyone yelling at the same time, that I could no longer use my skills and notice signals of the people speaking in the middle. I could not use my science or any CR training.

In the midst of the conflict, something out of the blue caught my attention. I suddenly saw that one of the conflicting politicians had a very red cheek and bright red neck. I am normally very good with double signals, but with all the screaming, I could not use my normal awareness. People were screaming about murder, "You tried to kill my group!" and "You tried to kill me!" and in the midst of that I relaxed for a moment, and saw that very bright red cheek and neck. I heard myself saying in the microphone to everyone, "Your cheek is so red, why is that?"

The politician arguing with another politician in the center of the room stopped and looked at me and said, "My doctor told me not to come because I have severely high blood pressure and I could die if I came to this meeting." The other man stopped and listened. Then he said, "You could die? I just had a heart attack! My doctor told *me* NOT to come here!"

The two men looked at each other for a few minutes as the whole group quieted down. Then, slowly, one came over to the other and actually put his arms on the other man's shoulder. The concept, experience, and fear of death helped them to come together.

They stayed together for the whole rest of the workshop as other people gathered around them to work on things deeply.

How did I notice that single signal in the midst of absolute chaos? Since I could no longer use my everyday mind and training, phase 4 appeared in that "emergency." Phase 4 is your most amazing "art." It is not only "empty mind" but also "creative mind" and knows how to do things. As I have said, phase 4 is linked to shamanism. Phase 4 is the "black box" and has nonlocal connections. What I saw was shared by both men. Phase 4 does not belong only to you, it is everywhere. It is the world around you. It is in politics, relationships, body problems.

Now you can try process-oriented, phase-aware meditation for yourself with the following exercise.

Exercise: Process-Oriented, Phase-Aware Meditation

This exercise can be done alone or with a partner. If you are alone, then read each step to yourself and wait to see your own response. If you practice with a partner, then one person will read the steps out loud, while the other is meditating. If you are reading, please read a little, then wait for the one who is meditating to respond. When she or he gets to the point where more information is needed, read the next sentence, whatever it is.

This *meditation method uses awareness of where you are at, by saying, "Yes," I am here, acknowledging it, and enabling it to roll and flow further.* If you get stuck, find your deepest inner facilitator, your own phase 4. Because your tensions may be in the air around you, if and when possible, invite others into your so-called inner meditation process—express it openly and notice the connections that happen.

Remember to be patient with yourself, experiment with this exercise, and have fun with it. Learning to work with the world and with yourself are very similar.

Process-Oriented Meditation

Reader, go slowly and wait for the person meditating to go to the next step.

Dear person meditating, what is your normal energy like? What is your most troublesome energy, "X," like? Notice the channel used when sensing "X." Are you feeling it? Seeing it? Are you moving to its energies? What do you smell, if anything?

Notice your distance from phase 4—from detachment, flowing, and "not-doing."

Now make a sound expressing how you feel in the moment and then perhaps you can notice your momentary phase.

Are you in phase 1, cruising? Phase 2, tense and disturbed by "X" energy in self or others? Phase 3, open to role switching with normal "u" energy and disturbing "X" energies? Or in phase 4, moved by the universe (processmind)?

Go more deeply into the phase you are in and express your experience in that phase through movement, feeling, sound, ideas, etc. If you are stuck in phase 2, "burn" or amplify the "X" intensely and notice any phase changes. (To repeat: *Burning* means amplifying the "X" energy beyond what seems normal and reasonable, while being careful not to hurt yourself.)

Amplify the "X" and follow any changes, including phase changes.

If you are still stuck, or at any time when ready, explore phase 4 and let the universe move you. One of the easiest ways is simply to relax and let the universe, that is the force field around you, move you spontaneously. Then try to notice the "u" and "X" energies in your movements. Note any insights.

If and when possible, write down what you learned. If there is time, meditate further, let yourself be moved to not-doing, to move spontaneously, when sitting, getting up, etc. Afterwards, make a note about your insights, your channels, phases, and sounds.

Demonstration: Arny's Meditation

Here is what happened when I practiced this meditation in one of my classes, with Amy as the reader.

Amy: Arny, what would you say your normal "u" energy is like?

Arny: My ordinary "u" energy is more or less open, moving along.

Amy: What channels do you notice? Hearing, seeing, moving, aware of tastes or smells?

Arny: I am most aware of movements.

Amy: How distant do you feel that is from phase 4—from detachment, flowing, not doing? Make a sound expressing how you feel and note the phase you think you are in with that sound.

Arny: I am not far from phase 1. And the sound that arises is Yippee! *I seem to be cruising in phase 1 for the moment.*

Amy: OK, go to the phase you are in now, and express your experience in that phase in movement, feeling, sounds, or ideas, and notice and follow any phase changes that occur.

Arny: I am in phase 1, so I will dance along like that. This phase reminds me of the client I spoke of earlier who almost died. Death? Oh . . . that sounds like dum, de dum dum . . . going downhill . . . well, I had my 75th birthday five months ago but am in good health. But I notice I am in phase 1, I want to avoid aging, so I notice now I am moving into phase 2. I had one of my first symptoms, a little pinched nerve in my carpal tunnel area. I got that climbing trees. I can't climb trees as much anymore. Phase 2 is here. Some "X" says, "If you get older, don't climb trees so much!" Perhaps I should not climb trees so much?

Amy: Express your feelings in that phase with movement, feeling, and sound, and follow the phase changes. You mentioned death . . .

Arny: Aging feels like letting go, dying. So I will move from that phase 2 directly into nothingness, phase 4.

Amy: OK, in phase 4, let the universe move you. Do you notice the "X" and "u" in your movement?

Arny: Yes, aging-dying-quietness, then climbing and wildness are now occurring. That is surprising. Wonderful . . . something ageless and detached is happening for the moment. Feels great . . . hmmm, phase 4 and peacefulness, at least for the moment. I got the point about agelessness. Thanks, Amy, for the awareness support!

Here are some of the discoveries shared by people who tried the exercise in my class.

B: I discovered that the dissociated feeling that I live with most of the time is a safe hiding place.

Arny: That is deep, I never heard that before—a troublesome feeling is actually there to create a safely hidden place.

R: I cannot jump and stomp and do those things because of body symptoms in my ankle. That phase 2 symptom experience then seemed like a sense of harnessing or focusing that I have been calling "the symptom." That phase 2 "intensity" brought me to phase 4, and helped me bring all my life together into a more focused direction.

Arny: Wow! Any other questions or insights?

L: I learned that I will fuck up again and again and again. And instead of getting stuck in the sadness and self-criticism, I can let go in phase 4 and just notice things. Exasperation directed me to let go into a kind of dying that brought me into this peaceful state. So when I get exasperated and uptight in the future, I will remember the process and can enjoy, relax, breathe till the next thing pops up!

Arny: Inner work helped you find your inner guru, and there is no better teacher on this planet than your own meditation.

Things to Remember from Chapter 7

1. Recall that all things change, that phases depend upon the moment.
2. Process-oriented meditation is about consciousness, that is, awareness of awareness.
3. To help recognize the phase you are in, make sounds to identify it.
4. If you are close to your phase 4 center, you are able to experience compassion for all that you notice, the phases you go through, and for yourself.
5. If you get stuck in phase 2 moods, bring out the diversity of internal conflicts, and use phase 4 as a facilitator.

CHAPTER 8

Recurring Problems? Great! Use "Not-Doing Inner Work"

• • •

In this chapter, we'll look at how to use meditation, awareness of your awareness, to help with your most difficult and recurring problems.

In the last chapter, I shared my basic approach of process-oriented meditation and added the awareness of process phases. I recommended allowing yourself to make a spontaneous sound in order to identify which phase you are in.

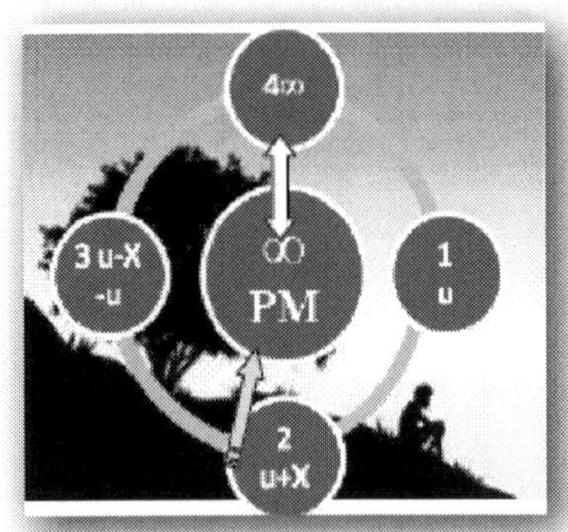

***15.* Process phase oriented meditation.**

In this chapter, I focus on phase 4, which is the phase we normally think of as meditation, and show how this phase of detachment and "not-doing" can facilitate your most difficult inner conflicts. Most exciting, perhaps, I present a technique that allows you to follow your process from phase 2 to phase 4 by "burning" your most difficult energy to move from conflict to detachment to flow.

Along the way, I'll talk about recurring problems and edges, the boundaries created by our familiar identity. Our edges can be seen in our earliest childhood dreams or memories, and both create and escalate troublesome "X" energy.

Like many meditation teachers, I often stress the detachment of phase 4 as if it could be permanent condition. It is true, we need it sometimes. And, we need compassion to notice that *everything changes*, including detachment! This is paradoxical, because it is a form of detachment to be detached even from detachment, noticing it is a phase!

With process awareness, you see all phases as part of your remarkable nature.

Some meditation experience is wonderful, some begins in hell. From the perspective of phase 4, it's OK to be in hell (of course, from phase 1's and phase 2's viewpoints, it is *not* OK). Remembering the phase diagram and that the center is in all phases, you might develop a more compassionate, processmind-oriented attitude. Taoists said long ago, "everything changes," nothing is fixed.

Our Biggest Human Job Is to Get Along with Ourselves and Others

To get along with ourselves, some of us go to therapy or to meditation teachers, many take drugs or use other methods. Living day to day, moment to moment, is our major human occupation! Have you noticed? It is a full-time job!

So even as I live day to day, I can also ask myself, "What state am I in today?" I have so many things to do—conferences, seminars, meetings, sessions, countries, and more. Yet in spite of all those things, I notice that something in me sounds like "mmm, oommm, nnnnn"—making me realize that I am in phase 4. As discussed in the last chapter, that sound represents the phase I am in.

Process-oriented meditation is a really helpful way to get along with yourself and with others. To briefly summarize, here is what we discussed in the previous chapter.

Remember to check your own sounds. Before you do anything, before you look at your dreams, before you try to understand anything about yourself, before you go to work, before you deal with organizational or world events, make a sound that expresses what you are feeling and which phase you are in.

Recall channels. Am I feeling, am I seeing, is there something somatic or proprioceptive in my body that is trying to gain my attention? Those are very useful signals to notice, as is which phase am I in with all that? How close am I to my center? Remember, being a person is a natural, spontaneous, ever-changing, timeless process.

Remember, phase 1 is cruising with who you are. I made a sound "Aba daba daba," like a child. Watch kids walk on the street—that is you in phase 1—you don't walk, you hop!

In phase 2, some "X" is bothering you that is often seen as a problem. A recurring "X" problem can often be seen in early childhood dreams and is often connected with your family's personal history, possibly even with world history.

Phase 3 is that rare moment when you can pick up the "X" energy that is bothering you and use it for yourself. In this phase, you are in the midst of an open forum and can feel or even identify with and use that "X" energy. Here, you may profit from what is bothering you. In phase 3, the "u" and "X" are almost interchangeable. It is where nonlocality in quantum physics occurs, as we discussed in Chapter 5, where you and the thing bothering you interconnect, almost without doing anything. Physicists themselves don't completely understand the quantum world or how something here can be found to link to something over there . . . without any known field or thing connecting them in between.

"X" and "u" are interchangeable in phase 3. Erwin Schrödinger, a discoverer of basic quantum theory, asked, "Can you be dead and alive at the same time?" In phase 3 the answer is YES. You are this, and you are the opposite of this, at the same time.

Phase 4 flows without parts. Sometimes I wear a tasseled hat to demonstrate phase 4. The tassel hangs off the top of my hat on my head. In phase 4, you are as loose as that tassel. Phase 4 is your natural ability to facilitate, and it often appears at first as a sleepy, tired, relaxed, or depressed feeling, or even a fear or sense of dying. If you are feeling that, I encourage you to let go, and let "It" move you. In this sense, fear of death can be a great gift. It allows you to enter into the realm of nonlocality, so what you do is influenced by and can touch upon others at a distance.

"*Not-doing*" occurs in phase 4. This means you are being dreamed; the power of the universe in the form of dreaming is moving you. Not-doing is the central theme of this chapter because it is the most creative conflict resolution facilitator we can find.

To practice not-doing, allow your body to do spontaneous things as a practice. For example, *I* can pick my coat up: That is "doing" the coat pickup. I intentionally reach down and pick it up. At the same time not-doing will also pick up the coat, but I don't know when or exactly how, or even *if*. . . . So I let myself go inside and allow my body to move spontaneously, and I wait. Suddenly, something moves me and I pick up the coat in a most unexpected way. This is *not-doing*. You are always a bit surprised, because something else moves you in a creative way.

Edges

In phase 2, "X" often seems to be the energy that is against you, as something present or past connected with cultural or family issues. But, at the same time, what appears to be a recurring "X" problem is linked in part to your own rigid view of yourself. By rigid, I mean the idea that, *"I am this, and not that!"*

Although that self-definition is "normal," we see that over time, a rigidity in our self-definition only increases the troubling power of the "X." Some of our recurring problems are created by our rigid identification only with "me" and not with anything else.

So, problems may be connected with past problems, family history, etc., but are also connected with edges, borders to what we consider to be "not me." The edge or border says, *"this is My territory, and get out of here!* Others don't belong here!"

Edges are not just a personal issue. In the world, "edges" to inner experiences appear as borders, a major world problem! Edges are related not just to government and personal problems, but in your psychology, they relate also to body problems. Some recurring body problems could be made easier if your identity was more relaxed and you could pick up a little bit of the "X" in your sense of identity.

Burning Your Edges

Edges separate our "u" from "X." Edges make "X" a disturbance. But this disturbance is not just a bad thing, it helps us to become conscious of "X." Edges create the possibility for awareness of awareness or diversity consciousness. In a way, problems can be good because they make us face our own internal (and external) u + X diversity issues.

In Chapters 5 and 7, I briefly mentioned the inner work practice of "burning" a troubling experience. Here, I want to show how burning can be used in a meditative practice to help with chronic, recurring problems.

Having an edge is natural, but it can be transcended by the technique of "burning" to get through that edge. As I have said, burning means *amplifying*—intensifying an "X" experience in movement and sound so much that it burns up and everything can relax.

If someone is stuck as "u," exaggerate or "burn" that "u" till it relaxes and moves along. BURN! Exaggerate the experience of "u" in phase 2 until new phases appear. Even though you do not like an "X," you can *burn* it to create a new relationship with it.

Burning means to AMPLIFY ALL SOUNDS, MOTIONS, and EXPERIENCES of "X." Make them more and more until you burn the "X" and get to its essence. This technique allows you to go from phase 2 to phase 3 or 4 and feel relaxed—at least temporarily, long enough to get some tips.

For example, someone I work with has a heart problem that terrifies her. The heart problem increases her blood pressure, which increases the heart problem. She did not know what to do. I asked her, "Can you take your hand and show me the experience of the troublesome energy in that heart problem? Can you show me that with a motion on the desk where you are sitting?" I waited a minute, and then she *rhythmically knocked on the desk.* I said, "Can you burn that and make that knocking stronger?" She knocked harder and suddenly said, "Oh! It knocks me out! I am knocked out, and . . . *I can relax*!!" In other words, she went from phase 2 to phase 4. I said, "Let's be knocked out, together" and we were just quiet for a while. The heart problem relaxed for some reason, she felt better, and we could talk about other things.

Burning is a meditation technique to help us with our biggest and most chronic edges. I want to encourage you to dramatize THINGS YOU ARE SHY ABOUT MENTIONING EVEN TO YOURSELF. Burning makes transitions happen so that process flows. Become an improvisation theatre for yourself and the world.

Your biggest edges can be seen in your childhood dream or your first memories. The very first memory predicts recurring diversity situations you might be working with again and again in your everyday life. If you ever get stuck in life, under stress, or faced with a big problem, *your basic childhood dream or early memory is a central tool to work with anytime you get stuck in life. It shows the problems and the potential solutions.* For example, a participant in my classes shared the following childhood dream.

> *U: I am standing on the balcony, and I start falling down, and I see a tree. I am flying, the tree is all I see, and I am going down-down-down, and I always wake up just before I hit the ground. I would step over the balcony and fall down, and I would wake up just before hitting the ground.*
>
> *Arny: Do you have any edges about bringing your spiritual experiences to the ground and making a "boom!"*
>
> *U: Yes, always!!* (laughing)

Arny: Just before you hit the ground, you awaken; the edge is portrayed in the dream as the thing you "almost" do. So you can be very spiritual "in the air and universe." I would guess that you have a tendency to step out of known reality and to dream, and be spiritual, but that it might be an edge to bring your spiritual experience to earth and meet everyday life with an "in-the-air attitude."

This example reminds us how edges are related to diversity issues. For this person, the edge helps differentiate one part of her that is very spiritual and another part that is concrete. We are born with diversity issues with two or more very different energies.

Another participant shared this early childhood memory.

P: I am outside our apartment building in Brooklyn, NY, and the woman who is living in the fourth floor in the same apartment building is called "crazy" by my mom. She throws candy out the window, and my parents say, "Don't eat the candy!" That was reality, not a dream.

Arny: So there is a crazy woman from the fourth floor who throws candy out of the window. And the mother says, "Don't eat the candy!" What do you think? Do you have a tendency to be reasonable and a little shy about your sweet dreamy nature?

P: Yes, WOW!!

Arny: The edges in your first memory or dream say a lot about what will possibly be a recurring theme, so don't be surprised when it comes around again. Say, "HI," instead of, "Not again!"

In working with that early memory, I suggested that the person might need to cruise as a happy, candy-sweet, crazy person and appreciate the diversity within, including the more reasonable motherly part! "I am like my mother to some extent, reasonable and rational, and I am full of sweet, flighty thoughts, but I don't want them all the time."

To know yourself best, play out how you avoid different parts of yourself. Notice your edges and how you avoid certain forms of behavior. Once in a while, love both your normal self and the other more marginal experiences in you.

You can try burning your edges yourself with the following meditation exercise. Directly below, I share an example of doing this exercise with a participant in one of my classes.

Exercise: Not-Doing with a Recurring Problem and Its Story

If you do this with a partner, have one person be the reader. *The reader should go slowly and wait for the dreamer to complete each step before going further.*

A. Which one of your recurring or chronic problems bothered you recently? What phase are or were you in with it: phase 1, cruising; phase 2, conflict with problem's worst energy "X"; phase 3, rolling with u + X energies; phase 4, detached?

B. Right now, how close are you to phase 4? That is, how close are you to feeling centered, to being moved in a not-doing way?

C. Act out your normal "u" energy and the recurring problem's worst "X" energy. In phase 2 amplify "X," BURN it, notice what happens, and notice what its biggest purpose is or was.

D. In phase 3, explore and play, move and be the "u" and the "X," one after the other as dreamlike roles. When you sense yourself flowing, explore phase 4. Let go and be moved . . . notice u + X energies in your "dance" and let the dance spontaneously do things. Continue dancing, and when an insight, relaxed, quiet moment or "cool spot" happens, note what you have learned about the "X" problem. If possible, explore the "u" opening up more to the "X" energy.

E. Go back to your processmind center, phase 4, and feel moved. Let the movement create a story about your recurring problem. Once upon a time, *"There was a 'u' who was troubled by 'X' and who learned to move with 'X' energy and occasionally to flow with all energies and to embrace not-doing with 'X.'"* How did this help that u + X conflict?

Demonstration: Recurring Problems and Not-Doing

The following example from one of my classes is a demonstration of working on a recurring problem. I helped the participant to burn the "X" energy in order to find phase 4, and then to use this phase to facilitate a better relationship between "X" and "u."

Arny: Can I give you a hug? You seem a little nervous. What is it about people that makes you nervous? Are some of them pretty bad?

H: I think I sometimes see my critic out there. She says, "No good!!" She won't do it right, she won't do it well!

Amy: Sounds familiar!

Arny: How many people have a critic like that? You are not alone! 85% of the class! That critic is nonlocal. And a great power.

H: And I am excited too, I should say that as well.

Arny: Let's relax and walk around. Let your body do whatever it feels like and then we can start to work on things.

H: (Walks, then wiggles around.)

Arny: Aha, that wiggle I did not expect! Is it a dance? (They dance and wiggle together, whistling a tune.) . . . *Shall we now go on?*

H: Yes. I have a chronic problem. My sinuses have been bugging me recently; it is congestion. That means I feel pressure in there, and it is a little hard to breathe. I also have a headache (coughs).

Arny: What phase would you say you are in with your symptom? Make a sound about your momentary symptom feelings.

H: (Makes spluttering sound with her lips.) *I have worked with this sinus problem a lot and it keeps coming back. I am sick of it!*

Arny: (speaking to the symptom) *I don't want to say I hate you, I am just frustrated by you!*

H: (answering as the "X" in the symptom) *What do you want?!* (splutter, splutter!)

Arny: (as H's "u") *Get out of here! I am depressed and exhausted by you and in phase 2.* (to H) *How close to phase 4 are you right now with the symptom?*

H: Not too far.

Arny: That is good to know. That gives me the hint that I am allowed to move more fluidly than with somebody else I might be more firm with.

H: Yes! Let's be fluid.

Arny: What does that congestion feel like to you?

H: Right now it is a pressure in the sinuses, behind the eyes, where it is a little dull, foggy. It is a restriction, not watery or drippy.

Arny: If you think of how you would like to be normally, how might you appear now?

H: (shows) *I am usually happy, feeling really present and well, and I like what I am doing. I like my processwork studies, and things are going well.* (Moves arms in cycling motion.)

Arny: Can you act out the recurring problem's worst energy, the "X" energy . . . the pressure maker?

H: Definitely compacting pressure (pressing her hands on her face) *Pfffffffff!*

Arny: Can you act that energy out on me?

H: (Moves sneakily around him, and as Arny plays, she puts a great pressure on the top of his head, exclaiming "yeah, yeah!") *Go back in your box! . . . Oh! I did not expect to say that . . . Yes, go back in your little box and stay there—you should not be out!*

Arny: (Tries to sit up.)

H: No! You don't get up! Stay in your box!

Arny: Now let's amplify that "X" energy. I will play your "X": "Get in your box, lady! Get in that box and stay in that box! Don't you dare fight back or you will be in trouble!" . . . (Now to H) And if you are still stuck in phase 2, burn this "X" energy, amplify it till transitions occur and go directly to phase 4.

H: (Playing the "X" energy, jumps up at Arny!) *Pft! Yeah!*

Arny: Go all the way with this "pft!" energy.

H: (Chases him with fists.) *Pffwwwwwww!!*

Arny: Pretend that "X" is not just a person and burn it.

H: (Swings and spins around with her fists and arms, uses big movements.). . . I am shy! I got to an edge!

Arny: So, go over the edge!!! BURN . . . until you burn it out.

H: (Comes at Arny, who is playing H, then moves around with arms out and hands shaking and waving! The class of people join in, their arms and hands reaching out and meeting hers, joining her sounds!) *I feel so good! . . . I feel so free!*

Arny: You look very free. Phase 4 looks good on you.

H: Thank you, I like being there now in phase 4.

Arny: After phase 4, we are going to go back to phase 3 to explore it; let's first explore now "X," then "u."

H: (Demonstrates in movement, going from bowed over as "u" to being the crushing "X," back and forth.) *Wow . . . that "X" is pushing me out of the box. . . . The "X" was pushing me through the bottom of the box and out!!*

Arny: So let's be free, sense phase 4, let yourself be free and moved around.

H: (Moves and finds unpredictable, creative movements in her floating motions.) *Mmmmm* (smiles). *Yes. I notice the "X" pusher in my dance, and the quieter "u" in there too.*

Arny: And if an insight or cool spot happens, just notice what you learned about the "X" problem.

H: There is something about floating freely and being free. I imagined when I was out there that there were forces that were pushing on me, like electrical forces and light and all of those things, and they were trying to move me freely to play even in relationships . . . now being permitted to play with big things.

Arny: Playing with big things! OK, now let's make a little story about the "X" problem: "Once upon a time "u," a normal person, was troubled by an "X" and learned to flow with the "X" energy."

H: Once upon a time there was a little "u" who was troubled by an "X," and the little one said, "OK" to the big one, because she was only little and the big one seemed to know what it was talking about. Much of the time the "u" would just be in the box and do nothing, was very quiet, and "X" kept pushing and pushing, and one day it pushed so far in, that she exploded out!

She was freed! It was great to be free . . . just following the currents, the solar winds, and it was great to float because she could see so much. Since she wanted to do all this on earth, she came back to do it spontaneously on earth with people, with lots of energy. She used the sunlight and the moonlight and the birds to move with.

Arny: Yes, sounds like she began not-doing!

H: It was great! She was very, very happy, and her nose felt better! The end!

Arny: Thank you!

This demonstration shows how the technique of burning the troublesome "X" can allow someone to shift from phase 2 (conflict with the "X") to phase 4 (detachment), and then to take that phase 4 state of mind and use it to facilitate a more fluid interaction between the "u" and the "X" (phase 3). At the end, phase 1 naturally arises: happiness!

Another participant reported their learnings after trying the exercise: My symptom and the "X" are trying to wear me out, and "X" says,

"If I keep pushing on you, you will have to give up, and then you will have to surrender and relax!" And I just flowed and moved, relaxed, and I even flew!

When you practice this technique, remember to exaggerate, to burn the "X" energy to be free and to jump over the edges into phases 3 and 4.

Things to Remember from Chapter 8

1. If you have an edge against an "X," intensify and burn that "X" to get its message and notice the possible next stages in relationship with that "X."

CHAPTER 9

Elmo and Kermit Introduce Loopy Relationship Meditation

• • •

16. **Elmo and Kermit.**

In this chapter, I explore meditation for relationships before we get back to world issues in the next section, Part IV: Your Deepest Art and Best Science for Our World. If we want to work on world problems, we can explore resolving our own relationship difficulties with a close partner or friend, family member, or extended family. I share a new relationship meditation to bring more joy and creativity to your relationships by accessing phase 4 fluidity.

As many of us know from worldwork, what is bothering an individual is rarely only her or his own business. Some of the problems we suffer from are impersonal and need to be handled as world or universal issues, not only internally. This is what I called *nonlocality* in Chapter 5, when we explored how our body experience connects with relationship troubles. Nonlocality is the experience in phases 3 and 4 that we are connected, and that whatever bothers us about the other person also belongs to us!

One of my points in this chapter is simply that *life is loopy!* The word *loopy* means crazy, silly, circular. Loopy is a very interesting word; some people say that *loopy* means nuts or weird or strange. Life is loopy because it can go forward, appearing as if it is going in a straight line, and then it loops backward before going forward again. As discussed in Chapter 6, process is cyclical and there appear to be timeless process patterns that make our lives a little loopy.

Life is loopy. When most people see themselves twist and turn in life, they often cry, "What?! That's weird." Or, "Wow, can't life be straight and easier?" Organizations get even more upset when "loopiness" occurs. Most of us complain and say, "What, the same problem coming again?"

Amy taught me that Jim Henson, the creator of the Muppets, said, "Puppets can do what people can't!" So if you ever can't express yourself, use a puppet or a sock to speak for you! Two Muppets, Elmo and Kermit, are going to help me introduce meditation as a creative relationship practice.

Kermit the frog is similar to all of us, getting upset about the loopiness in life, as you can see in the following dialogue.

Kermit: Hello! I am Kermit, the green frog.
Elmo: Hi! I am Elmo.
Kermit: Hi, Elmo. Don't be confused, and don't be afraid, life is reasonable and linear!
Elmo: No, Kerm. Life is loopy, not straight! Life loops around and around.
K: I don't believe it. I never saw that! I want people to be reasonable, rational, and comprehensive in all that they do. People must not be loopy!
E: But, Kerm, I thought that as a frog you would not be so linear. Your hope that people are reasonable, rational, and comprehensible doesn't work because people are not only straight.
K: People MUST NOT be loopy!!!
E: Wait a minute, Kermit, haven't you said, "People MUST NOT be loopy" before to me?! Haven't you already said that? We are cycling.
K: Ahhhhhh. OH no!!! . . . we are cycling.
E: You see, life is loopy!!!
K: Hmmmm . . . ohhhh . . . got it!

It seems paradoxical, but you see, Elmo and Kermit actually agree. We cycle through phases. Life is loopy but we rarely laugh about it—we try to control life, and become shocked at how out of control life is. We are all like Kermit and Elmo. We try to aim carefully and proceed straight ahead, but then we loop. After a moment or a few years, we cycle back to where we were, before going further.

Elmo must have been in phase 4. In that center *and* the phase, he realizes that we can be detached and flow, and then before we know it, we are looping around into phases 1 and 2 again.

Fortunately, the detached processmind, empty mind, or phase 4 is behind and in everything. That is why, with a little practice, you can usually feel the universe moving you, and from phase 4's viewpoint, things flow and are loopy.

This viewpoint can be particularly helpful for dealing with trauma in our personal histories. Many of us have had mild to heavy traumatic "X" energies in our lives, which were personal, familial, social, and global. The worst of your problems are yours; however, from the phase 4 nonlocal perspective, they are not only yours. You may feel that an "X energy" uses or abuses you, and that is uncomfortable. Then, without realizing it, the very thing that bothers you is the thing that you do to yourself, and sometimes to others.

Nonlocality is a core aspect of process-oriented relationship work since what bothers you may also be in the "air." So awareness of awareness—that is, of how your experiences touch you—may help you understand others around you.

Nonlocality is a phase 3 and phase 4 sense. With awareness you can sense the nonlocality behind phase 3, phase 2, and phase 1 in relationships. When I am "me" and you are "you," we can be in phases 1 and/or 2. In phases 3 and 4, there are shared experiences between us as well.

Process Phases in Relationship

Here is a brief overview of how the process phases can be observed in relationships.

> *In phase 1,* You are you and I am me, and we are different. Don't mix us up! Yes, we have a relationship, and in phase 1, we think, "Let's have a good time, let's *not* think about any problems!"

In phase 2, something between us or from the outside bothers us. It is "you" (or "me" or "them")!

In phase 3, relationship flows between you and me. Sometimes your view comes forward, sometimes mine, and we are aware that *we share* each other's views.

In phase 4, "we" are in a wonderful atmosphere, with the feeling and field between us creative and open. Awesome. We feel we are "one," so to speak. We feel something universal between and moving us. Call it love, luck, life, or the universe.

A lot of people project bliss, unity, or sexual ecstasy onto phase 4 in relationship. That is beautiful when it happens. Phase 4 in relationship is not just a personal experience of ecstasy, however, but the sense that you and the other are aspects of something infinite. We are not just individuals; the universe is doing something with us that connects us to one another and to our whole planet and solar system. Call it *trans, bi, gay, hetero, friendship, love,* or whatever you like in consensus reality. In phase 4, it is the infinite that moves us.

There are many kinds of relationship problems that I have seen over the years. Here are some of the main relationship problems in relation to phases.

In phase 1, people say, "Everybody bothers us! We just want to forget the world and only talk to people we like."

In phase 2, you often hear one partner or the other saying, "You drive me crazy! You must CHANGE!" The response is often, "No, you are the problem!"

- *Or* I have often heard, "You remind me of one of my parents that I can't stand!"
- *Or* "What happened to our intimacy??" There is an "X" in there that has not been addressed.
- *Or* "If you don't love me . . . if you don't quit seeing this other person, I am leaving."

- *Or,* one person feels downed by the other's unconsciousness of her or his power and rank. There is too little diversity consciousness. In other words, one person feels that the other does not recognize her or his abuse of personal, financial, social, or psychological rank. Other phase 2 issues include diversity issues around race, sexual orientation, age, health, family background, and unshared interests.

In phases 3 and 4, I rarely hear about problems, only about shared understanding and good feelings.

Process-oriented meditation in relationships depends upon the phases of the individuals in the relationship. To notice these phases, sense the feelings and moods and the partners' SOUNDs.

As you experiment with this practice, you will notice that different sounds come up in you when you are near different people. Notice the sound and its phase. Notice and enjoy one another in phase 1. Share doubts and avoid or fight it out in phase 2. In phase 3 pick up the "X," the ghost roles and problems in the air, or the problem in the relationship, and play it out in an open forum. In phase 4, if possible, you might enjoy exploring a first experience or dream at the beginning of your relationship. Bring that up and explore it deeply as a symbol of the field and phases connecting you.

In all relationships it is helpful to talk about experiences. Dramatize them; make life and relationship more "dramatic" if and when possible. Everyone, in every culture, often represses talking about problems. Rarely do people speak about the "X" that is bothering them.

Instead, most of us choose to be moody and create double signals in which we say one thing but signal another. You don't have to talk about everything, but you can try to express your feelings in sounds, with or without the other person.

I demonstrated this idea in my class by focusing on myself and talking to myself in front of the group.

"Arny, what is bothering you today?! Come on! Did you say everything! Are you making yourself look happier than you are? Are you totally happy?"

"Yo! That means, yes and no."

"Well, what is bothering you?"

I hear an inner voice saying now, "This group wants you to go into things, and it has got to be done right away!" (laughter) *Dear group, please join me in this inner–outer dialogue for just a minute with sounds of "X" kinds of things that are bothering you!"* (the group makes HUGE sounds!!)

Amy asked me, "Do you feel better?"

"I feel A LOT better! My process is mine, but when shared, I always feel better. That is what I hope will happen in the following exercise. Become aware of awareness and share it as part of relationships."

The important point is that the "X" thing that bothers us is almost always shared with others. This is nonlocality. Do an open forum for yourself with it, and if possible, for the others as well. To explore this process for yourself, try the following exercise with a partner if possible.

Exercise: The A, B, C of Creative Relationship Work

Choose a partner with whom to work. Then, meditate at first individually and then together with the person you will work with in the following dyad. It might be someone you like or don't like, you know or don't know. Meditate out loud with your partner, together. Then, discuss things. Here are the details of the exercise.

The A, B, and C of Relationship Meditation

Share the "u," "X," and the infinite in relationship. Meet the other person and chat for a few minutes. Choose one of you to read the instructions (and both participate). (Reader, go slowly and wait for both yourself and the "dreamer" to go further.)

> *A. ALONE, both meditate. In which relationship phase* do you sense the relationship with your partner is in? Make a sound to

indicate what phase you are in (phase 1, cruising along with no need for any "X" problem; phase 2, conflict/tense with an inner and/or an outer "X" energy *in self or other*; phase 3, *flowing* with your u + X energies; phase 4, feeling *infinite* connection).

B. *ALONE,* relax and each, alone, let the universe dream and move you in phase 4 for a minute. Then, still working alone, go to phase 1. Go inside and appreciate what's good in the relationship. Next go to phase 2 and note and act out your typical "u" and a possible "X" trouble (in self or other). Now go to phase 3 and try, if possible, to flow between the u + X. Be "u" then be "X" for a minute. Back in phase 4, be moved by the universe and note if any insights appear about anything in yourself or the relationship. Write down those insights.

C. Now both *TOGETHER, first meditate together quietly,* with each person sensing her or his inner experience, feeling, movement, body signals, and visual flirts. Now s*hare your experiences OUT LOUD* with your partner. Both speak about the phase you are in (alone or with other): phase 1, cruising; phase 2, u + X diversity issue; phase 3, dialogue + FLOW between u + X in self and/or other; phase 4, detachment-dance.

D. *Finally, creatively process and flow* with your relationship experiences together by discussing and exploring and feeling into oneself and the other. Both speak out loud, naming the phases occurring inside and/or between you (e.g., phase 1, cruising; phase 2, u + X conflict; phase 3, flowing between the "X" + "u"; phase 4, feeling *infinite* connection) and notice how the phases flow. Speak with one another, and also feel free to sing and dance as well.

After about 10 minutes, *both relax and discuss,* "Did phase 4 flow freely? That is, did you have the sense of being moved spontaneously and unpredictably by the universe?" Whether or not this phase 4 occurred, both *e*xplore phase 4 now; let the universe dance you, and let feelings or songs arise. Perhaps one song will arise that you can sing together.

After the dance, share what, if anything, the song and associated feelings say about relationship. Discuss and show one another how the *u + X + all experiences* may be diversity issues, problems, but also potential powers that belong (at least in part) to both of you.

I demonstrated this exercise in class with two colleagues who were soon to co-teach together. The relationship meditation allowed them see that they shared the "X" energy of a perfectionist critic that put down their teaching styles. In the later part of the work, they danced and sang together, and realized that "just being" is the core of their relationship and the power of their teaching. Some of the teachers' students were present and observed, "Remarkable, this is the first time we ever saw the inner life of teachers who would soon be teaching us."

So, what do our relationship experts, Kermit and Elmo, have to say?

Elmo: Well, Kerm, did you get something linear out of this?
Kermit: Yes, I am learning all about following feelings that you cannot always comprehend.
Elmo: Kerm, you got it!! Relationships are loopy, and if you follow that loopiness, you can relate in the best possible way!

Relationships are loopy in part because of our shared interconnectedness, because of the potential song and dance between us waiting to be discovered. Remember, no one person in a relationship has a problem "alone."

The nonlocality of relationships makes me remember an African teacher whom I love, Sobonfu Some, and her native African area, Burkina Faso, a country in West Africa.[32] In her community they understand that you cannot keep secrets, because *if somebody keeps secrets, the whole community is affected. They also understand that anytime there was a problem between two people or when one person was sick, it was the community's problem.*

My social action is to ask you, dear reader, to bring this relationship awareness to your lives and streets. Bring it into your bedroom, your living room, bring it into your friendships and organizations. If you see somebody on the streets who does not know how to talk to people, if you feel safe enough, please use the exercise to help make more relationship in our world.

One of my class participants asked, "How would you do that with a street person that smells of drugs and looks collapsed and dazed?" They enacted a slumped figure, dazed, confused, silent. Using phase 4 and not-doing, I modeled a radical possibility.

> *I would say, "Boy, I am in that same state of mind too. I hate facing reality, and oh, I wonder if I can dance, if we can dance"* (*reaches out and touches J.'s finger*)? "Oh*oooo*" (*J. smiles, fingers touching*). *"Maybe that is enough contact. I like your smile, and I am going to give you a kiss from a distance."*

With practice, relationship meditation can allow you to enter the "other's" state of mind, speak her or his language, and still be self-protective as well.

In reality, I had recently met such a drugged person on a popular shopping street in Portland, Oregon, and I went one little step more. I touched his finger gently, to let the person know he was not alone, and I spoke, sang, and danced with him. At least for that time he felt that he wasn't alone. We are also all together in whatever is happening to one person. We need to "dance" and "sing" and "improvise" with one another.

In process-oriented relationship work, one party makes a move and the other creates another move. This leads to forms of dancing, singing, and "jamming"—and that is creativity in relationship. Relationship meditation is a wonderful challenge that will help you appreciate who you are and the awesomeness we can all create and share with one another.

Things to Remember from Chapter 9

1. Develop your awareness of awareness to appreciate that "everything changes."
2. Process-oriented meditation is simple yet subtle to explain. Notice what you notice, notice the phase you are in, and when possible, use phase 4 to follow and appreciate all phases and experiences as parts of a larger flow process.
3. Remember nonlocality in community. Shared experiences bind us together in relationships and can create a sense of wellness. Nonlocality can be experienced in part through singing, jamming, dancing, and letting life and community create the way.

PART IV

Your Deepest Art and Best Science for Our World

• • •

THE FOCUS OF PART IV is developing your "deepest art" to assist you in using the knowledge and sciences you have learned to help our world. This is the second training that we discussed in Part I. It includes the phase-aware bodywork and meditation techniques of Parts II and III, and these new techniques to connect you to your deepest art.

As I have stressed before, the essence of deep democracy is the processmind, or phase 4. It is the experience of letting yourself be moved by the universe. It appears to be a "black box," as we discussed in Chapter 2, governed by quantum theory, a "quantum mind" with nonlocal characteristics, and is your greatest shamanistic ally.

Now I want to speak of this processmind in terms of your "deepest art." Your deepest art is needed to work with tensions that bother you inside and outside.

CHAPTER 10

Your Deepest Art and Best Science for Helping Our Planet

• • •

The Edge to Living Your Dreaming

I HAVE EMPHASIZED THAT OUR world needs deep democracy to unify inner experiences, dreaming, and world issues. In my private practice these days, I am in contact with a number of world leaders who are interested in their inner life. However, like most people, they hesitate in bringing their inner work out because they fear the public will not accept their fluidity.

We are all like those leaders. We mostly develop "realists" through our educational systems. Yet we know from our dreams that the monsters we fight outside are similar to what we all must deal with inside. Hatred, diversity unconsciousness, and self-dislike are all world issues. Just admitting that you and I are somehow like the monsters we are fighting—saying it just *one day a year*—would bring a needed global paradigm shift.

Our present world is at an edge of realizing that we must not only fight the "X" that troubles us, but also experience it as part of ourselves. We need an open mind to bring forward our deepest selves. If you fear showing your deepest self in public, then speak against yourself, have a dialogue between the u + X in public. Why? Because a public that is focused mainly on overcoming some "opponent" becomes, in many ways, the opponent itself.

Recall that in phase 2, we must speak against the other, but then if you forget phase 3—namely, that *we have the other in us*—the result will be a form of war. Putting psychology and politics together, bringing phase awareness to inner and outer work is something Amy and I have done for the military, for United Nations groups, for politicians, and even for terrorists in different parts of the world. I have learned that phase 3 works, but it takes your deepest art to make it work in the heaviest circumstances. It is this deepest art that I want to focus on here.

Your deepest art comes from phase 4. If we can bring this deepest art to our facilitation practice, it is possible to enable the transition from heavy phase 2 conflict to the role switching and fluidity of phase 3.

In this chapter, I share two exercises that may help you to find your deepest art, and illustrate with a demonstration of my own inner work to show how connecting to a place in nature can help with inner and outer tensions.

The Importance of Double Signals

Remember that dreamland's phase 3 is filled with marginalized, invisible, and visible "double signals." As I mentioned in the book's introduction,[33] one of the leading people at a United Nations group told us that "knowledge of double signals could change the U.N." I often share an example of two parties who are about to make peace. One shakes hands but has a hidden grimace on the face. The other has a double signal around his mouth because he is grinding his teeth. You can guess that the peace treaty they are shaking their hands about is not going to hold very long.

It is relatively easy to see double signals in an ordinary state of mind, but under tension, it is more difficult to let go and experience your own or others' double signals or other things you have learned. So let's explore how to work with this tension using phase 4 and your deepest art.

What we do as facilitators, therapists, coaches, organizational consultants, and world leaders works best with these three steps:

1. First, ask about, explore, and discover people's needs.
2. Explore the dominant phase of the group with which you are working. Are people relaxing in phase 1, in tension in phase 2, able to

switch roles in phase 3, or feeling at peace with what is happening as in phase 4?

3. Enact *your* phase 4 *deepest art to work best.*

Discover People's Needs

Before working with people, ask about what *they* need. Facilitators are often more interested in applying what they *know* than in finding out what the people actually *need.* So even if you work with familiar people, ask about their needs, for needs change from day to day. Ask directly, "What do you need today? What does the group, or different parts of this group, need?" There is always a diversity of needs. Learn about that diversity of needs.

> *The needs of a group depend upon the culture. If you work in Europe, Africa, or Asia, be aware that cultures and communication styles are different. Can you understand their needs? Can you speak that culture's nonverbal languages(s)? Do you know about the diversity problems within their own cultures and in the larger world as well?*

Remember their problem and needs, not just the problem you think you should solve or were hired to resolve. Listen carefully to what the people ask for. The culture, the problem, the nationality of the group, the race or racial identity of the people that you are working with are all *very* important and *very* marginalized. Remember the diversity problems connected to gender, race, sexual orientation, nationality, age, wealth, appearance, etc. Listen to their dreams and notice their health issues. Health issues are often repressed. Remembering needs can sometimes be a matter of life and death.

Explore the Dominant Phase of the Group

Next, explore the phase your people are in. As I have said before, the basic principle behind process phases is that *everything changes.* In phase 2, when you or your organization or clients are in a tense situation, it is natural to feel stuck and that NOTHING will work. So respect that feeling, but watch—just about everything changes. If someone says, "Oh, no, not again, I am or we are such idiots for having this problem again!" remember Kermit and Elmo from Chapter 9 who taught us that "life is loopy." Remember phases 1, 2, 3, and 4 and your timeless process pattern from Chapter 6 and recall how to discover, explore, and enact phase 4 deepest art.

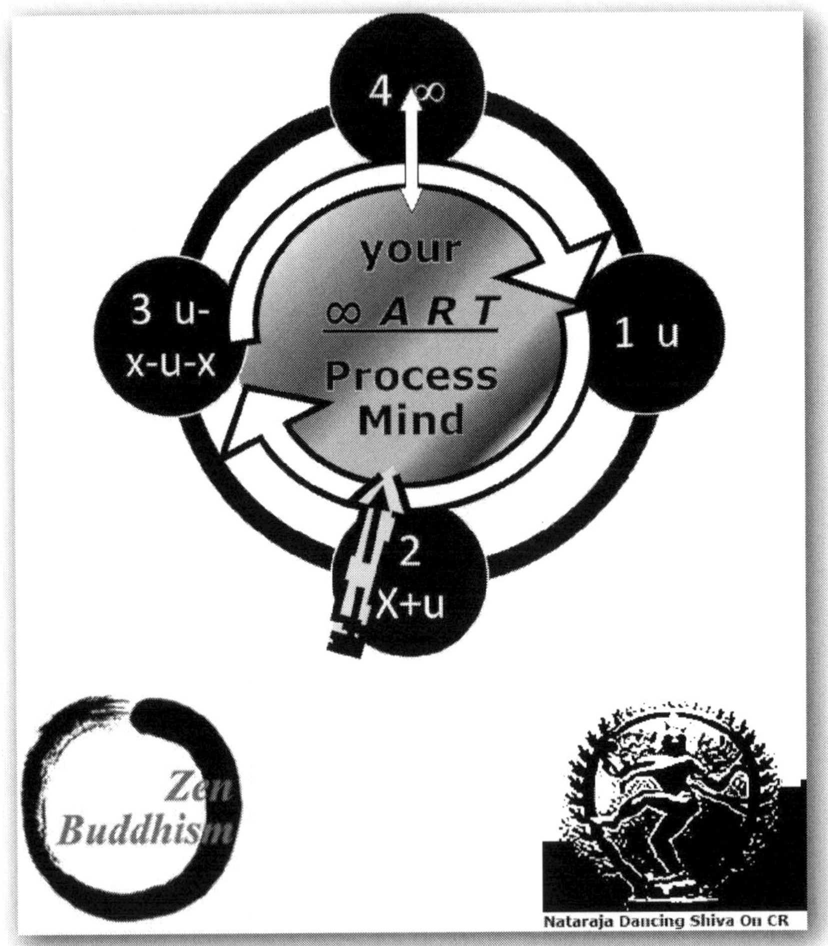

17. **Your Deepest Art and Processmind**

Here is a brief review of some ways to work with groups in each phase.

In phase 1, when "we" are cruising and happy, remember we may have had some problems yesterday but need time to enjoy ourselves today. So forget problems for the moment; we don't want to talk about our problems! In phase 1, listen to people, ask them about their natures, their first dreams, their organizational vision, etc., to support them more. What is the group's mission statement? In phase 1, help them realize it.

In phase 2, overt or covert tension and conflict are present. People who are afraid to speak of tension may look away or appear tense, angry, or afraid. Often people are hurt because of social rank and power abuses. In phase 2, explore rank and power differences. Help people who feel victimized to defend themselves and take a stand. What is bothering them most? Medical problems, people from another country, climate change, etc.

In phase 2, people often suffer not only from being downed, but also from the feeling of worthlessness. In phase 2, strengthen the people you work with so that that they may eventually have the courage to facilitate a dialogue with the "X."

The biggest recurring problem for most organizations often appears as it is developing its first vision. Very young organizations often say, "We want to be more successful than our competitors," the "X." Expect that the "X" will appear again in their process. Our everyday minds are phase-ist, we tend to favor one particular phase, but process is loopy and cyclical.

In phase 3, we often hold on to consensus reality while repressing the sense of being moved between energies as in dreams. Yet people need the chance to experience themselves as "X." In phase 3, people can flow between the "u" and "X." Help your group's "u" gain some of the power in the "X." *Demonstrate* how to do this yourself first, and then suggest an open forum with the individuals and groups.

Phase 4 is the deepest art, a background to all experience. Most of us hope that *we will stay in phase 4*, but as we know, it is a phase as well as a permanent background. I love Hinduism's Nataraja or Dancing Shiva, the cosmic ecstatic dancer, as a symbol or embodiment of this phase. In phase

4, we flow beyond the parts as we are moved. This experience leads to our deepest art and makes it more accessible.

Phase 4 is what Chinese Taoism calls *Wu Wei* (not-doing). Wu Wei means that it is not "you" but "it" that does things. In this phase, there is little struggle or effort.

Often I feel that I have a thousand things to do. But in phase 4, I have *nothing* to do; "it" does the things. In the other phases we get stressed out. Phase 4 helps gives us access to everything we know.

Phase 4 is important for your whole life, and it is needed to make your science work. As I have said, phase 4's nonlocality reminds me of quantum mechanics. Richard Feynman said the heart of quantum mechanics is a "mystery."[34] We cannot know cognitively what is happening in this quantum world, and for me, this is the space of dreaming. All we know is that there are waves of something that quantum mechanics describes in its wave equation.[35] Before you observe something, it is a mysterious non-locatable wave. Einstein refused to think that "God throws dice," or that nature could be so mysterious or capricious. How could nature be both particle and wave-like? But apparently it is (Thanks to http://www.physicsoftheuniverse.com/topics_quantum_probability.html).

In phase 4, you are everywhere and anywhere. As you may have experienced, to know phase 4, relax and use your spontaneous movement (or wave-like undulating dance) that may suddenly become a "particle" as a particular "idea " pops up. When you decide to look into that dance, a particle may suddenly appear! What was the particle before it was seen? Feynman said, "Don't think about it!" That was 1948, or 1950, and since then, physics has thought about it, but has not yet come further.

Phase 4 is a blurry mind experience. It is empty, and at first blurry, and when you intend to look at it, *blip!*—you get "it" but you cannot track where that thing was before. This blur is the key to understanding the nature and background of what Jung called synchronicity: events that seem significantly related but are not connected by any physical means.

Remember my story in Chapter 7 about our experience in Ireland some years ago?[36] With all those hundreds of people in that room in Dublin, there was so much agony and tension we could not think straight or use our science. Yet because Amy and I were supporting each other, I could go into that blurry space and without even thinking about it, suddenly had thoughts that began the resolution just prior to the peace accord that was voted for the day after the seminar. Phase 4 nonlocal connections and synchronicity occur when your deepest art is present, even when you are in tension and can hardly use the science you have learned.

Developing your deepest art is a kind of second training needed to make your science work. We have all had times of being in a scene where we cannot think straight and we just don't know what to do. We cannot use what we have learned, our normal science. Phase 4's deepest art helps. It is unpredictably creative.

In one of my classes, a participant commented, "But I sometimes feel it is impossible to use it." And, I understand completely! I can't use it either, if I begin from a normal state of consciousness. It is impossible to get there using your intention! What I have discovered is that "it" happens. I do not know how to do that phase 4 experience, but *it* does.

And, I think you can sometimes do it even when you are very depressed and miserable and hopeless. Maybe even especially then. Fear, hopelessness, and depression are terrible, but if you go into them carefully, you might end up in phase 4, and this can be very helpful.

Another person had a question about our experience in Ireland with the two powerful leaders of each side screaming at each other in a public meeting. Did this phase 2 phenomenon take me into a phase 4 experience and allow me to bring an unexpected facilitative intervention to this tense and frightening conflict scene?

It seems so, yes! The tensions of phase 2 knocked me out . . . in a positive way. Then the process did the rest. My point is that there are many good business methods and conflict resolution procedures that work beautifully if groups are in phase 1, 3, or 4, but very little really works well in the severe conflicts of phase 2.

If the conflict is not too wild, many things work. In a wild conflict, take one side and then take the other. If you cannot do that, then let go so that your own creative unpredictable phase 4 art can help you and others more deeply express the viewpoints of the "u" and the "X."

You might be wondering if you can be in more than one phase at once. And the answer is *yes*. Hot days occur in the winter, cold days in the summer. For example, you can be totally detached and you hardly notice the difference between phase 4 and phase 1. If you are in phase 4 and in the center of all things, you are totally detached and dreaming, moved by the field. There is an overlap between phases. The essence level, phase 4, is at the center and behind everything. So, you can be in conflict and yet you can sense a bit of this deepest part of yourself, and this seems to make phase 2 conflicts a little easier.

Depression and tiredness point to phase 4. Every time you feel tired, let go of your regular self so you can relax and "dream." In this way, tiredness can lead to phase 4. Phase 4 is an essence-level experience; it is one of our most altered states, the state of *letting go*.

Compassion

To develop your deepest art, explore phase 4 and notice, if you can, a compassionate attitude towards yourself and others. A phase 4 attitude towards our planet is one that recognizes conflict as a natural part of relationship processes that can be mitigated by phase awareness and intentional work with phase 2.

Also notice that *how you are moved by the universe* is one of your most amazing characteristics, yet one you probably need time to discover. Your natural behavior in phase 4 is often projected upon a place in nature that you love. You think nature is beautiful, but forget that YOU are that nature as well.

Developing your deepest art is the central part of your *second training*. Recall that the skills and science you have learned comprise the *first training*. The second training, however, includes experiences from the nonlocal quantum realm.

The second training connects us to the "field" in which we live—which is *a phase 3 and phase 4 ability.* Being moved by space, by the field in which we live, is something that happens to all of nature. Recall that the very same wind or field can create very different behaviors in each of us. Remember seeing grass and trees in a windy field. The same wind or power-field creates two entirely different motions in the grass and in the trees. The grass is like one kind of "person" in the field, and the trees represent a second kind of "person."

Every person, like the grass and trees, behaves differently in the same field. Each of our motions and behaviors may differ in the same field. Yet *we are all moved by the same* power. We are different but sense the same thing, each in our own way.

A big point is that we might look like a person, and in consensus reality we are people, but from a deeper viewpoint, we are a ribbon in the field that is "moving us," each in her and his own way.

To begin developing your *deepest art,* you can try the two exercises in this chapter. First, I illustrate with my own inner work demonstration. Then, below, you will find the exercise to try it yourself, on your own or with a partner.

In the following example of my own inner work, guided by Amy in one of our seminars, I illustrate how I found my deepest art through a connection to nature.

Demonstration: Deepest Art Earthspot Inner Work

Amy: What would you say you need these days?

Arny: We have so much stress, I would like something that lights up to show me the way. The thing that troubles me most concerns this large commercial group in the world that has some problems and would like our help. It is connected to three major governments, but we don't have the time to work with it. We need help with that, because some of the things they stand for are things I don't totally support. A big business group, let's call it that, is pressuring us.

Amy: What methods do you have to deal with that problem?

Arny: My favorite method has always been following my dreams, and I dreamed about having fun—that looks good—but I don't yet feel that "fun."

Amy: And what phase would you say you are in with that organization, the "X" that is bothering you?

Arny: Phase 2, feeling conflicted between what I call their "X" and my "u."

Amy: So, let's work on the "X." Can you feel and show us and act out with your hands your normal "u" energy?

Arny: My normal energy is mostly wave-like (shows with hands).

Amy: Feel and act out motions for this "X," this organization that is pressuring you. How would you show that?

Arny: (Shows arms coming down and pointing directly forward, straight at him.) *Their energy is, "You come now! You have 3 months to do this!"*

Amy: Sketch these two energies. (Arny sketches.) *Now, Arny, we are going to get to your deepest art, so take a minute now, putting aside the sketches, relax a little bit, and let yourself drift into that blurry, quantum realm. Go into a foggy state, where you relax your mind.*

Arny: The word blurry *helps me relax my mind.*

Amy: Relax your neck a little bit, your shoulders, your arms, your pelvis, your legs. Let go carefully and as you do that, imagine, sense, and feel that the universe around you begins to move you about like your ribbon in the wind. Be careful of your own body as you do that.

Arny: (Begins to move, flowing, sinking, a wave-like flowing, then suddenly a jerking motion appears, and the wave motion comes again as well.)

Amy: As you are moving, notice a couple of recurring motions.

Arny: (Continues moving and finds a repetitive movement.) *Yes, there are recurring motions. There is sinking and then this wild splashing or rising up.*

Amy: As you do that, notice if the u + X energies of your sketch are somehow present in those recurring motions, in that dance. As you are doing that, ask yourself, "What nature, quality, and spot on earth reminds you most of that dance?"

Arny: In Yachats on the Oregon coast, there is a hole in the rock that the waves surge into, creating a big spray in the air. Yesterday we saw that big spray; we saw a big rainbow in that spray. When the tide comes in, it makes a big spray in that "blow-hole." With the sun at a certain angle from behind your head, there is a rainbow. Yesterday was a king tide, a very high tide, and the rainbow was constant.

Amy: Now let yourself be moved again as if you were dancing on that earth spot, with the spraying water and rainbow, and while moving, remember the "X" energy. Notice if your dance gives you a spontaneous tip about how to deal with that "X" energy and that conflict. Use your attention to catch really quick tips that come up, that may suddenly arise.

Arny: (Makes more movements, repeats.) *Oh, my god! I got it! Oh, yes . . . "Use your energy, your timing, and their energy"* (rising up motion)—*oh, my god, I got it!* My *timing,* their *energy!*

Amy: Can you imagine what it would be like to use those tips in reality?

Arny: Let's use our timing—maybe next year! And their energy! Yes!! Do it next year! We can be a little bossy like they are. I notice, I am too humble. I need to be more like they are—big director types! Yes! Our timing! Their energy! I need them: I need to integrate their energy myself. I can now think psychologically. Well, they are a group of many thousands, but we can direct things too.

I am touched and almost want to cry because I found what I was looking for, near that rainbow. The spray that comes out like that, for me was more than just water and rock . . . it is a living power coming from the quietude of the non-stormy sea. Our timing, their energy! Thanks!

What I hope this example shows is that your deepest art is *yours* and it is also none of your business—it belongs to nature. It is given to you—that is why it is hard at first to believe in it. How can we believe in funny little wiggles?

Exercise: Your Deepest Art

Read through the exercise and reflect on the questions in each step. You might like to take notes about your answers. Immediately following the exercise, you can read some comments from seminar participants who tried the exercise themselves.

A. What do you need these days? What bugs/bothers you *the most* recently, from inside or outside yourself (we'll call it "X")? And what methods do you have to deal with it?

B. What phase are you ("u") in with the "X" that is bothering you: (phase 1, happy, cruising, supporting your basic nature, forgetting "X"; phase 2, anxious, tense, conflicted, troubled by "X" as a figure or energy; phase 3, role switching with u + X problem energy, sometimes being "u" and sometimes "X"; or phase 4, exhausted or peaceful, detached, moved by the universe)? Make a note about the phase.

C. Let's work on that "X." If possible, stand and feel and act out with your hands the normal "u" and its type of energy. Then feel, act out, and make motions with your hands to express the "X" energy. Make a note and a sketch of each type of energy on paper.

D. Now find and use your deepest art. Stand if you can, relax, relax your neck, your arms, hips, legs, let go carefully, and let your mind be a bit blurry, and imagine, sense, and feel that the universe around you begins to move and dance you about. Be careful of yourself and those around you. As you move, notice *how* you move and especially notice *recurring motions* that you make. There may be a couple of recurring types of motions.

Take your time to notice this. And while you dance, notice if you feel/see/sense the u + X energies somewhere in those recurring dance motions.

E. What quality of nature and spot on the earth reminds "u" of your dance energies? Finally, imagine that you go to that earth/nature spot and let yourself be moved again by your art-dance with its recurring motions and—while moving—remember the "X" energy and wait and notice if your art-dance gives you a spontaneous tip about dealing with that "X" energy and conflict. It may surprise you. Use your attention to catch quick tips that suddenly arise. Make notes about your art-dance and the tip you got from this dance.

Some participants in my classes shared their experiences after practicing the exercise, and we saw the connection between their deepest art and their earliest childhood dream or memory.

> *In my art dance movement, I became leaves blown about by the wind, and in my childhood dream there is a tiger in the bakery chasing me around and around—and I have never, never worked on that aspect of the dream, being blown or chased round and round.*
>
> *I also saw a part of my childhood dream that I had never worked on—the message that I got from phase 4 was "roll with it." In my childhood dream, there was a rolling figure with no arms and legs that was chasing me, someone in a wheelchair rolling after me!!*
>
> *In my childhood dream, I was being chased by a monster, and I fell down and was paralyzed and could not move any more. The message I got from my art dance was "give up, let it go"—it was the same sense of release, fall, stay there, and don't get up.*

Many people's experiences echo these comments, and I have learned there seems to be a connection between your deepest art movement and your most basic dream patterns, just as we saw with your timeless process pattern in Chapter 6. It seems that the same powers that gave you your life myth, the pattern leading you through life, are saying, "Hello, remember me! I am part of your phase 4 dance."

What I am also suggesting is that your deepest art is a key to relationships. You can explore this for yourself by applying this deepest art to relationship work with a real or imaginary person. The following exercise gives you guidance. You can try it alone or with a partner who can play out the difficult "X" person so that you can practice bringing your deepest art into everyday life. Have a piece of paper handy so you can sketch your energies and make notes of any insights that arise.

If you try this with a helping partner, the trick for the helper is to notice when the person working describes the monster that she or he is in relationship with. Then the helper makes a note about the monster's signals so that the helper can play out the monster as authentically as possible.

Exercise: Your Deepest Art in Relationship and/or Organizational Practice

1. *Think of relationship problem* with someone (a personal friend, someone in a group you are part of, a family member) who has a disturbing "X" energy. Make a note about "X" on your paper. Stand, if you can, and act out that "X" person's *most difficult energy* with your *hands, body, posture, face.* (*Helper, notice the "X" energy* so you can play it out later.) Make a note and sketch of the *"X" energy* on your paper. What is your normal *"u" energy* like, or *what's it like in relationship to that person? Express* that *energy* with your *hands, body, posture,* and *face* and make a note and sketch it as well.
2. *Let's assume the relationship is in phase 2.* Think of the u + X as an unsettled diversity problem and note rank differences that may be related to the tension.
3. *Now find your deepest art.* Stand, if you can, and relax—relax your neck, your arms, hips, and legs; let go carefully and let your mind

be a bit blurry, and imagine, feel, and sense that the universe around you begins to move and dance you. Be careful of yourself and others. As you move, notice how you move and especially notice recurring motions and qualities. Take your time to notice these movements and their qualities. While you dance, notice if you feel/sense the u + X energies somewhere in those dance motions. Then ask yourself, what quality of nature and spot on earth reminds you of your dance or dance energies? (This could be the same or different than earlier experiences.)

4. *Now, go to that nature spot* and quality + let yourself be moved again by your dance-art. . . . Now remember the "X" person and energy while moving, and notice if your art-dance gives you a tip about how to deal with that "X" conflict. Make a note about the tip and your deepest art and imagine using the tip with that "X" person.
5. *Then, Helper, play out the problem person* in her or his "X energy state" and, Dreamer-Artist, apply your deepest art to the situation. Watch for a relaxed, quiet spot where tension is reduced and note the feedback from "X." Make notes about what you learned.

Things to Remember from Chapter 10

1. Record the sense of your deepest art and consider that it may be "synchronistically" or nonlocally connected with the earth spot and problem on which you are working.
2. Your deepest art is your "earth spot," a guide for you in difficult situations when your first training, the "science," can't be accessed.
3. Use your second training to live a more artistic life, and to make your science work in whatever situation you encounter.

CHAPTER 11

The Elder and Shaman in the World

• • •

IN THE LAST CHAPTER, WE explored two exercises for connecting with what I am calling your deepest art, a phase 4 experience. Now, we'll explore how to use your deepest art to work with organizations, businesses, family relationships, and world issues.

First, I review the overall approach and go further into the characteristics of each phase and ways to work with it. Then I share an exercise for preparing yourself to facilitate an open forum, and share an example of an open forum from one of our seminars. Being an elder and shaman in the world means using your deepest art—your own ability to connect with phase 4—to facilitate all the other phases.

As I described in the last chapter, facilitation works best by focusing on these three steps:

1. Discover people's needs.
2. Explore the dominant phase of the group with which you are working.
3. Enact your phase 4 deepest art.

Discover People's Needs

In the last chapter, I described the importance of adapting your work to the needs of the people. Don't forget to ask all the personal and business details about what an organization needs. Remember to ask the many people, parts, and members of families, groups, and organizations, "What do you need?" One will say, "I want to play!" Another, "That kid is a monster, tell her to shut up!" Still another person will say, "I just need more love from my partner."

Listening closely to needs is equally important in business. Listen to the organizational bosses and world leaders about what they need. They may speak in terms of economics, but be sure to also ask what they *personally* need, and note what the people in a given land or organization need. In any and all cases, don't forget to note if and how sexism, racism, and homophobia are affecting them.

One of my goals is to remind you that we are all walking diversity issues. All inner work is a diversity issue. It is facilitating an inner conflict between two different energies that do not get along with each other. Without realizing this, work on diversity issues in the outer world may have good results but will not remain in everyone's mind as an ongoing issue. We are all diversity issues, every moment, all the time.

What do leaders, parents, politicians need? I have a lot of feeling about this question because of my experiences working with leaders. Ask them personally, "What do you need?" Some may speak in terms of the need for rest, which can point to the need for detachment. Others ask, "How can I eventually get out of my job?" or "How can I be stronger than my opponent?" Some want to know how to get their partner to understand them and be closer. Some say, "Free me from conflict." Everyone says, "How can I find the child within me once again? I want to play," and so on.

If you talk with leaders who are not open to sexual orientation issues, you might discover that a member of their family fell in love with another person of the same orientation. What a shock that can be. In any case, take the time, if possible, to look into the needs of the people you work with and their organizations before you do a group process with them. Then, after exploring personal needs, take note of the process phase.

Notice Organizational Phases

In phase 1, as I have said, people don't like talking about problems. This is extremely important. For example, in Haiti or in the tsunami areas of Japan, or other sections of the world that have suffered immense catastrophes, after a couple of years, people turn away from the agonies they have had. "I don't want to talk about it, I just want to have a good time. Leave me alone!" That is phase 1. "Leave me alone—I don't want to look again at trauma." Even if there has been terrible radiation, hurricanes, and tsunamis, it is natural to first be depressed, and then to try and forget and have a good time.

Remember that anyone who has suffered trauma or abuse of any sort often needs years to be able to look at the trauma. That's phase 1! You can even predict it. If you don't live in the country or area of tragedy, you might think, "Oh, my god, there are so many remaining problems—why can't they work out the details that were behind the most dangerous elements?" For example, I personally did not remember anything of the trauma that happened to me as a 5-year-old child until I was 37. I could not remember those terrible street conflicts, I could not, or did not want to think about all that until I started to develop worldwork.

You can see this delayed recall with children. As a seminar participant commented, often after a parent leaves, "the remaining parent thinks the children should be grieving the loss, but they don't want to do that, and will only grieve later, if at all." We know this delay was true for Carolyn Kennedy, the daughter of President Kennedy. Her father was shot and killed when she was 6. Today, she speaks about how it took her many years to remember that terrible event.

Another participant mentioned her work with veterans and confirmed seeing the phases: "I have many veterans in my life, as well as friends who served in Vietnam, and only now, after 45–50 years of carrying that pain are they finally ready to talk about it."

Similarly on a societal level, certain social problems can be overwhelming—for example, climate change—and lead people to want to forget it. To respect phase 1 means to say, "Forget climate change! Let's have a good time, enjoy ourselves, but be careful about the stuff you throw out." The point is to understand phase 1 and not to insist on trying to work on such issues at first. Then 10 minutes later, you might begin to address the problems. Follow the people and the process phase; do not fight it. That is worldwork.

For example, we have been working in Japan with the help of our Processwork community, Kumamoto University, and the United Nations University. In 2011, in the Fukushima area of Japan, that terrible tsunami and resulting nuclear reactor breakdown and subsequent radiation leak hurt and killed many. Today, even though many children from that neighborhood have thyroid cancer, people can hardly talk about it. We are in the midst of working on that reluctance.

Thinking about this work in Japan, I feel a huge thank-you for so many people and all their different kinds of work with the agonies of the world.

But back to working with phase 1. Underline the importance of supporting people until they have the ability and the distance to work with problems. It's OK to challenge phase 1 if you are in phase 2, but if you want to make a sustainable change, at least *start with appreciating where people are.*

In phase 2, in the midst of tension, remember your own deepest art and then bring awareness to social and psychological rank issues in conflict areas. If some people have more social rank than others, ask them to notice it, and eventually to listen and be open to everyone. How you do these things is up to your deepest art. Don't just proceed mechanically; let your deepest art work with the group more spontaneously to avoid unnecessary conflict.

People often ask me about the problem of social justice conversations and how to communicate with people of high social rank about the impact they have others, without alienating them. It is a common experience that if those of higher rank feel put down and not understood, then they stop listening and don't come back to the conversation.

Understanding phases means that we know that a push coming from those with less rank and power is part of the story in phase 2. "Woof!" Wake up! A push can be important, but a big bruise makes matters worse. Your deepest art will help you to take all sides and move from phase 2 to phase 3 where at least you, as a facilitator, can also speak for the person or people who have been unconscious of their rank and power. As above, asking about everyone's needs, especially those with the highest power, is really important and can be transformational. As someone commented,

> *I remember the first time I saw you do this work—it blew me away. We were in a racism forum, and you went over to the guy who was identified as a racist, and you said to the guy, "I think you need some soup," and after that, you asked him what his needs were. I will never forget that moment! It changed how I saw worldwork.*

As an activist, it is normal to be in phase 2 and want to wake people up, and then to be temporarily unconscious of your own power in that moment, which is what I call your "spiritual rank." If you feel spiritually "superior," as many of us have felt at one time or another, then you have some spiritual rank and power that you could use against others as unconsciously as social rank. An aware facilitator knows that it is natural to be unconscious about rank—*on all sides.* Facilitators who do not notice their own power may abuse it by favoring one side or another and inadvertently perpetuate abuse issues.

Understanding as well as fighting are keys to transforming our world. If you can, *feel into* the person you are working with to understand her or his side, and then bring in all the other voices to the conversation.

Again, the big point is to have phase awareness and appreciate where people are at. Appreciate phase 1 and phase 2. If the leader of the organization is in phase 1 and says, "I don't want to think about too much, let's have dinner," then have dinner, and be gentle about phase 2 discussions. You will be asked to help more, and your work will progress faster!

Suicidality, Terrorism, and Phase 2

As I said in Chapter 2, in phase 2, the sense of aloneness and the drive for change can even be a matter of life and death. An activist can be suicidal if she or he implies, "I'm willing to give my life for this! I don't care if it kills me!" A lot of the problems in our world are related to people saying, "I will give my life for what I believe in!"

I learned about this issue for the first time from one of my Jungian teachers who died fighting for Jung. My teacher, Dr. Franz (Nicklaus) Riklin, was president of the Jung Institute in Zurich many years ago. After Jung's death, many "followers," including Riklin, fought against being dominated by those who did not like Jung. The institute had just begun and there were many people at that time who did not want to follow the spirituality of C. G. Jung. They wanted to be more oriented toward consensus reality.

There was a meeting of the institute people who wanted to move away from Jung's more controversial ideas. My teacher, Dr. Franz Riklin Jr., stood up on stage to speak on behalf of those ideas of Jung. I wish I had been awake enough at the time to help him. Riklin had a heart attack while speaking on stage for Jung. He died in the hospital two weeks later. Just before he died, he told me a dream. In that dream Jung came to him, saying, "I told you, you did not need to speak up so strongly." Riklin said to him, "Yes, live and learn."

The day of Riklin's funeral, I dreamed that I took a breath and he came out of his grave and through the air into my lungs. So I have Riklin in me too. My own inner activist is always trying to learn; we need awareness of social phases, and to remember phase 4 as well.

If you and or others feel strongly about things, take care of yourself and your opponents. Find more sustainable, phase-oriented ways of doing things. Remember, many so-called terrorists often say or feel, "What's the difference? My life does not have any value anyway—my violent struggle will give life meaning even if it kills me!"

Stopping terrorism will never work sustainably without making social reforms and helping everyone to feel that life is worthwhile. Fighting terrorists is natural, but it's not sustainable. We must help ourselves and our opponents to feel that life is worthwhile beyond the present circumstances. It was really heartening to hear President Obama say, in a speech, that we cannot just go after terrorists. We have to ask them what made them so upset, and try to make a better world around them so that they don't feel so disenfranchised and disrespected. I feel hopeful about how our process-work community values are being shared more and more. Perhaps the problems of our world will eventually help us all awaken and change together.

Amy and I recently worked in Colombia while peace talks between the so called "guerillas" and the mainstream government were beginning. In our seminar, I spoke about the potential suicidal nature of the activist. At the end of a big conflict forum, a woman grabbed me by the arm and said quickly and dramatically, "Don't tell anyone my name, but when you spoke of suicide, you were speaking to me. Thank you!" She then ran off. It was a very touching moment and I will go more deeply into this encounter in Chapter 15.

In phase 3, when a group is ready for an open forum, don't just suggest possible roles and ghost roles but model switching roles for them. To begin with, act out possible polarities for others, demonstrate what might be in the background as the open forum begins. Remind folks that your demonstration is not necessarily correct, and that they will have to step into the roles and complete the discussion authentically. You are merely opening the door.

While working in open forums, make sure you *show* double signals, rather than just pointing them out. Rather than saying, "I see you doing this . . . what does that mean?" say, "I notice you making this motion, and if I made that motion, it would mean this to me. What does it mean for you?"

In phase 4, notice cool spots and quiet moments that occur in the midst of small and large group processes. Those quiet moments are important because participants may be close to phase 4—to insights and resolutions. Ideas for system change can emerge in those cool spots that often happen after conflicts. This is a time for new ideas to emerge. Hold the group briefly to this quiet moment.

In phase 4, when things are quiet, all the good methods you learned—such as nonviolent communication, using your own spiritual tradition, open-space work, story creation, consensus work, and more—will work wonderfully.

In summary: Remember phase 1 and support people to relax and forget about problems. Recall in phase 2 to help folks stand and fight for themselves and get others to react. Be aware of social rank and spiritual power for all involved. Almost any business or organizational method works in phase 3, and all conflict resolution methods work beautifully, but in phase 2 they may not work if things are too intense. If things are too intense, or whenever you are stuck, remember phase 4 and use your deepest art to find unexpected, spontaneous solutions.

Now, I share an exercise for finding and using your deepest art to facilitate an open forum on a social issue that matters to you. You can use this exercise to prepare for facilitating any group working on an issue that troubles you. Then we will see an example of an open forum that occurred in one of our seminars after people had completed this exercise.

Exercise: Practice Your Deepest Art to Help Family, Organizations, and/or Political Problems

A. Choose a relationship, family, organizational, national, or world problem on which to work. Write down the problem. Think of someone or some "X" energy you dislike that is connected to that group issue. What "X" energy in that issue don't you like? Stand, if you can, and act out this "X" energy with your hands and body. Really get a good feeling for this "X" energy and make a note and a sketch of it on paper.

What is your typical "u" energy like in such a situation? Act out this "u" energy with your hands and body and make a note and sketch it.

When did you last want a little "revenge" against this "X" person or energy? Or, if you *could get* revenge against the "X," what would this be or feel like? What kind of energy did/does your anger or revenge have? Act out that energy. Does it have a similar quality to the figure or group "X" energy? (It may or it may not.)

B. In what phase is your relationship with the "X" energy, person, or people (phase 1, cruising, enjoying, not really caring very much; phase 2, hidden or overt conflict; phase 3, you are in the midst of a u + X dialogue + role switching fluidly, going back and forth between the "u" and the "X," inside or outside; or phase 4, relaxed and shamanistic, being moved by nature)? Make a note about the phase you think you are in with that "X."

C. Now let's try to use phase 4, your deepest art, with this "X." Stand, if possible, and relax into that quantum world, let go for the moment. Let your mind be a bit blurry, and let yourself feel and be moved by the universe around you. Be careful of yourself and those around you. As you move, notice any recurring movements that are happening. When you notice them, ask yourself: What piece of nature reminds you of your dance? As you dance, do you notice the u + X in your movements?

D. Continue to dance your deepest art and, while dancing, feel and imagine using it in that relationship with the "X." Perhaps it will give you a spontaneous tip about how to do that. Use your attention to catch it, as it may be very fleeting. Make a note about your learning and imagine how you might apply it in the actual outer situation with that person or group.

Demonstration: Open Forum on Climate Change and Extractions from the Earth

The following open forum occurred in one of our seminars, after participants had practiced the inner work presented above. Here, I present certain highlighted moments to show the unexpected fluidity that the facilitator and participants' deepest art can bring to complex and difficult world challenges.

The first step in an open forum is to find the topic that will be worked on, and to bring awareness that it is an *umbrella* topic. Under the umbrella there are always various sub-issues. If you, as a facilitator, mention those sub-topics, it usually makes things easier so that these other topics don't have to pop up or push themselves forward.

The next step is to notice the different sides in the issue, and ask someone to speak on one side and another person to speak on the other side. After a few minutes, the facilitator can invite the whole group in for dialogue, as she or he notices roles and ghost roles, hot spots, cool spots, and momentary resolutions.

In this example, the group brought up a variety of important issues before choosing to focus on climate change.

Sorting: The group process begins, and the following issues arise.
PTSD and the overlooking of veterans.
Vaccinations and whether or not parents are free to not have kids vaccinated.
Sexism and violence towards women, including rape, domestic violence, slave trafficking; and the agonies of men as well.
Refugees in Europe and the treatment of asylum seekers by governments.
Ageism and the perceived redundancy of older people, their pain in becoming invisible, and how the history of the older people becomes marginalized by youth.
Unborn babies who don't have a choice to have natural birth.
Dubai/Middle East, where there are no rights for 80% of the people and slavery is practiced around the world.
Anti-mining, oil wells, and economic interests vs. ecological view.
Animals dying—half of all animals and insects and plant species are going extinct in our lifetime.
Climate change—the issue that overlays all.

Group Process: Climate Change and Extractions from Earth

In this process, some people played the mainstream role wanting to ignore climate change and extract oil and gas and coal from the earth. Others challenged these practices. One person played the earth itself. The resulting group process is simplified and shortened below.

Mainstream: We want to heat our homes and think first of today!!

Activists for implementing changes to reduce climate change challenged the mainstream view with scientific information.

Extractors: Dig up the earth, get what we need today, think of now, and not the future!

There was a lot of debate in the group between the "green movement" people and the extractors. At one point, the Earth—which had been a theme but also a ghost role until now—appeared in the group process.

S: (crying, speaking as the earth) *I want you to know how much I love you all. All of you. I exist for you, really. My whole being just exists for all of you. I have given everything, always. Please wake up, pay attention to me before it is too late.*
T: We are your children, and some of us hear you crying, Mother. I will breathe in your pain.
S: I don't want you to breathe in my pain, I want you to breathe in love and awareness.
T: Can you show me how to breathe that in?
Arny: Notice that breathing in love and awareness is a moment of phase 4. . . . Let's not rush it. Look—S., as the earth, is nodding "yes" to that, to more awareness of community and love.
S: Now all of a sudden, I feel the starlight coming in from the universe, starlight bathing the earth.
Arny: Starlight is a phase 4 ghost; she is speaking for the earth, for all beings, all women, men, animals, sea creatures, insects, and even the microbial world.
S: Yes, for all beings, all animals, all beings.

The group is quiet for a moment.

Arny: OK. Notice the cool spot.

Amy: There is so much feeling in the room.

Arny: There is a sense of love, of working together at least temporarily, and of being more aware of the larger things in which we are in the middle.

K: In the role of the extractor "X" of gas and oil, I just want to say: "You are just a hysterical woman who does not know what is going on; you create disasters. I know what is going on, I am in control, I want to extract whatever I want from you earth mothers. I will take what it takes to heat homes and run cars."

R: Yes, somebody needs to be the boss and heat houses.

S: And I am the earth—I am not a woman. And I still love you, dear extractor, I love you the same way I love everybody taking from my body. If that is where you are in your development, I love and accept your development as bosses and extractors. Yet, I am still going to be myself. I am still going to say, I need help.

Arny: I notice that those who played the earth and all the bosses are nodding, agreeing. . . . Let's talk about it more. What allowed you, S., to love those hurtful figures even though you were suffering from them?

S: Because the earth exists only for everybody here; she exists since the beginning of time for all of our development. Humanity has gone through good and bad phases, and she loves every phase, she has no judgment or criticism. She just needs people now to understand the consequences of their choices.

Amy: She is there for everybody, even the ones who seem to some of us to be really impossible.

Arny: I notice everyone's silence. Perhaps I can speak for a moment and say that S.'s earth nature is an aspect of phase 4, a detached universal sense.

J: When the seminar began this morning, I noticed that there was not enough gas needed to heat this very building we are in. Interesting that the topic we chose is not just in the world out there. The gas–earth problem is here right now; it is both local and nonlocal . . . it is right here in the building and town we are living in and it is on the other side of the planet.

(At this very moment, the group process stops as a big gas truck with gas for the building drives up outside the seminar house in Yachats, Oregon!)

Arny: WOW, nonlocal synchronicity! This particular group process was in Tao. Perhaps it was a manifestation of what is needed for our planet—namely, more phase 4, the deepest art in all of us.

This open forum gave us a touching example of the unexpected insights and resolutions that can arise from your deepest art connection to phase 4.

Things to Remember from Chapter 11

1. Recall and sense your deepest art, your deepest metaskill, to create community.
2. If you're not in touch with that art, you are "normal," incongruent, and get exhausted or burned out.
3. In a group process about the earth in this chapter, the "earth" was at first discussed and then enacted as a "ghost role" to create solutions.
4. The earth encompassed and had compassion for all sides, and was the key to helping with its own future.

CHAPTER 12

Your World Leadership Myth

• • •

In this chapter, I want to support you in finding what I call your world leadership myth by connecting to your deepest art. We will see how your deepest art is connected to your life task in the world, to your world leadership myth, and how it can help you overcome the challenges of what you are here to do. Phase awareness brings a new dimension to grappling with the process of living your myth in the world.

Phase 4 deepest art experiences are surely localized in your body, but they may also be nonlocal and connected to all that is needed. It seems that phase 4 is a "spiritual" power at the center of all our phases *and* our deepest art, which makes our sciences and trainings work.

What do I mean by the nonlocality of your deepest art experiences? I can illustrate with an example. You might recall from Chapter 10 that I worked on my experience of being pressured by a large business organization. My deepest art gave me the message: *"Follow your timing, using that organization's energy."* I made this discovery while working with Amy to demonstrate the exercise during a seminar.

Later that very night, around midnight, I got an email from that business leader and he literally wrote, "Dear Arny, take your time." It was amazing—a synchronicity, as Jung might say. The person actually used the phrase I heard when I worked in the middle of the seminar and connected to phase 4. My experience over years of practice in many different contexts teaches me that our deepest art is nonlocal. Your life is not just yours; it belongs to you *and* is intertwined with our world—and perhaps the entire universe.

DISCOVERING WHO YOU ARE

Now, let's discover who you are. Is there a reason why you are here on earth, besides just taking up some time and space and having a good time or whatever?

Shamanism and phase 4 are at the very edge of the focus of our normal, everyday mind. But our need for that phase forces us to look for it in others or to project it, feel it, or experience it in terms of some deity that others believe in as well.

On the right you can see pictures of various divine beings. Top left is Apollo—see the circle behind his head? Next to him is a picture of Jesus with a kind of circular power behind his head! Then in the middle on the left, you see a symbol for the Islamic god Allah, also with a circular form. To the right in the middle you see a picture of Yahweh, also as a circular power. Below on the left you see Zen's empty (enlightened) mind idea, and on the right you see a goddess, possibly from India. All have circles in the foreground or background. There are many more such circular pictures portraying spiritual experiences, including in aboriginal/indigenous traditions.

18. Apollo, Jesus, Allah, Yaweh, Zen, Goddess

My point is that our peak experiences are often sketched with a circular form and a theme of universal power.

We all experience a unifying cyclical field around us, at least sometimes. I am pointing out something you might already sense, but you probably rarely allow yourself to feel: phase 4 spinning you about in everyday life. It is "edgy" to realize how you, too, have this undulating and cyclical behavior. In those moments, you are connected to the ordinary part of yourself, and at the same time connected with something universal . . . like compassion.

I love all our aspects and phases . . . and, of course, sometimes I don't! For most of us it is easier to identify with problems and often harder to say, "There is something amazing in me that I often marginalize." The gods are one of our biggest edges! It is this "spiritual" power at the center of all our phases that is our deepest art and that makes our sciences and trainings work.

In the first training, you discover and notice double signals that don't go along with your primary process; you try and notice how ghost roles are mentioned but not explored. In your second training, you contact this deepest part of yourself and feel how you are also the "X" from your double signals, relationship troubles, or the ghosts in a group. Even if you seem to lack energy, you can sense the Tao that can't be said, the power of the universe and its various phases.

***19.* Bagua, 8 trigrams flowing.**
(thanks https://en.wikipedia.org/wiki/Bagua Wikimedia)

This universal power is symbolized by the various trigrams of the "Bagua diagram" describing the *I Ching*. This symbol, symbolizing the Tao, represents phase changes from summer, summer changing, autumn, autumn changing, winter, winter changing, and spring, spring changing.

The swirling movement you see in the center with the yin and yang energies is the center of the phases, the power of the universe moving us. This Bagua diagram is yet another symbol of the phases of nature, and of the Tao that can't be said behind your deepest art. It gives answers to life in the form of sudden ideas or trigrams of the *I Ching*.

Your Deepest Art and Your Life Myth

Your deepest art seems to appear not only in the typical movements you make throughout your life, and in your childhood dream, but also when faced with uncertainty about the future. In the following exercise, I ask you about your childhood dream, the earliest memory or dream that you can think of. In those memories and dreams I want to search for phases—which may be clear or embedded and implied.

For example, let's say you are being chased. In Amy's childhood dream, for example, she is being chased by the Mafia. She rushes to an elevator to escape. Phase 4 is implied by the height of where her elevator is headed; she is not there exactly, but phase 4 awareness is implied.

> *Amy: Since I was a little girl, in phase 1, I was happy just being myself, this happy little girl. In phase 2, I was in constant conflict with an inner critic! Phase 3 is only now happening to me consciously as I find the power of that critic in myself. And phase 4 is implied by the "elevator" rising upwards.*

Where do these childhood dreams come from? After thinking of your personal and family history, also think that the world or the universe (the Tao) needs you to have that specific childhood dream pattern for reasons you often discover much later on. In other words, your dream is not just yours, it is not just psychology. Your life is your responsibility, but—especially in phase 4—your life, we might say, is "none of your personal business." From this perspective, it is as if something mythical was given to you without your asking for it, and part of your life is about realizing that myth.

Try the following exercise to find out more about yourself. You will need a piece of paper for notes and sketches.

Exercise I: The World Needs Your Art for a World Task

> Part I: A. Recall a childhood dream or first memory. Make a brief note about it. Which phase or phases are seen or implied in that dream memory (phase 1, cruising; phase 2, tension or conflict; phase 3, flow between "u" and "X"; phase 4, sense of the universe moving you somehow in the background)? Make notes about this.

B. Now relax or stand, if possible, and let the universe "dance" you. Be careful with your spontaneous movement. Your "deepest art" dance may be a little different or the same as earlier experiences. As you are dancing, let recurring spontaneous movements imply or tell you what world task the universe wants you to do, if any. What is it? Make a note. Explore/imagine/ feel doing that "task" now. Make notes.

Part II: Sense your dance again and recall the task it just gave you and apply it to the phases. That is . . .

Phase 1: Stand, if possible, and re-experience your deepest art-dance and imagine feeling, cruising, and enjoying your world task. Make a note, if you want to, or just continue cruising.

Phase 2: Imagine meeting a problem or "X" energy associated with that task. What would it be?

Phase 3: While continuing your art-dance, go back and forth between the problem energy and the dance you are experiencing. Imagine that your inner experience is both inside of you *and* outside in the world and model this nonlocality; that is, feel "I am the 'X' *and* I am this whole dance in the world around me." Make notes.

Phase 4: Then, just let go and move with the universe. More insights may arise, and if they do, write them down now. Also write down your nonlocal experience and eventually share it with a friend. Tell this person your myth, and how your "X" and your "world dance" are both you.

Some seminar participants shared the following insights about their world task experience after completing this exercise.

L: Oh! I am very shy. My image was rolling back, "unraveling," and my sense was to get out of consensus reality, to go into the universe—that is the essence behind consensus reality. But then IT was rolling, diving in and out while I am dealing with consensus reality things. Thus, I must go deep within and then outside again and again.

A: My world task makes me shy. In my dream, a grizzly bear grabbed me out of my bed, but had a travel pack with the cubs in its pockets! The bear grabbed me out of the bed and started chewing my fingers, but she had soft leather teeth! My world task was to come out as a big, open-chested protective bear. I have to say, "I am here, I am this bear for everyone."

C: My world task is to notice the tunes and their rhythms behind everything, and to replay the songs of the world for the world to help others hear their tune and the other tunes of the world around them. (People in the audience began clapping, feeling the "tune in the wind.")

The next exercise may help you take the next step by exploring what stops you from living your world task and by integrating your experiences into everyday life.

If you do this exercise with a partner, one person will be the helper, and should observe the person working (the dreamer) carefully. The helper should notice how the dreamer describes the "X" energy so she or he can play the "X" energy and encourage the dreamer to use her or his deepest art to deal with it.

Exercise II. What's in the Way of Doing Your Task

A. Dreamer, re-feel your shamanistic deepest art dance again, and as you are moving, let it define the *same or another* mythic world task for you. Note this task on paper. What phase are you in now with this task (phase 1, cruising; phase 2, tense, fear of/struggle with an "X" that might be present; phase 3, feeling and imagining flowing in an open-forum manner between "u" and "X"; or phase 4, depressed, tired, sad, but relaxing into the infinite)?

B. Regardless of your present phase, imagine, act out/speak for an "X" energy associated with that task. *(Helper, please note the "X" energy in order to play it out later.)* Now, Dreamer, stand (if possible) and let yourself be moved again by your deepest art-dance, note its recurring dance motions, and then add sounds to it. Associate your motions and sounds with some quality of nature and spot on the earth. Feel this dance and its earth area's nature, and write down in words its deepest art.

C. Recall the world task and its "X" problem or energy. And now, re-feel and dance once again as you imagine using your deepest art to work with that "X" (also recalling "I am 'u' and I am the 'X'").

D. Finally, the helper should recall and play the "X" for the dreamer so that she or he can experience working on the real-world problem. Dreamer, let your shamanistic art dance relate to this "X," and remember nonlocality: *"I am you,"* or perhaps "I am the world." Then make notes about your insights and review them tonight before bed to understand your dreams in the morning!

One of the participants who shared his childhood dream above also discovered an unexpected way that his deepest art could help him live his world task.

> *When my partner was playing my "X," bullying and criticizing me, I become the bear protecting the children. As she kept criticizing, my*

bear-like arms were held out to hold her. At first they were a barrier and then they became a bear hug, and I reached out and grabbed her, the critic. I realized I can hug the bully. My art is more powerful than the bully! Something said, "Yes, love in the form of bear hugs is what bullies need!"

Please bring your insights onto the streets and into your home and to all your communities.

Dear Reader, If you need a specific example of how to do this, see the text in the end note.[37]

Things to Remember from Chapter 12

1. Your greatest wealth is your deepest art.
2. Your inner experiences, childhood dream, and worst fears or problems seem to be aspects of what the world gave you and with which it needs help.
3. Your life is both yours and, in a way, *none of your business.*
4. Process phase awareness is like the Bagua diagram. So, sense the Tao, notice the rotating core expressing itself in terms of flowing polar opposites, and realize how it needs all these "opposing" energies in its flow.

PART V

Preparing for Group Work

• • •

PREPARING FOR RELATIONSHIP, GROUP, BUSINESS, or government work requires your "facilitator's meditation" and deepest art in order to be able to recognize your "X" as an ally. In the next two chapters, I focus on process-oriented meditation practices to access your deepest art in preparation for your work with groups.

CHAPTER 13

The Facilitator's "X" as the Ally

• • •

PREPARING FOR RELATIONSHIP, GROUP, BUSINESS, or government work requires your "facilitator's meditation" and deepest art in order to be able to recognize your "X" as an ally.

What we have learned over decades of conflict facilitation is that peace itself is not a sustainable goal. What *is* sustainable is learning to process the relationships between the parties. This requires your deepest art.

In this chapter, I give examples from our work in the world, and share two exercises to help you transform your "X" into a facilitator's ally.

Part of Amy's and my work is traveling to different places in the world and facilitating for groups and individuals. We rely on the facilitator's meditation to deal with some of the agonizing and intractable conflicts where people have asked us for assistance.

As I briefly mentioned in Chapter 11, we recently worked in Bogota, Colombia. It is an amazing country, as you may know, which has suffered one of the longest civil wars on this planet. In 2015, the conflicting parties were on the verge of coming together. This meant, of course, that some were also *not* coming together, and some were fed up and did not want to think about war any more. It was an awesome experience to teach a seminar there.

Prior to the seminar, we had been connecting with people from certain underground guerilla groups, and some of them came covertly, "undercover," to the seminar. I was really happy to see people participate from some very marginalized groups—people who have been seen as the "bad guys" from the mainstream viewpoint. It was there that I met the woman I mentioned in Chapter 11, who was touched by my message about the suicidality of the activist. It was an amazing moment, and in Chapter 15, I share my inner work about this encounter.

While in South Africa, we worked on immigration problems. The polarity there was between South African people of all colors who are against immigrants from other African countries who are fleeing problems in their homelands, hoping to come to South Africa. As we all know, refugee problems are universal on our planet.

In Moscow, we facilitated a large group process, and I saw things I have never seen before. Not surprisingly, with all the tension between Russia, Ukraine, Europe, and the United States in 2015, we worked with dozens of Russians who talked about being depressed and about suicide and death. When Amy suggested they explore that feeling, suddenly many people lay down on the ground, quietly, and hummed as if bringing up sounds from the earth. They were doing that partly because they were depressed by the way the West and rest of the world are perceiving them, and in part to go deeper and feel more detached. Amy explains,

> *They had the sense of being hated as a country, and they were filled with pain and anger. We heard all the different sides, and then when they lay down as if they were dead, the sense of going beyond the present boundaries became possible. We all found a way to go beyond the boundaries and reach out to all people, to everyone. Even non-Russians who had traveled to see us work there ended up falling in love with this aspect of Russia.*

As mentioned previously, in Tokyo, we worked for Kumamoto University at the U.N. University. We told them the story that I shared in the Introduction, about our encounter on the canal in London, where Amy and I used our deepest art to intervene, through singing, in a potentially dreadful street scene.

As you might remember, on our walk, we saw a young man threatening and trying to rob an older man. So we recalled our deepest art, we felt that dance, and out came a song that Amy and I created in the moment: "Give me your money! Grrrr, give it now! Give me your money! Money—money—money now!!" To all of our surprise, the thief stopped threatening and began singing too. He actually started jamming with us, "Yeah! Yeah-yeah! More money now!" and he seemed almost happy. The older man who had been attacked, listened, looked at this scene, and took money out his wallet and gave the "thief" some money! All this happened while we and the so-called "thief" were still singing.

We told this story in Japan during our seminar, and afterward we received a letter from a wing of the Japanese government. This seminar participant wrote to tell us about how he thought Japan should use processwork in what comes next in the future.

Our hope with this work is to show you that although policing, arrests, and jail/prison can be important, they are not a sustainable answer to worldly troubles. When the man from that agency in Japan heard that story and told us, "this is how Japan should deal with problems," we realized that our deepest art may be like quantum mechanics. It allows us to connect nonlocally to all involved in problems and relate to everyone in the best possible way.

Just another word about the story in the London canal. How did we have the courage to intervene? What about the danger that the thief would turn on us? It is true that he could have attacked us; this was a possibility. I am very careful to watch for signals, especially in extreme-state situations (when people are in so-called psychotic states). It is very important to watch people's feedback: Someone in an extreme state often relaxes if her or his state can be expressed creatively and without any apparent effort to change anything. If someone in an extreme state feels that she or he is being "joined" and dealt with in a humane way, change can happen, as it does with everyone.

The point is that to work effectively with conflict, we must do so in a deeply democratic way. Use your first training studies and background as well as your second training, your deepest art. When your first training does not work for you in extreme situations, recall phase 4 and your deepest art essence-level dance. This shift in focus will give you a non-cognitive, shamanistic connection with the world.

Your Best Teacher

Only your body can really teach you about your deepest art and how to work with situations in the moment. Outer work needs inner meditation to access guidance from the true teacher, your body. In Part III we looked closely at process-oriented, phase-aware meditation practice, and now we will take this work further by applying it to group work.

Recall how meditation can be understood across the four phases.

In phase 1 people don't want to talk about problems. In large group work following very traumatic events—for example in Japan, in specific areas such as the Fukushima region—people don't want to think about radiation anymore. It was a painful mess; they don't want to think about it.

Facilitators of course, hope to clear up the remaining radiation problems. After all, kids are getting thyroid cancer, but you cannot work on change with the general population if they are in phase 1. Similarly, right after the Second World War, nobody talked much about bloodshed. You know that attitude in yourself. Sometimes you feel, "I am sick of problems, I do not want to hear about them, I just want to have a good time, I just want a breath of fresh air."

In Japan, the activists wanted to say, "Let's change this and that," but the people were not ready. So we suggested that the activists relate to that phase 1 collective mindset by saying, "OK, let's have a good time first. How do we make more money? How do we get better food here? How can you bring your kids to school in the morning?"

Then try bringing in the more difficult topic: "There's still radiation around here, shall we deal with it now? Or forget it? Or talk about it next week?" *My point is, don't press a group into phase 2.* "For now, let's first celebrate that we have survived." As a forum leader, you can try saying, "How can we make money in this city? How can we be happier and stronger?" And *then* work on ecological problems. This approach is different from the normal activist in most of us who says, "Let's get the bad guys, let's change them." That is OK too, but it will burn you out if that is not the phase the public is in. Following the process phase paradoxically means that change happens sooner.

Recall that the news media loves phase 2, because it makes money from war and hatred, from talking about the "bad guys." The news says, "Everybody is killing everybody!" That creates only more war.

In phase 3, people are ready to switch roles. You can give them a hint about how to do that by doing it yourself in front of them. Phase 3 is an amazing moment; it is what many therapists hope for and are trained for. Phase 3 allows for easy open-forum discussions in groups. Don't forget that even though the ideal phase for an open forum is phase 3, many groups in open forums are in phase 2, *not phase 3*! So don't put down aggression, but try to understand, and even take the aggressor's side, at least temporarily in order to elder the whole scene.

In phase 4, when you are open and flowing, you can connect with just about anyone, locally and nonlocally; you can do so shamanistically and eventually, cognitively as well. When possible, remember to bring your dreaming and meditation out PUBLICLY during group work; model checking-in on personal needs in front of the group. In this way you may be relating to others as well.

From the phase 4 viewpoint, problems can become gifts. I spoke earlier about my childhood street conflicts. People wanted to kill me as a child for religious reasons. Even though I forgot that as I went into phase 1 until my late 30s, it came back as I began to develop worldwork. When I began worldwork, I realized that those problems within me drove me to work on and help with world problems. Things that are bad for us are horrible to experience; with enough time, however, those very experiences might eventually be helpful to ourselves and others. Diversity and conflict can lead towards world unity!

Work for Better Relationships, Not Only Peace

As I have said, a permanent state of peace is not a sustainable goal. We all want peace and should fight for it, but peace, as with all states of consciousness, is usually temporary. What is sustainable is learning to process the relationships between the parties. Don't only hope for the handshake between two parties; work towards helping all to make all the channels and phases of relationship flow better.

Follow your own and the group's awareness. Model meditating until you get an insight or a momentary awakening happens. *Awareness allows process. Just noticing what is happening* allows things to change. That is nature. The goal of inner and outer work is *not* just one state of mind or another; it is to *flow better together*. You can begin by noticing channels and watching things evolve.

But what if you get stuck somewhere? Or, what if it is too hard to fight the monsters? Notice and respect the phase you are in. If you are scared, then run away. Or be depressed, and collapse and sink into phase 4. Notice dreaming again. Or say, "I am confused and stuck, so I am going to have compassion for myself and go straight to phase 4."

Sometimes your meditation process skips right over channels and phases. If you go deeply into phase 2, sometimes you skip phase 3 and go to phase 4. If the monster tends to kill you in phase 2, that is not good. Protect yourself. But there might be one tiny, good thing about being down and not feeling well. If you are depressed or even feel dead, it might be a shortcut to phase 4. If you go deeply enough into the depressing feeling, you may possibly "die" and then bliss out. That is another possibility. Of course, be careful, and if you are seriously depressed, don't hesitate to get help.

Sometimes one part of a group will try to take this shortcut from phase 2 to phase 4, but it does not work and actually irritates other parts of the group. In some spiritually identified or New Age groups, this has been called "spiritual bypassing." As one of our seminar participants described it,

> *"You get into conflict, things get very bad, and the idea is to drop out and go to essence and, 'Let's just be all spiritual' and try and resolve things there."*

As a facilitator you can watch the feedback. The phase 2 to 4 shortcut is great when it works. Try it and if it doesn't work, then realize that other phases are insisting upon recognition. What is important is to elder all the phases. Begin with the phase 4 needs. "OK, let's imagine going into phase 4. Smile at yourself and others, everybody be nice, communicate, put your hand up before talking, behave properly." But then as a facilitator, if people start growling again, say, "Oh, the monsters are back! Welcome back to phase 2!" Then use phase 4 to go into phase 2. Don't fight the primary group process; if you do, you will probably lose the fight.

Remember that all groups get caught in phases. Do not put them down for this—I would clap for them! With such groups you can also try modeling phase 3. Do not ask them to do it, but show them how. Say, "I want to show you how to do this. I want to pick up some of the energies that I would expect you to do. I know you don't want to do this, but just let me do this for a minute and then perhaps we can discuss it. Otherwise we can forget it, and I can bring it up tomorrow, if needed." The point is to *follow the process*. The New Age culture is also just another culture, neither good nor bad.

In part, I describe the difference between eldership and social activism. The elder loves social action and is an activist, but not *only* an activist. She is there for everybody and for the planet and universe. His or her focus is on "burning awareness," letting that awareness burn through and move with relationship between the sides and the phases of nature. To elder conflict is to change the world sustainably by following nature, acknowledging what is present.

The following meditation gives you a chance to practice connecting to the phase you are experiencing in the moment.

Exercise: Phase Meditation

You can try this meditation sitting at the edge of your chair or standing. Read it through first, or have a friend read it to you slowly.

1. You have a thousand and one needs. What is one of your biggest needs these days? Name one to begin. You may have a couple!
2. What are you noticing in your body right now? Are you feeling something? Or is there a little movement or jitter? Are you remembering or seeing something? Are you hearing something? Just notice what channel or channels you are in. Are you in a relationship channel or a world channel where you are talking to someone or to a group?
3. Explore that channel of awareness a little bit and watch channels change.
4. When you are ready, ask yourself, "What phase am I in?" Are you just enjoying yourself in phase 1? Are you in the middle of tension or conflict or worry about something in phase 2? Are you in phase 3, able to pick up the energy that was bothering you? Or are you just blissed-out in phase 4, being moved by the universe, so to speak?
5. Just follow your phase experiences, exploring them as they come and go. Maybe an insight or understanding will pop up. If some understanding or insight occurs, don't hesitate to write it down.

One seminar participant shared the following experience in the meditation, and then I worked with the person to deepen the experience.

D: I found I needed help with a symptom and my phases came up very quickly. . . . I felt the conflict about my body symptoms in phase 2; it was very easy to pick up that body energy as an "X." Then the tension of my "X" energies was so disturbing, I just wanted to kill myself—and in the killing I was in phase 4. But then my body symptoms were so intense I could not detach all the way, so then I am back in phase 2, and again then into phase 3 trying to get into the different energies. Not easy! Phases kept coming, going, and returning.

Arny: Phases move around, and that swinging process is often the point. But I hear you talking about your process as phase 2; the symptom itself is a problem in the moment.

D: Yes, I am against it and need help.

Arny: OK, what is the "X" energy like there?

D: (Shows a hand motion.) *A gnawing energy in my stomach, but at the same time my bladder is burning and I need to pee so badly. It's a war in there, I tell you!*

Arny: Can you show me that war, that gnawing and burning? Can you give it to me?

D: Grrrr! (Gets up and grabs hold of Arny with her hand.) *I don't want to take up too much time in this class . . .*

Arny: Thank you for saying that, but what are you doing to me when you grab my hand?

D: I want more, more! I can never get enough! It is so tiring. There's the edge. I am shy to take up time. I was really just asking a question!

Group: (yelling to encourage her onward) *Grrrr, we want more!!*

D: Really? OK, I want more of everything! I want my world visions! I want the depth of my connections with people! I want to eat the food I want to eat! I don't want to have to limit it! No limits! I hate the limits! I hate the difficulties . . .

Arny: Yes, we want what we want and we want it NOW, dear world!

D: YES!! That reminds me of my friend's project, and how he engaged everyone. (to the group) *"Yes, we want it?!"*

Group: (joins her yelling) *"NOW!!"*

D: (to the group) *How will we do it?*

Group: Who cares! Just do it!

D: (laughing)

Arny: D., you are laughing. You look well when you do that. Your phase 2 led us into the public arena. Your body phases temporarily have become a nonlocal community process. "We want it now! JUST DO IT!"

D: Aha! I see! I need to do things more as a galvanizer, as I did just now, and have more fun! I got it! Thank you! . . . So when you don't go far enough in phase 2, and come back with the conflict—"Oh, fuck! I don't want to have a body, I want to kill myself"—I should have gone further with that!"

Arny: Yes, exactly. Your "X" wants to kill your normal identity.

D: The one who suffers. I don't want to have a body . . .

Arny: Yes, and it wants to free you from identifying only with your more conservative, quieter nature.

D: Thank you, and thanks, group, for galvanizing and helping me get there.

In this work, the person's phase 2 contained a lot of "X" energy. Like most people, she had an edge to the energy of that "galvanizer," the one who wanted to electrify and arouse consciousness not only in herself but in the world. When she "burned" that "X," it connected her to the entire group.

In the following exercise, you will have the chance to work on transforming your worst "X" energy into your facilitator's ally. Remember, if you get stuck in phase 2, take a stand against the "X" and at the same time *BURN "X" as much as possible*, as described in Chapter 5. "X" is often nonlocal and wants more global connection.

Exercise: How "X" Can Be the Facilitator's Ally

In the next meditation, I ask you to find your facilitator's ally. By *ally*, I refer to the spirit helper of the shaman. I recall such figures from the shaman Don Juan, in Carlos Castaneda's book, *Journey to Ixtlan: The Lessons of Don Juan*. There the shaman Don Juan spoke about the ally. Don Juan often said to Castaneda, "Death is your best ally." Don Juan did not really mean *death*; he meant that sometimes the "X" looks devastating and can possibly be useful, just as we saw in the example above.

In this exercise, I am asking you to remain open to the possibility that your "X" may be a potential gift, an "ally." Don Juan speaks about how the ally is "always waiting for you." I would add, *your ally is knocking on your door to help you also relate to the world.*

This exercise can be done with a partner as the helper (or alone as inner work).

The Ally: How Your Powerful ART Explains Reincarnation and Your ALLY

Helper, ask the dreamer: "What is on your mind or in your body these days? Use your hands to act out your most troublesome energy "X," and then your normal everyday identity ("u") energy."

1. Follow the channels you notice now—proprioception, movement, visualization, sound, relationship, world issue, etc.
2. Note and follow the phase you are in, and its main channel. Now when ready, intentionally move to other phases (i.e., phase 1, cruising and enjoying; phase 2, tensions/ conflict with an "X" energy; phase 3, flow or dialogue between "u" and "X"; phase 4, detached and following flirts, i.e., things which quickly catch your attention).
3. Explore phase 4. That is, let yourself be moved by nature and notice "u" and "X" energies in the dance. *While dancing*, ask yourself, what is the significance of the "X" energy, and why does it sometimes return, appearing as a problem?

What is possibly OK about "X's" reincarnation? Is "X" possibly an "ally," a spirit helper for you? If yes, what does it look like? How can that "X" be "burned" or amplified to serve not just you but the world as well? Make notes.

These facilitator meditation practices connect you to your deepest art and will help you do more sustainable work in the world. Phase 4's presence, compassion, and encouragement conveys belief in your own and everyone's process and awareness. Remember that "X," when burned, can be an ally for your public work. Believe in process and flow. Why? Because you are a piece of nature.

Things to Remember from Chapter 13

1. Practice asking yourself and others: Are you in a process of detachment, phase 4; or phase 1, just cruising; phase 2, in conflict with "X" in self or others; or phase 3, flowing, as in an open forum or as an Aikido master, with u + X polarities?
2. Follow the process in terms of the momentary needs and signals, channels, and phases.
3. Note: In phases 3 and 4, your u + X are NONLOCAL, connected to the world. So your "X," when processed in relationships and in public, may become your greatest ally.
4. Remember, your "ally" often appears as a "critic" at first; later it may appear as an addictive substance or a body problem.
5. When you wrestle with your ally, "burn it," exaggerate it to sense its power. It will bother you less, and your worldwork will improve.

CHAPTER 14

The Meditator's "Nonlocal" Process

• • •

IN THIS CHAPTER, WE FURTHER explore how your inner work and phase awareness can prepare you for outer facilitation challenges. Then, I suggest an inner work exercise to prepare you for group work by using the nonlocality of your meditator's experience.

We have seen how your deepest art nature, your inner work meditations, and your recurring "X" often seem to have a nonlocal connection to the world. The field and polarities you are working on "inside" yourself are yours, and, at the same time, might belong to others. To notice this nonlocality and to help yourself and others, explore sharing your "inner work" wherever and whenever you feel this is possible.

Consider the idea that perhaps you are a shaman, aware of spirits in the field. This awareness can make things easier for others. The normal phase 2 psychological viewpoint is, "Let's heal and change." A more detached phase 4 process-oriented view of the same thing is this:

Problems awaken you to your diversity
and
to your potential for meditation awareness
and ability to work in the world.

You cannot get away from yourself or the world. The existence of a problem implies something that disturbs or "awakens" you. A phase 4 viewpoint is that if you have a problem, perhaps you are lucky! Problems can force you to notice them, and if you notice that you are noticing, if you become aware of your awareness, then you have the opportunity to metacommunicate with yourself.

"Solutions" are important. But what is wrong with this normal facilitation and therapeutic attitude is its missing appreciation *of nature and phases.* To understand meditation, work with your awareness *all the time.* This is like dreamwork; did you dream last night? A lot of people do not dream dreams, per se, but you can still ask, "Did you notice what was happening in the night? What was it like? Did you catch any funny feelings? Can you remember a song that describes an aspect of the night?" Sound and songs are like dreams.

A Unified Approach to Human Consciousness

Processwork, a work we are creating together, should work for your inner world and outer worldwork, for yourself and for your organizations. It aims to provide a unified approach to human consciousness. As we have seen, what is happening outside is also an inner process, and what is inside can be outside as well. Problems may or may not get permanently resolved. But problems can make us aware that we are all part of a learning community, that our world itself is a learning community, and we are all in it together.

This idea of the world as a learning community reminds us that our so-called problems might be connected nonlocally to the people around us and the world. The concept of *process phases* allows us to have compassion for the times when we do not want to learn from our problems.

In phase 2, work with the "X" that is bothering you. When you are in phase 3, begin to role switch with the "X" and consider "X" to be nonlocal. Do an open forum with the u + X for yourself, and when possible, for others. In phase 4, flow and contact the universe. You may have more compassion for all the other problems and phases. In phase 4, there may not be any absolute life or death; there is just movement and awareness of awareness.

Years ago in my early 30s, when I was living in Switzerland, I had an attack of gout and could hardly walk for a few weeks. At that time, I was also working with a person who had a disease which disabled her from walking. She asked, "What is that like for you not to be able to walk very well?"

I began to tell her, "I have this problem, and it hurts, and medical people have told me that I will never get over it." She started crying and said, "That is what the medical people said to me as well! They told me I would never get out of this situation that I am in. What are we going to do?" she cried. My answer was, "Follow dreams. Dreams are as important as reality." She loved that approach.

My gout/pain problem helped me develop the concept of the dreambody. I thought later that gout attack was a kind of "gift." Having been crippled at 30 was not only bad! It was an ally! It helped me discover the dreambody, and in the course of several months, my gout problem left, and has never returned.

Exercise: Inner–Outer Preparation for Group Work

Now, I want to present an exercise for you to explore how the facilitator's process is nonlocally connected to the group's problems. This meditation practice will help you feel closer to the groups you work with, which in turn will make your facilitation more effective. I will be asking you to meditate on the phases of a group in which you are interested.

The world has problems, and many of them seem totally independent of you, but in some ways *the world has problems in part because we are all working on the same stuff.* Consider the idea that *your group can't have a problem if you don't have it.* This implies that if you can solve your problem, you can help your organization!

1. Choose an organization, a group, or a family system you are interested in, or a group that is troublesome for you. If you don't have any of those, you can think of a relationship, but I would prefer you thought of a family, small group, a cohort, bank, or organization.
2. What is one of the group's main needs? What other needs might be present? What is the group trying to do? What does it want to be?
3. What are some of its diverse, often unexpressed, needs? There may be a lot of them; there may be as many needs as there are people, but choose one or two of the main needs that come to mind.
4. Now, what overall phase would you say the group is in? It can be in many phases at once, but what is the main phase? Is it discovering itself? Finding or following its vision, as in phase 1? Or is it tense, as in phase 2? Is there a hidden conflict with some sort of difficult "X" like energy? Or is it in phase 3, able to switch between energies? Probably not, if it is on your mind, but it could be possible. Or is the group in phase 4, detached or potentially detached, depressed, afraid of going downhill?
5. Now, act out the present phase with your hands or any way you want in your imagination. Imagine exaggerating that phase for participants. Sitting is good, but sometimes you need to stand. Imagine acting out that phase for them in movement, and unfold an "X" energy. Imagine unfolding some "X" energy for yourself and *for them*, in front of them. Imagine it.
6. Follow the process, that is the parts, the people, and the phases. Imagine acting out the biggest problems for them and following whatever comes next. Imagine using your hands, your face, and your voice.
7. Notice phase changes. Do things switch? If you were in phase 1, does it move onwards? Are you in phase 2? Does the conflict begin to flow to phase 3? Does phase 4 occur? Really intensify and burn until things change. If you get close to phase 4, or a more relaxed cool spot comes up, notice what you are learning. Keep your inner focus on that group. If something relaxes or changes, make a note about what you are learning. What did you discover? Write it down.

8. Ask yourself, in what phase was *your* biggest edge? What do you imagine would be *the group's* most difficult phase?
9. Explore in your mind sharing that troublesome edge work with the group. Work on yourself internally before you work with a group and discuss your experiences with them. In your imagination, do you feel closer to the group? That feeling of closeness can be important. Do you feel closer to where they are at? If you feel distant from the participants, they will feel distant from you. What you do for them won't help as much. This is one of the reasons I suggest meditating *before* you work with groups, in order *to feel closer to them*. Imagine sharing that difficult spot.
10. Finally, imagine the problem coming back again. Imagine the reincarnation of that problem and consider, what could be good about it? What can you recommend to the group? Imagine saying, "If this comes back again, perhaps it is an ally. . . . What, if anything, might be good about the problem returning? Could it be a helpful spirit trying to awaken us to our process?"

After completing the exercise, one participant shared the following insights about a new way to deal with the organizational "silo effect."

P: I saw the energy that disturbs the group was actually something that I had experienced myself recently, so it helped me dream right into that energy. I would not have made that connection without the inner work.

I had some awareness about the government organization that I work for. I became aware that we bring in consultants that do team and relationship building, because we have this problem we call "silo-ing"—that means that subgroups retreat within their own boundaries and become separated.

So there is a lot of discontent and not much flow, but we bring in a consultant to help us and what happens is, some feel, "This is great!" They love this new energy and things flow. Then a few months go by and the love disappears as everybody retreats back into their own holes again. So it has been like a recidivistic process. We fall back into the same problem!!

Then we bring someone in again and this honeymoon phase returns, and then we go back. I realized personally that was familiar in my own family. That was the connection I made between my own personal life.

Arny: Did your meditation help?

P: Yes, I felt at first that they were in phase 1: "We do good stuff." Then I realized that they were in phase 2, in conflict with failure! They are innovative and hoping to succeed, but they marginalize times of failure. When I started there, I got depressed so quickly because I kept feeling I was such a failure at this job! So I went with that tiredness energy, and I felt, "Oh, my god, thank god for the 'X' that puts everybody down—it helps us get in touch with something deep, so we can bring out our big vision. So, now I even hope the problem will come back again to remind us of our visions!"

This was a wonderful example of the compassion and flow that phase awareness can bring to facilitation. Many businesses and organizations often begin to fail in part because they get caught in doing things and lose track of their common vision. "Why are we here? What is the meaning of the life of this business or organization?"

Remember, if you get stuck with yourself or a group, try the technique of burning the problem. Use your meditative awareness to get into the "X" energy problem so intensely that it burns itself out. If you get stuck with an "X," burn the "X" in your imagination. For example, I worked with a medical organization. The "X" for that group says, "Work!" So burning that, I said, "Work, work, work, ahahahahhhaa—it is too much! We cannot take it anymore and need a temporary detachment so we can see new things." The "X" burned itself out, so to speak.

I used the exercise above to prepare for a community meeting at our Process Work Institute in Portland. Before the meeting, I explored an "X" that had a lot of energy. For me, this "X" said, in essence, "We have got to make it; we have to get this and that, become this and that, get this license and that." Another voice of that group was, "How about the feeling and friendship part of things? How about the love that was there between us?"

One part of my meditation said, "We've got to make it, get our license, do this and that, *woof, woof, woof!*," and the other part was, "Yeah, but we used to be more interested in dreaming! Is that going to leave?" I went further and burned the "X" energy (*stomp-stomp-stomp!*), "Do this and that!!" I really went into the "doer" until it was exhausted, and then I relaxed and to my surprise, the dreaming reappeared and said, "Let's cuddle and be friends." Suddenly, the "X" came back in me, the doer came back, and both parts *flowed* more—*relax and then "woof"*! There was no longer a conflict. Instead there was a flow.

Then the next day, when that conflict arose during the meeting, I remembered my inner work. So I was not surprised when it came up and was at least temporarily resolved. The problematic split between pushing and relating awakened me to the process: PUSH, then RELATE! I have that split inside me; everybody has a split between feeling and working. Phase 4 often sees conflicting parts as one flowing process. My point is, do your inner work before a group process, and you may be a little more fluid yourself and be better able to connect nonlocally with the group as well.

Things to Remember from Chapter 14

1. Inner work is needed for your worldwork.
2. Help organizations to flow by modelling their flow process yourself, using your own "inner" work.
3. If and when you and/or others get stuck with that troublesome "X" energy, burn the "X" to gain "freedom" from it.

PART VI

From 360 to 721 Feedback

• • •

In Part VI, I share new tools and ideas that you can use with your deepest art to create more sustainable change and better relationships for the groups and organizations that you live in or work with.

In Chapter 15, I address the problem of groups splintering into factions that fight with each other about the way to reach their goals. The ideas of a *metaview* and *metamovement* can allow groups to get along with and appreciate different approaches.

In Chapters 16 and 17, I introduce a new feedback method that I call 721 feedback, or *721* for short. (I'll explain there why I have given this feedback method a numerical name.) Dealing with critical feedback is one of the most difficult challenges for individuals, relationships, and organizations. 721 uses our understanding of deep democracy levels and process phases to create a practical method for feedback that supports sustainable relationships and creative organizations. In Chapter 17, I focus specifically on how 721 feedback can be used in teaching and learning interactions to revolutionize our educational systems.

CHAPTER 15

Your "Metaview"

• • •

AROUND THE WORLD, MANY PEOPLE and groups trying to fight social and economic injustice often lose energy fighting with one another and fail to deliver their greatest common dreams. Why? A main reason is that they are missing a "*metamovement*" that would help similar and related subgroups work sustainably TOGETHER.

Often groups fighting for the same cause do not get along together. For example, some say, "Change the mainstream by giving them a push!" Other groups say, "Follow God, and all will be well!" My goal in working with these groups is to discover how they can collaborate and not exhaust themselves by fighting and criticizing each other. I call the solution to such problems, the *metaview*. In this chapter, I focus on this metaview. In the next chapter, I introduce 721 feedback, which is a technique for dealing more creatively and productively with criticism in organizations, businesses, government, and your own personal life.

Relationship Work for Sustainability

Around the world, most activists aim at particular goals and often forget relationship. However, without ongoing relationship work, activism is not sustainable. Leaders obviously need goals. But to realize those goals, leaders need to relax and relate to all the different directions in their groups. In government, the shortest path between today and tomorrow is not a straight line, but often a zigzag line. I'll talk more about working with that zigzag process using the BIGWAY technique in the last chapter of this book.

Since my early 30s, when I was living in Switzerland, a range of leading government people have asked for my help. Switzerland has been a place where people from different governments would go to seek support. Questions would often come up about their personal histories, about how to be a public person, about what skills are needed to resolve conflicts. They often asked about resolving historical issues in their countries.

I think about group conflicts when I think about combating racism in the United States. Some activist leaders say, "Forgive and forget," whereas other activists say, "NO!! Fight and wake everyone up." There are always various, and often conflicting, ways of helping to relieve social issues.

Or, for another example, we know that the EU today is suffering, trying to pull itself together to help refugees from other countries. Some of the problems involved in achieving this goal are connected with historical relationship issues—the ghost roles from the past are still haunting us. Similarly, as I began writing this chapter, Greece had a new leader who brought hope for unification. However, this liberal party was splitting because the leader took a more conservative direction without relating to others in his party. By 2016, the party was beginning to split into parts. In the moment, Greece has conflicts with itself and also with the rest of the EU. At the end of this chapter you will find one participant's unexpected insights into the Greek situation after completing the metaview inner work.

Many people have their own stories about social groups that struggle with internal conflicts or corruption, leaving their members feeling exhausted or betrayed. For example,

R: Any social action group I have been in has always had many different opinions about how to go forward, and usually the ones with the strongest voices or who spoke out most strongly to get people on their side led the way.

T: Five years ago I was involved in the Haiti earthquake recovery process and the efforts to bring awareness of that small country's desperate needs to the world. Recently I have read about the Red Cross

> *absconding with $1 billion—while I was working there! They were supposed to build habitats, but with that billion dollars, they have built all of SIX houses. Now, I hear that soon they are pulling out of Haiti because they say they cannot find people to do the jobs. I want to murder people! There was so much effort to raise awareness and nothing happened!*

The Metamovement

In my view, the problem is not that there are always diverse, separate apparently impossible movements within any large movement like the Red Cross. The problems arise in part because the different movements do not communicate, though all are saying they intend to help. They lack an overview, a "metamovement," so that members and subsections of groups can work together rather than against each other. We need a *meta*movement that expects and includes both old and new "sub" movements of the main way of going forwards.

The term *meta* in metamovement means an overview movement. The metamovement is able to include all the other movements with their different approaches. Metamovements help various approaches work together. For example here in the US, I have been involved in raising consciousness around racial problems. One group says, "Let it be, forgive!" while the other says, "Wake up the idiots!" Without a metamovement, these different approaches can fall into conflict with each other. We see similar problems everywhere with social and financial metamovements.

A metamovement has more power than do the several different directions within one large movement. Metamovements require awareness. You will see that a metaview values social action, including awareness of rank, double signals, and roles. For example, the activist with a lot of "Woof!" is needed to awaken people to rank unconsciousness. "Wake up!" But we also need to relate to the "other side" for sustainable change to happen. One direction to do that (but not the only) is a spiritual direction, for example, "Forgive and forget."

The metamovement person is able to be in phases 1 and 2 in consensus reality, but also include phase 3's role switching and phase 4's detachment.

What? Normally we are against becoming the thing we are against! We have to switch roles with monsters we hate?! We refuse! But in the metamovement, there is a perspective that says, "We don't like it, but we will try it!"

Metamovements need all directions, and all phases. The phases of the metamovements are similar to those involved in personal and group phases.

Phase 1. Take it easy, relax with the world of problems. Don't think about rank! Don't think about oppression! Take it easy.
Phase 2. Now push! Wake people up!!
Phase 3. Switch roles and "recycle" the enemy's power. The enemy that gets thrown into the "trash" carries a lot of hidden energy that we need.
Phase 4. Now leave things up to nature and the gods.

You might have experienced people who are particularly able to flow between the phases. For example, one participant shared the following story.

> *This past weekend a bunch of us were with a group of shamans, and I was studying the way a native woman, a spiritual woman with a lot of rank, would go from one state to another congruently. Watching the way she did that was amazing! What an indigenous leader! She would go from one to the other, then just relax. She would move from one to another like a child playing. I feel we are going back to that kind of wisdom.*

From the deep democracy perspective, leadership means saying *yes* to action, and *yes* to role switching and *yes* to relaxation—that is what I would call *community eldership.* Elders have metaviews and can see different phases as natural and needed: It is OK to fight, then relax, be at peace in phase 4, and then return to phase 2 and fight.

However, without awareness, we unconsciously zigzag, and the "u" becomes the "X." Like individuals, groups who have been hurt often become the "X" that they hate. A group that at one point is oppressed by something else and does not pick it up, eventually becomes oppressive towards others without realizing it. Groups are often united as allies against a common enemy, but eventually they should pick up that energy with awareness, or they will unconsciously *become it* at another point.

It seems there are health benefits to this ability to consciously work with the "X" energies that have hurt us. In other words, there are health benefits to avoiding getting stuck in phase 2, where we fight and reject the "X" unabatedly, and instead to flow with the other three phases. Countries wanting good health should pick up and use the energy of their opponent's viewpoints. All of us need the same thing. Everything that bothers us, even if it is a sore foot, is a crucial "X."

Deep democracy means saying *yes* to resolving body problems with phase 2 methods, but at the same time, consciously using phases 3 and 4 to work with the troubling "X" energy of the dreaming process, so that you don't unconsciously become the very "X" that is disturbing you. Get in touch with all your energies *before you unconsciously become them with others.* Integrating those "X" energies is relieving and can improve your health. Picking up the "X" is a form of preventative medicine, and helps you flow better with your entire nature.

But can you get people to switch roles in the midst of a real negotiation in a relationship or organizational conflict? As a facilitator, can you move people from phase 2 to phase 3?

The answer depends upon the issues, the timing, the people, and your own state of awareness. Switching roles depends upon the awareness and eldership of all present. It is a matter of timing. Your body will teach you how to facilitate. Facilitating is an art, a body experience, and a *metaview* that allows you to model phase 3 and phase 4.

Within social justice struggles, there is often a painful split between a role that wants to forgive and move on, and a role that is furious and hates the one who is doing harm. One participant asked me,

> *I am thinking about the fury coming out of the heartbreak of racism. I think of the activist who hates the cops who hurt others unnecessarily. My question is, how do we support the one who forgives but also the one who is feeling, "Fuck no! You have to stop this!"*

One answer is to remember occasionally to have a metaview that understands that both sides are needed and can flow into one another. The metaview remembers that, "Yell, forgive, yell, forgive" is part of a natural cycle of process phases. Befriend the entire process!

I now share an inner work process focused on finding a metaview that you can use to transform your relationship to troubling approaches within a group in which you are interested. I illustrate using my own inner work practice, facilitated by Amy.

Metaview Inner Work

First choose a social action group, or a person, that is most difficult for you in connection with that given social issue. You can work on any social action group working for a better world, for more diversity consciousness around racial, religious, environmental, health, sexual orientation, or economic issues.

Choose some group that is working towards helping those with less social rank and power. Perhaps you like them, but are disturbed by the way they are working on that issue. For example, maybe you feel they are too spiritual and you would like them to be more powerful, or maybe they are too powerful and pushy and that bothers you. It could be a million other things that disturb you. You can work on a person that bugs you, or the whole group that bugs you, or a subgroup of the group. If you cannot think of a social action group, you can choose any group or organization, or somebody in it, that is disturbing you.

Demonstration: Inner Work with Arny

In this example, I work on my encounter with a woman in Colombia that I mentioned earlier in this book.

Amy: Alright. Here it goes, Arny. What social action person or group troubles you the most? It could be someone who disturbs you who is fighting or working for a particular social issue.

Arny: This person who bothers me the most is a terrorist. She has been on my mind since I met her for twenty seconds in Colombia. We were leaving the seminar, after having helped everyone work on the "guerilla" activists—a forceful group that has, for many, many years, kidnapped people, extorted money, and done other things to many including upper-class Euro-Colombians. The poor felt the rich were racist towards others with less social rank. I had said that activists often feel they must awaken the mainstream, even if they will die doing that. Activists must be careful about suicide. Social change is the point, not the loss of their lives.

I told the group that what they are hoping for is important, and can be done in a way that doesn't harm others and will not be suicidal. I said all this in a lecture and then the group worked together well.

While we were walking out of the seminar after a large group process including many sides of Colombia's conflicts, a woman grabbed me by the arm and said, "Suicide! You were talking about me—don't ever tell anybody my name," which I didn't know anyway. That was it. She held on to me for 20 seconds and then she disappeared. She could not say more because she was a guerilla and was afraid of being arrested. Some people who had been guerillas (including her) were at that meeting, and she was thankful for what I had said.

Today, I am thinking about her again and asking myself, "What else could I have done?" What is my metaview? I am an activist, but I also want to hear all sides. She was apparently a more violent activist. What could I have done to help her by bringing our approaches even closer together? What's a possible metavision here?

I know I wanted to do more besides saying, "Thank you." What could I have done better?

Amy: And what would you say was her larger goal as a guerilla?

Arny: Economic and social equality, recognition and change. Down with the mainstream that is unconscious of social rank and inequality.

Amy: What would you say is her worst or most disturbing or difficult energy?

Arny: The energy that bothers me is violence. It seems that she was willing to kill herself to accomplish her goals. I don't want that to happen. I guess she came to that seminar in order to find new ways.

I wish I could have said something. I only had a few seconds, yet, even with that time I could have done better. It just takes a second to say something. I want to work on that.

Amy: What is the most disturbing "X" energy?

Arny: For me, her "X" was her potential violence: "I will do what I have to do even if it kills me. I don't care about life any more. My life is possibly worthless anyhow, so let me at least achieve my goals. If I lose my life doing it, so what?"

Amy: Can you make a little sketch of that energy and maybe give it a name? Or make a note about it for yourself?

Arny: (Makes sharp-angled squiggle and writes "Smash! Crash! I must succeed!")

Amy: What part of you doesn't like or has trouble with this energy? We call that the little "u."

Arny: My "u" is, "take care of yourself, let's talk about it" (draws a wavy squiggle).

Amy: Now let's think about rank. Do you think that person is unconscious of rank in some way?

Arny: Yes, she is driven by a spiritual motivation to correct the world. She does not have social rank, but she has a lot of spiritual rank that she may not have been conscious of—enough spiritual rank to possibly kill herself and others.

Amy: Do you think you were unconscious of rank in this situation?

Arny: I always need to remember that I am a white male teacher from the United States in South America. I try to be conscious of my social rank and use it well, but I can always do better.

Amy: Now take a moment in phase 1; relax and forget it all—and be happy if you can.

Arny: Yes, ah. The sea is so beautiful today. The beach. The sky is blue. I saw a whale the other day.

Amy: And let's move to phase 2. Remember and show again that difficult "X" energy. Act out that smashing, crashing "X" energy.

Arny: (throwing his arms up) *"Get back! Here I come, a suicide bomber! Kill the other! Knife them, what is the difference if they get me back?! Who cares about that, my life is hopeless anyhow! This way my life will have some meaning! This is the way—I will sacrifice my life for something! Who cares if I die?"*

Amy: Remember the "u" and the "X" energies and let them dialogue.

Arny: The "u" says, "I don't want you to have to die. You look like a potentially very fine human being. Perhaps you can get what you hope for without having to die for it! I don't want you to die. The "X" says, "There is no other way!" . . . but . . . hmm . . . your teacher (Arny) implied that there was another way! I was touched by that."

Amy: In phase 3, do role switching to work beyond polarities. See if you can express the "X," and really go deeply into what it is expressing. Then do the same thing with the "u." Express each side, moving back and forth, if you can.

Arny: (Takes roles, one after the other in phase 3.)

- *"X" She, the guerrilla: If you have been through the hell that I have been through, then you would understand better.*
- *Arny: Yes, you remind me of my own background, wanting to get back. Hmmm . . . I could not say this to her then. I was not aware of it at that point. But now this exercise helps me say to her, "I do understand a little, a tiny bit—yes, I understand."*
- *She: Understand me? Nobody understands me! People just want to imprison us, to shoot us!*

Arny: I do *understand. I can feel into your activist role. Now some understanding is beginning.*

Amy: Relax again for a moment, and while you are relaxing, sense the universe around you, the big space. And imagine that the universe starts to move you . . . let the power of the field move you spontaneously.

Arny: (Lets go into movements, wiggles, a leap, arms flying up.)

Amy: And while you are dancing, notice how the "u" and "X" energies are somehow appearing in that dance, in those movements.

Arny: Yes! The "X" in my dance makes a big smash, and the "u" is quieter.

Amy: While dancing and feeling both, find a metaview insight. Sense how both energies are useful for you personally and imagine how your insights might be useful for that that person.

Arny: (dancing about, after a while) *Yeah! I got it, here is what I didn't say to her! "You are great, but I want you to be even more socially powerful! If at all possible, please speak out or learn to speak about social issues publicly! Don't be so shy of the public. I want you to speak out more, come out from the background. Come forwards and speak, then take it easy. Get over the shyness! You are strong and have a lot to say."*

My phase 3 and phase 4 experiences put together her power with our shared hope for social consciousness. My process showed me that there is neither a "no" nor a "yes" to radical activism; instead my metaview includes supporting her to be a bit more fluid as an activist in speaking out. It also supports me to speak out more on these topics! I feel I understand her and other radicals better. Like many of us, they feel that only in extreme states can they achieve change. But the metaview shows that all of our states of consciousness need more support and encouragement, both the extreme side and the moderate side. Her way and my way are both right, and can come together to support one another.

If we had more time, Amy could have taken my inner work further by role playing the troublesome "X" person for me, and allowing me to practice relating to her with my new approach.

My inner work gave me insight into the possible experience of the activist driven to acts of terror, and it made this radicalism feel less alien and "other." Most importantly, it gave me a direction for how to facilitate a dialogue with this difficult role. The phase 3 and phase 4 role switching and relaxation in my metaview inner work made me realize that people who are shy and hopeless may be shy about coming out strongly as activists, and instead end up doing so secretly in a violent manner. If I could support her to come out more publically, I imagine that she might say, "Thank you, you are really talking to me," and I would reply, "You can and should be an important leader, and I will try and grow as well to bring out my most radical views!"

Some activists might be even more powerful and successful in getting their messages across by speaking up more instead of doing life-threatening things. It is not easy, but it is possible that if that woman could speak out in a metaview manner in both phases, 3 and 4, she could achieve what she hopes for and not fear for her life.

It is interesting to know that in Colombia now, some of the the general public is beginning to relax, and some background radicals are beginning to come forward and speak out publically.

To explore this process for yourself, try the following exercise on your own or with a friend.

Exercise: Metaview Inner Work

This exercise gives you a chance to work on your own experience of somebody who disturbs you in a particular social action group you support. You will need some paper and something to write with. Sit in your chair or stand, and be open to movement.

What social action PERSON or GROUP troubles or bothers you the most (e.g., too spiritual or too powerful/pushy)? What is the larger issue or goal? Stand, if you can, or sit at the end of your chair, and describe to yourself that person or group's worst energy. We'll call that "X." Act out this "X" energy with your hands and body. Make a note and a sketch of this "X" energy on your paper. What part of you doesn't like that "X" energy? Call this part "u." What kind of energy does it have? Act out this "u" energy. Make a note and sketch of it on your paper. Now think about rank. Do you think the other person or group is *unconscious of rank* in some way? If so, how, in your mind, is this person or group unconscious of rank? Make a note. Are you *unconscious of rank* in some way? How? Make a note.

Now explore the phases.

Phase 1. Forget the problems and relax, if you can. Be happy for a moment.

Phase 2. Recall the difficult person or group, and act out that "X" energy again.

Imagine "u" discussing/conflicting with "X."

Then, move to the metaview of phases 3 and 4.

Phase 3. Try to flow between the two polar opposite energies "X" and "u." Here's how: Stand, if you can, and become and express "X"; then move and express "u." Now go back and forth between "X" and "u," sensing deeply and playing both energies as a kind of dialogue. Now, let's move to phase 4.

Phase 4. Still standing (or in your chair), relax for a moment if you can and imagine that the universe around you begins to move you about. Let it dance you about and wait until you feel it moving you a little spontaneously *(be careful of yourself and those around you).* While dancing, notice how the u + X energies somehow *appear in your movements.*

While dancing and feeling both the "u" and the "X," *find a metaview* in which you sense how both energies are useful *for you personally.* Can you imagine how this insight might create a metaview for you, to deal better with that issue and that person or group? With these insights in mind, imagine talking to "X" and notice what happens. Make notes about what you discover.

Metaview Relationship Work

As a final step, share your experience with a partner/friend. Tell her or him about how you might use your metaview experiences to collaborate with the real outer people and situations. *Then, have your partner play the "X" individual or group.* Use your phase 3 and phase 4 metaview experiences to relate to and interact with that "X." Your partner should notice when these interactions from the metaview begin to change her or him. Ask your partner to give you feedback about how your metaview state affected her or him.

The following example from a participant in my classes illustrates how the exercise can help you to find a metaview. This participant was able to find an eldership state of mind and feel less conflict with another approach within the same social movement, even though it was an approach with which she disagreed.

> *L: I worked on my liberal views, and the Greek government's conservative way of doing things. In Greece, we had many years of austerity, and finally we have a government that grew out of social movements. So we put a lot of hope in this government, and things did not go the way we hoped.*
>
> *The "X" energy of the leader for me was conservative and rigid. Though he came from an activist background, when he got into power, he suddenly closed down and disconnected from the liberal and social movements that had brought him to power and became more conservative.*
>
> *When I played that leader, I felt afraid, and that the responsibility lay heavy on my shoulders. I felt up against forces much bigger than me. I felt retreating was the only way to survive. I became more conservative. The new thing for me is to let that be, let him be, to see that view without only fighting it. I can withdraw my projection of the liberal leadership from him and relax and accept that I can nevertheless continue to hold an ultimately liberal view. Now, I am no longer only against him. That changed. I can now accept*

> *his way and my more liberal one as well. This lifts my depression and changes, in a way, my sense of being in conflict with that leader. I am still in conflict with him politically but something in me also understands him as a part of me. It's a subtle change in my feeling attitude toward him that has happened, which I feel has an effect in my inner relationship with him, and would have an effect on an outer interaction with him.*

This work illustrates how the metaview can allow you to accept and live with viewpoints very different than your own, and move forward with less conflict.

Things to Remember from Chapter 15

1. Activist groups aiming at similar goals often conflict, reducing everyone's ability to resolve social problems. Metaviews help those activist groups work together.
2. Use your metaview experiences to enable social action methods to co-exist and work constructively.

CHAPTER 16

721 Feedback for Business and World Issues

• • •

IN THIS CHAPTER, I INTRODUCE you to a new form of feedback that I call "721 feedback" or 721 for short. This type of feedback is a creative and sustainable approach to dealing with criticism or critical feedback in relationships, small and large group work, and business and government contexts. Though I have been using 721 for some years, this is the first time I am introducing it in book form.[38] As I explain below, I developed 721 after examining the 360° feedback method being used in organizations.

In this chapter, I especially relate 721 to worldwork for both small and large groups and share an example of an open forum that occurred at one of our seminars. In the next chapter, I show how 721 can be applied specifically to education and the feedback process between teacher and student.

721 is based upon the deep democracy structures found in your dreams, groups, and the world. As we know, everything goes through phases, and all are important at one moment or another—at least from the phase 4 metaviewpoint, the detached overview of all views, a creative, shamanistic part of life. Similarly, we all experience each of the deep democracy levels of experience. During the day you are in CR but then going to bed at night, you usually relax and enter into dreamland and the essence level.

721 can be written as 360+360+1. As you know, there are 360 degrees in a circle. "360" is the name given by the business community to the process of getting a full 360 degrees of feedback from around, above, and

below you (peers, superiors, and subordinates). My 721 feedback concept is an update of 360.

721 includes 360 degrees of feedback from those around you in consensus reality, but adds another 360 degrees of feedback from role switching in dreamland. Finally, it seeks feedback from phase 4 and your deepest art to provide the final 1 degree, symbolizing the unifying feedback from the essence level.

721 is a Combination of Deep Democracy's Reality Levels: Consensus Reality + Dreamland + Essence Level

360 consensus reality feedback from all u's + X's of people "above" and "below" you

\+ **360** dreamland (role switching feedback)

\+ **1** your essence level, processmind's experience and metaview.

= **721** *a new organizational and worldwork feedback method.*

I have found that 721 is a basic structure of just about all human and natural processes. It is something that you can use all the time. For example, I can use 721 with myself right now to work with an experience I had this morning. I woke up and had a critical voice giving me feedback. I looked in the mirror, and the critic said,

> *Critic: Look at that face?! What is that red spot on your cheek?! Hide it!! You had better hide that red spot!*
> *I said, Why should I hide it?*
> *Critic: You don't want to appear to others and show that you have a red spot on the cheek of your face—it's ugly! Ask Amy for some makeup!*

So to practice 721, first I consider 360 at the surface. I ask myself, what is that spot? It is a dry spot of skin. Just dry. I've had dry spots on my knees sometimes. Since I was a little boy, I've had little bits of psoriasis, dry skin spots. Nothing very serious.

> *Critic: You don't want to show that, it's gross!*
> *"u": It's just psoriasis!*
> *Critic: You can NOT show that, you must look just perfect! You have to get some makeup on your skin.*

This dialogue is 360 in consensus reality. There is the critic's feedback saying "You have an ugly red spot!" whereas the "u" is saying, "Come on, what is the big deal? Forget it!"

To continue, I go deeper by exploring 360 in dreamland. This means feedback and role switching between all the different CR parts, including fantasy figures. It means I can *switch sides.* I can take the "X" role of my spot, and say to myself "Hmmmm, red spot!" By role switching in dreamland, I suddenly have a brand new idea that came out of this phase 3 activity: "Red spot means, *bring your insides out more, show the blood inside of yourself!*" And I realize that sometimes I don't show the deepest part of myself.

Then I go deeper to the "1" of 721, the essence or "oneness" level. It is the processmind or deepest art experience. Here, I can let my body be moved by the universe and pay attention to "feedback" or messages arising from that dance experience. As I relax and let myself be moved, I hear a sentence, "Bring it all out, tell the world about this." So now I share it in my classes and this book.

The following diagrams describe 721 feedback and show how the deep democracy levels and the phases of process are connected. Notice especially that in dreamland, you can bring in ghost roles, people and things mentioned but not acted out, double signals, etc.

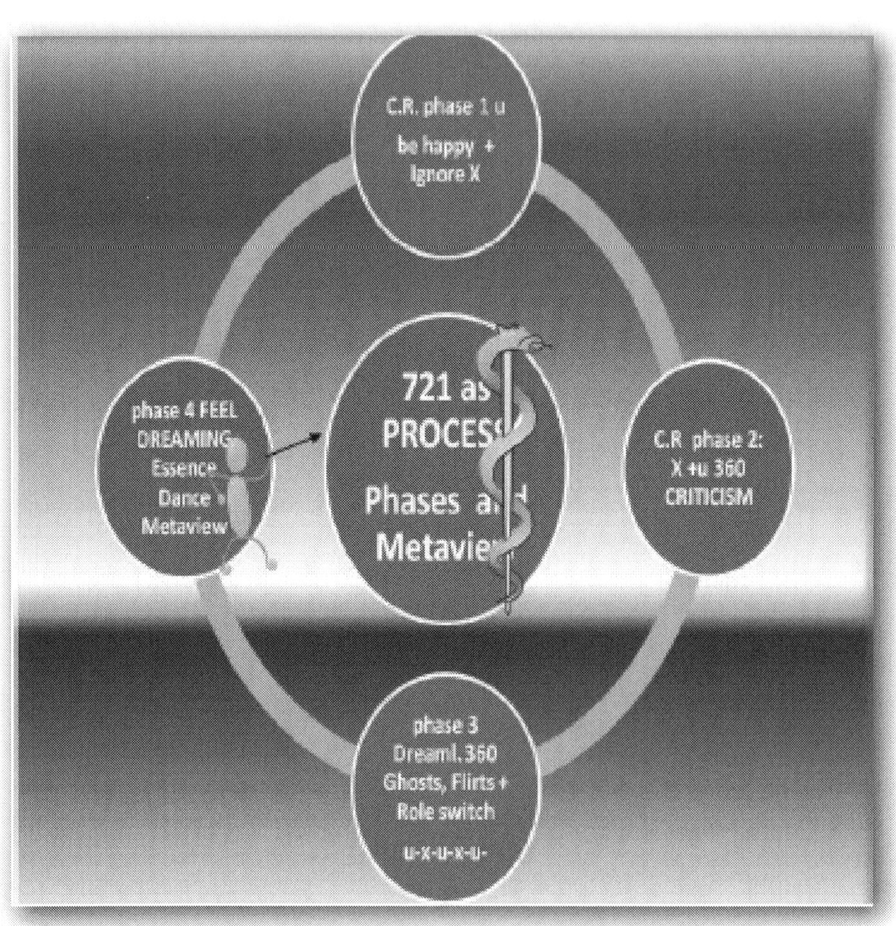

20. **721 as Levels and Phases for Self, Business, and World**

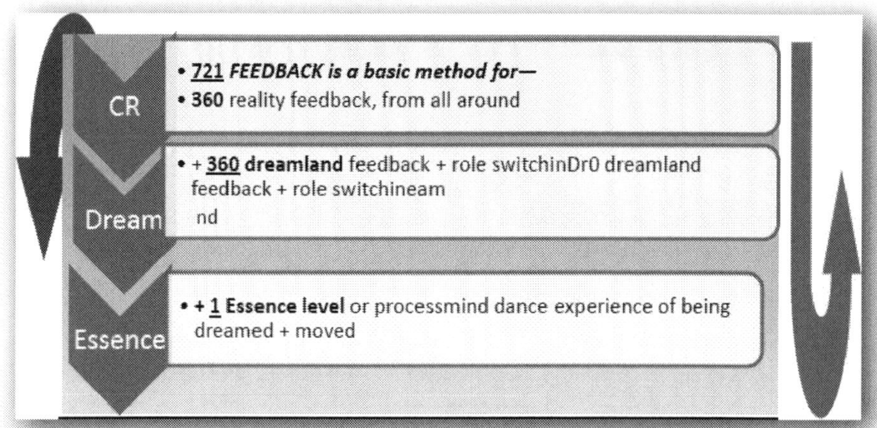

***21.* 721 as Forums and Process Levels**

721 is a basic pattern of our nature, as individuals, groups and nations. 721 can be used as a powerful structured method to deal with criticism or any kind of feedback

721 is a pattern behind all internal and external criticism and experiences. Every tension inside and outside yourself can be connected to internal negative feedback from some part of yourself. If you are in a group or organization, all possible tensions can be understood as part of a conscious and unconscious feedback system.

721 ideas began to dawn on me when I first heard about the 360 feedback method used in business, thanks to my friend, Dr. Max Schupbach of the Deep Democracy Institute.[39] The business world says, "Employees need feedback!"

As noted, the standard 360 feedback system in business gives you feedback from those above you, your superiors; from your peers, people who are on the same level; and from your subordinates as well. For example, some of that feedback might be, "Well, you are our teacher, our boss, or something like that, and sometimes you are good, but we do not like most of what you do, etc."

When 360 feedback became known in the business and industrial world some years ago, it was quickly very popular and still is today. One reason is that it encourages people to give mostly written feedback so no one has to talk directly to the other. The benefit is that you hear all sides, and it can wake you up to things that you may not have seen, or that people could not tell you directly. It can break out of the stagnation of hierarchies.

However, *Harvard Business Review*, a scientifically and socially conservative business magazine, reviewed the 360 method, and concluded that its effectiveness "is in doubt."[40] Why? Employees often quit! People react negatively to negative feedback; they don't just pick it up and change the way the critic would like them to. Negative feedback complicates relationships. Some say that 360 is a "pot for relationship trouble." It can make it hard to maintain an authority role. It can be a vehicle for challenging the status quo, and yet much of the feedback is comprised of other people's projections!

So, in my view 360 is a wake-up call but not yet a final answer. Studies of 360 say that the method takes more time and money from the business! People get all upset, and they don't talk to one another, and teamwork suffers. The 360 method is good to wake you up: "Come on, Arny and Amy, you are giving a seminar—give others a chance to speak, do it this way, do it that way, more group process, less group process!" Those are great things to pick up. But what is missing? Role switching and processing the essence of it all. There is no *dreaming*!

Now, you might be wondering, how can we bring dreamland into business and government? We can! It is simple. Consider the outer critic as a figure you can switch roles with! This is a dreamlike principle you experience mainly in dreams, but which we try to bring closer to reality in deep democracy. If you don't pick up positive or negative feedback in the day, you dream about it at night. Maybe you need to fight with that "X," maybe not. Maybe you are a bit like "X"? Maybe you are too self-critical and need to take a stand against all that junk you are tossing at yourself?

Without dreamland and the essence levels, the feedback process is not fluid. So, we keep CR 360 *and add to it another dreamland 360.*

In 721, we no longer take 360 as a written or secret process, but as a possible inner or outer *open forum process wherein everyone* can be involved if they want to be. In an open forum, many unexpressed "X" factors and diversity issues can appear. Some criticism is related to unconsciousness about gender, race, sexual orientation, religion, etc. 360 dreamland realizes that the disturbing outer "X" is trying to standardize us, inside and out! As I reflect on my idea of 721, I realize that I am partly an activist fighting against this standardizing "X" in dreamland! If I bring this out even more directly, I can better explain the value of 721.

The conventional 360 feedback system assumes that we are a little like a machine that can take in feedback without taking things personally, and then mechanically change for the better. The assumption is that if feedback comes in, then you will change. But although there is something good about this thinking, human beings are not entirely machines! Businesses that focus only on production easily negate relationships. To help people really integrate feedback, we need the 360 dreamland level of feedback and role switching wherein I pick up the side that does not like the red spot on my skin and I discuss matters with it, so to speak.

In 360 dreamland, you can feel yourself into the "X," into the other sides, and play them out as you might do in dreamwork. It's rare to admit that you are like your critic, but please do consider that possibility. Then you can bring all that into an open forum for yourself, and for others, when possible.

In dreamland, there are not only critical voices but things that catch your attention suddenly. I call those "flirts." Things "flirt" with your attention, and you can catch them and let them speak. Dreamland 360 includes switching roles with consensus reality critics, with flirts, dreams, and even body feelings.

Finally, I bring in feedback from the essence level. I refer to the essence level by the number "1" in 721. Add this 1 to the original 360 CR + the new 360 dreamland to complete the 721. The "1" is my symbolic formulation of the oneness of the essence level. It unifies things; it arises from the oneness level. Your deepest art, your shamanistic processmind can change you and your organization.

So 721 accepts 360 feedback as it has been applied until now, and adds to it all the levels of our experience, including the open forum idea to let parts interact and role switch, and to open to the essence or shamanistic level.

Our idea of the second training can now be reformulated. First training skills deal with 360 CR, and second training focuses also on 360 dreamland and the essence level dance at the deepest level. Your second training is devoted to trying to use your deepest art to work with yourself, with individuals, and with small and large groups in psychology, in business, and in government.

We used 721 feedback when we worked with the American Chamber of Commerce in Japan. To present 721 in a corporate context, we told them to consider that there are three levels.

In reality, do an open forum.
In the second level, switch roles.
In the third, just relax and see what happens.

Remember when working with corporations that around the world, a major problem with corporations is sexism. Racism and homophobia are next to be addressed. Groups are just on the verge of accepting women as bosses. Accepting people from other races and cultures is the next step. These issues will almost always be in the background of whatever topic is being worked on.

Another way to bring deep democracy levels into mainstream government or business contexts is to work with the organizational vision. The part of an organization's vision or first dream that can be formulated is part of dreamland. The root of that dream is an essence-level experience, such as peaceful solutions to nuclear energy. In dreamland we can see parts such as peace versus nuclear energy.

Remember, the first dream is a vision or flag or motto, an essence experience of where an organization or country is headed. It is a guiding hand behind the organization!

In order to bring out phase 4 or essence-level experience for organizations, I recommend that facilitators not only ask the organization's members to do it, but to *model it for them*. In other words, facilitators ideally should *show their 721 to everyone.*

Remember to do 721 for yourself first before you work with people and model it for them. Then invite any and all who are able to participate to an open forum. Model role switching and go deeper with the forums. Sometimes people are not able to switch roles; they may not have seen it happen before, or it is too shocking for them to do this at first. But if you show and model 721 yourself first, then aspects of those levels become easier for organizations or groups, even those in wild conditions.

A participant shared the following example of modeling 721 for a group:

> *G: I was leading a seminar on shamanism, and one of the shamans was working and pushing the group really fast. Then it was my time to teach, and everyone wanted things fast, fast, fast, and I showed this conflict inside of me. I showed my conflict between the fast and slow. No one in the group had mentioned going slow, but afterwards a woman came up to me and said, "Thank god you did that—I was being pushed so fast, I was so scared, then you showed your own conflict and I felt so safe. So, thanks, it was really a great learning for me."*

Demonstration: Open Forum with 721

The following excerpts are taken from an open forum that occurred in one of our seminars. First we led all the participants, including the facilitator, through a 721 inner work preparation, which you will find below as an exercise you can try yourself. Then the group opened up to dialogue in the open forum practice.

The open forum began by choosing a theme by making sounds. I reminded the group that all topics that are chosen are really the name of an umbrella, and that under that umbrella are subthemes. Facilitators should remember to mention subthemes, because doing so can relieve people so the central theme can be focused on.

We asked the facilitator to try and show her 721 attitude—that is, "I am on this side, and there is another side over here that is totally different and that may be against this side"—and to bring in her deepest art, her processmind before going into the forum. Facilitators should try and drop down and show how to get deeper into both sides by starting to role switch themselves. With practice, all this takes is just a minute, and you don't need to make a big deal about it. Of course, you cannot do this with every organization or every group all of the time, but our practice in the seminar was to help the facilitator to show her 721, as it can be very helpful.

The group chose the topic of racism in the United States against African Americans and Asians, and the facilitator was the person who suggested the issue.

Here are steps we used to prepare for the forum. After the exercise I will discuss what happened in our forum.

Exercise: 721 Preparation All Together

If the theme is not yet clear, dear facilitator ask each participant to think of a most difficult group, organizational, national, or world issue on which she or he would like to focus.

Spin the pen and ask the chosen person about their topic and speak about the worst "X" and "u" energies in that issue for them.

Then facilitator, lead everyone through the following suggested 721 training.

I. 721 Inner Work + Metaview led by facilitator (10 minutes)

> *360 Consensus Reality*: Think about the chosen issue. Stand, if possible, and feel and sense the worst "X" energy *for you* in that issue. Make a motion to describe that "X" energy and sketch and name it on a piece of paper. Where did/does that "X" energy happen in *your personal life*? What part of you, "u," is most upset by that "X" energy? Make a motion to describe that "u" energy and sketch and name it on your paper.

360 Dreamland: Now, explore u + X transpolar role switching. That is, go back and forth, expressing the "u" and then the "X" *deeply* and imagine bringing in any ghosts or spontaneous flirts that catch your attention.

1 Essence Level Metaview: Relax, if you can, and let yourself be moved spontaneously. Sense if the u + X energies are part of your dance. Continue dancing and note any insights emerging about how to deal with "X." Make a note on your paper about any insights.

II. Group Process (30 MINUTES)

Facilitator, remind everyone of the issue and your u + X. Then *BRIEFLY* show *your* 721 experience, and *model it* before and during the group process if and when possible.

Group Process: *(Facilitator, read all of this section first before beginning.)* Everyone, use your 721 inner work to help elder what occurs, if possible.

- 360 Dialogue in CR: Someone speak for the "X," and someone for a "u" in that issue for 2 minutes.
- 360 in Dreamland: Introduce a level shift as everyone tries to play out and switch ROLES. Bring in any GHOST roles (roles mentioned but not there in the moment). Remember to go slowly at HOT and COOL spots or RESOLUTION moments.
- 1 in Essence Level: If needed, recall your metaview experience and use.
- Continue until solutions emerge and/or the time is up.

III. Discuss together (10 MINUTES)

Discuss the issue and its various CR positions, ghost roles, role switching, and/or metaviews that emerged. What are the possible next steps in this topic and in your learning?

The following group process emerged around racism.

Different people spoke about racial issues. For example,

I would focus on race issues in the U.S. and the world and my "X" energy would be stomping down on people. My "u" would be open-hearted.

My challenge is also racism, the white silence, and the challenge we white people face picking it up and working with it. My "X" feels busy with other stuff, getting on with other things. I am progressive and I am out there doing things; my usual "u" energy is super-fluid and liquid, but maybe around this issue there is a lot of anger: "Fuck! Let's do something! Face it and change it!"

My issue is the U.S. power around the world. The U.S. thinks it knows the right thing for everybody. The "X" makes movement throwing arm outward "Yes!" and my normal "u" moves on the spot, (quietly shaking) "feels very little."

My topic is also racism. I am normally able to speak out, but it is painful to bring up racism, and the deep feelings we have about it.

Racism is important, but I want to be more specific and talk about poverty—that is a big thing for people of color. Poverty is a big thing. It is a privilege to work on the environment, but some people don't have the luxury, they just have to survive each day.

I want to echo the race relations and the topic. I live in a neighborhood that used to be predominantly African American, and a lot of the community costs have forced out many people. I somehow want to bring in the personal as a light-skinned person living in that neighborhood. I want to be personal about the issue.

Once the topic was chosen, someone spoke about the complexities of different kinds of racial experiences.

> *D: I have a low dream that racism belongs to the white and black people and often the Asians and Native people are marginalized in that topic.*
>
> *Arny: Thanks for showing how one important topic under the racism umbrella is the marginalization of Asian and Native Americans!*

We spun a pen to choose the facilitator, and then Amy led everyone through 721 inner work, described above. The person in the group who was going to be the facilitator spoke of his inner work.

> *N: Wow, I am the facilitator! In my 721, I was thinking about all the various experiences of racism all around the world, in indigenous worlds, amongst all of us. Then when I went down to the dreamland level, I was thinking about hopes and repressed dreams. . . . Then when I went down to the essence 1 level, and out in my movement, one hand was on my center and the other hand open to the world. The new part for me is, that in the past I have always been trying to be so open, and this reminds me of the importance to keep my own center as I open up to the world.*
>
> *Amy: So, everyone, try to use your 721 to help, elder, and facilitate what is happening. Have someone speak on one side and the other side, consensus reality, then do 360 in dreamland to try and bring in ghosts and role switching, and bring in your "1" at any time.*

In the group process on racism that followed, one role involved the people who are hurt, ignored, impoverished, and another role was described as the sexist, racist, and money-oriented figure of the U.S. politician then running for president, Donald Trump.

Someone in the marginalized black minority position began to shake, move, and throw her arms and legs expressively showing the agony in her role.

Then suddenly, the person playing the white U.S. mainstream "Donald Trump" role (a person who was an African American) was so touched by the cries of agony, he had to leave that Trump role to care for the marginalized role. He said,

> *Even in this white racist role, I got to an edge and changed when I saw her having all that intense emotion. . . . Those feelings are in me too and brought me out my role. . . . I had to . . . dance with her!! . . . I see now we are connected, at least for a moment: I am and she is, we are both visible for a moment.*

The U.S. mainstream white role and marginalized not-white American roles then *danced together in such a way that both of them said,* "There is understanding" . . . and everyone was quiet as the group process completed itself.

What we saw in this open forum is that when the marginalized position exploded in shaking agony, deepest feelings, and dance, the "X" (Donald Trump) role surprisingly dissolved. All this must go deeper beyond the CR and dreamland polarities because of that essence level dance together. That was a rare, transformational group process experience. The dance relieved the conflict through essence level communication . . . at least temporarily.

For the CR level, this is a beginning; there is a world of things to be done. But this remarkable event occurred while doing 721. The people went deeply into the agony of the marginalized role, into the loneliness, pain, hurt and power where polarities danced together, at least for the moment.

In this seminar, the large group then broke up into small groups to work together. When all the small groups returned, we had the following discussion.

Arny: When I went around helping small groups, I saw many doing 721. I heard conversations I have heard in private but have never heard spoken so clearly before. In a Japanese speaking group, people worked on the pressure to conform in a certain way, and the need to be freer from huge social pressures in Japan. In another group working on children's issues, people went to the essence level and sang, "It's a small world after all, it's a small, small world." Many started to play with children's toys. I never saw that before!

R: Before we part this evening, I want to report an experience. I am shaking. I want to share about an "inner" group process that I did by myself on the beach—between me and different voices in my head. Arny said something about being your real self, and I feel I have not been able to be my real self the last two days in the group. Why not? I have been isolating myself from people because I am in the middle of a huge life change, and I didn't know how to relate to others from this place. Then I did this 721 group process on my own, and the ghost role that was wanting to come out was a "baby." I am pregnant, and have a baby growing inside me!

Arny: Perhaps in dreamland you are carrying a new little world nonlocally for all of us, a world about to be born!?!

R: Thank you, I feel I can be more myself now!

Arny: Thank you, everybody, for working together, for an amazing day, for helping new things get born.

Things to Remember from Chapter 16

1. Deep democracy can be expressed in terms of levels, phases, and forums.
2. 721 stresses that the three levels of reality in deep democracy are waiting to become open forums.

CHAPTER 17

Your Second Training as Activist and World Elder

• • •

THE METHOD OF 721 FEEDBACK, or 721 for short, can also be used to transform educational systems. In this chapter, I deepen our study of 721 by focusing on an exercise to transform the student–teacher feedback interaction. I also explain the relationship between 721, your deepest art, and the first and second trainings. Later in Part IX, Education for New Governments, we return to the use of 721 in education, and explore the transformation of your worst teacher experience.

In the previous two chapters, we began to see how 721 and its metaview can bring opposing parties closer together. It helps you have greater understanding and more compassion even for the monster critics inside and outside of you. In my experience, it just take a few seconds to feel, once you practice it enough. Even in the midst of an intense conflict, you can eventually use it for a few seconds quietly by yourself to help the scene. Of course, I should be mindful of my psychological and spiritual rank when I say you can do it in a few seconds. I can say that only after 76 years of practice!

Like all things, if you do this practice frequently, it gets easier. I do 721 many times a day, all the time. I love it; it turns troublesome things into something better. I might even do it when I am on the toilet! If I notice that I am pushing, then I ask, "What is that push for? What are you doing, Arny? What is the need? What are you pushing against? What's the 'X,' and so on."

Another way to describe 721 feedback is as the first and second trainings integrated into one practice.

A Second Training Teacher

A second training teacher is one who understands first training basic concepts—for example, roles, role switching, ghost roles, signals, double signals, and edges, or has gone through a first training in psychological and organizational or government work—and is also devoted to finding and using her or his deepest self, like the "1" in 721. In other words, devoting yourself to remembering and trying to integrate your deepest art makes you a second training teacher—not your success but your *devotion to* 721 is the point.

The 721 concept in education is this: Pick up 360 CR educational feedback, *do* 360 dreamland role switching between teacher and student (for example), and then be danced or connect to your deepest art. Use that method for working with yourself and with your students.

Now you can explore this process for yourself with the following exercise, intended to be completed with a partner. After the instructions, you will find different learnings that participants shared after completing the exercise.

Exercise: The 721 Student–Teacher Relationship

In this exercise, we explore 721 in an education or training situation. You will be recalling or imagining a teacher/student relationship you want to explore. When you play the "teacher," don't just be nice to the person playing the student getting feedback. Be direct; it could be more helpful for all!

Teacher, please read the following to the "student," and *both of you* take notes about these inner learning questions.

a. How are you doing with inner and outer critical "X" energies?
b. Can you sometimes move fluidly between the "u" and "X" energies?
c. What do you feel you need to learn to facilitate conflict in relationships and/or small or large groups?
d. What are your growing edges as a facilitator/elder? (Noticing people's needs, having more power yourself, awareness of phases, having more fluidity, compassion, ability to speak up, etc.)

"Teacher," ask the "student," "How are you doing with your access to your most fluid, 721 phase 3 and phase 4 metaview in:

- inner work? (1 = great, 2 = OK, 3 = not OK) Make a note.
- relationship work? (1 = great, 2 = OK, 3 = not OK) Make a note.
- group situations? (1 = great, 2 = OK, 3 = not OK) Make a note.

Teacher, say to student: Please *imagine the worst "X" feedback that I, the teacher, might give "u" about your work as a facilitator.* Student, make a note.

Then, Student, please do the following 721 process out loud:

360 CR: Let "u" and "X" both speak and dialogue about the imagined "X" feedback.

360 dreamland: Stand, if you can, and switch roles between the "u" and the "X" feedback, *speaking deeply* for each. Notice and bring in flirts (things that catch your attention) and any ghost roles (people or events mentioned but not given a chance to "speak"). Then,

1 Use essence field-dancing for more tips about how to deal with the "X" and your next steps in learning.

Student, rate yourself as to how you did with 721 (1 = great, 2 = OK, 3 = not OK).

Reader-Teacher, now give CR feedback and tips to the student about her or his development as a facilitator. *(If you don't know the person, use your intuition or your experience of him or her having just done the 721 work.)* Then explore *your own essence level dance* and let it speak spontaneously and shamanistically to the student about tips as well. *Don't be shy, try it!*

Then student and teacher, switch roles and *each* be the other and rate *the other* as student and teacher (1 = great, 2 = OK, 3 = not OK). Both make notes about your own learning and about your learning together. (Teacher and student now SWITCH ROLES in this dyad and repeat this whole exercise so that both get a chance to be the "student.")

The edge for the helper-teacher is to be concrete and clear in giving feedback, and later to drop everything and see what nature has to say to the other person. Teacher, be more of a teacher and also be a shaman, too. 721 can help you with this new form of education.

Participants shared some of their learnings after completing this exercise.

> *A: Self-criticism has been a big issue. I have been working on this a lot—self-love is hard. So in today's work I became the critic, and the essence of critic transformed, and to my surprise, became love and support. Until now, I have experienced criticism everywhere, in everything I do, every bit of me is criticized, and then in the exercise, all this turned into self-love. It flipped, so whatever I do I am surrounded and held by the universe and self-love and the critic.*
>
> *S: My partner's support and love was very helpful. I did not focus on the content but the energy of the critic, and that energy was trying to elevate me.*
>
> *M: My critic criticizes my dreamy nature and says I have to get my shit together and be more linear studying processwork, and the dreamy side actually became the universe and invited that critical energy in to be part of itself. Yes, the dreamy side invited in the critic. That was really powerful.*
>
> *Amy: Some people went deeper into death-like states and came back with a lot of detachment and openness to everything.*
>
> *K: My critic was pretty brutal, but had a lot of muscle. When I went into things, it was like I was out in the stars, and I could feel all these sentient beings and history blowing through my back and blowing energy through me to facilitate with, and it told me I don't have to read any more books, and I loved that! They said they would tell me what I needed to know—at the moment they had all the history in them. It suits my nature not to have to read too much.*

L: What we are doing is very nonverbal and primal and reminds me of the African culture and Ubuntu—the connectedness so many of us have lost in the middle passage here. I appreciated T. for that part of our interaction and I appreciate the fact that I felt very different from him, as if we are at the opposite ends of social strata, of understanding, of personal philosophy. But at the end of the day and in this process and with all this differentness, there came a nonverbal feeling of just being, "Dude, this world is going to work!"

It is very difficult to be black in this culture because you are in the minority. But if you don't have a choice and it is in your consciousness and you must sit with someone who feels very different from you, and with that processmind feeling, you realize, "Well, shit! We are all connected, as always!"

P: We were talking about that this morning in terms of an indigenous African American culture, Native American culture—if somebody is sick it is a communal experience, that's what came out for us.

H: Yes, how are "we" going to get well. The symptom belongs to the group and if someone commits a crime, it reflects on the whole group and world.

J: I often enter into a situation pondering how do I hold onto and recognize this deepest self amongst all of us? And when I name that, and trust myself, what needs to happen happens!

It was a great pleasure to hear so many people sharing the nonlocality of the great spirit and field between us. The work we are doing opens up the opportunity to transcend the usual educational dynamic between teacher and student, and create a more collaborative 721 forum.

Remember that your first training is about learning the skills, the science that you can know and talk about. Then the second training is the intent of going deeper. From your deepest art, we sometimes sense we are in this world and in the beyond . . . together.

Things to Remember from Chapter 17

1. Teachers and students, whenever possible, use 721 to update educational processes.
2. Remember UBUNTU: "I am, because you are" from the Zulus, from Nelson Mandela and Desmond Tutu in South Africa, and from your own processmind experiences.
3. Consider the possibility that everyone around you is a teacher giving you feedback, and then give them feedback with 721 . . . and (if possible) enjoy growing together.

PART VII

Bring Your Dreams and Dreambody to Life

• • •

In the Introduction, I mentioned that we need to connect with dreaming in order to help resolve conflicts in consensus reality. I asked, "Dreaming? Why is it important?"

I hope the previous chapters have introduced you to some of the practical ways that dreaming through body awareness and meditative states can help you prepare for facilitating conflicts. In the following chapters, I focus more deeply on the concept of dreaming both in nighttime dreams and in your daytime experiences, to promote the possibility of *dreaming as a lifestyle practice.*

CHAPTER 18

Basic Components of the Dream-Maker's Mind

• • •

***22.* Rumi's view.**

CONNECTING WITH OUR DREAMING EXPERIENCES is essential because we easily become possessed by, and in conflict with, "reality," and miss potential solutions that can come from deeper layers of our experience. I want to encourage you, the reader, to make dreaming and connecting with your dreaming body a lifestyle—something you do as often as possible! Dreaming connects you to a universal field with unexpected resources for life's conflicts and problems.

In this chapter, I elaborate on the idea and practice of *commune-ication,* which is the ability to use dreaming to commune with other viewpoints and experiences and communicate more effectively and sustainably.

I explore specific dreamwork methods for use with both nighttime dream images *and* daytime dreamlike experiences, using both first and second training methods.

Dreaming and Detachment

Why does worldwork need deep connections with your body and dream world? The dreaming intelligence you were born with is more detached and free from everyday reality than your consensus reality identity. We need this dreaming detachment and freedom to point the way to resolving inner and world conflicts.

But what is dreaming? As we've been exploring in this book so far, dreamland is not only what happens at night, but can be found in the continuum of experience: from body symptoms, to relationship troubles, to our own flirts and fantasies, and even within the painful agony of social issues.

So, dreamwork is part of worldwork. Dreaming helps resolve tensions and conflicts in consensus reality. What I have found consistently over more than four decades of practice is that the essence and dreamland levels of deep democracy are crucial to helping our consensus reality problems flow best.

For example, every time we mention someone who is not present, every time we speak about such a "ghost" role, we are dreaming. So gossip, and take note of it in the moment. For example, I suddenly remembered and began to speak about an African American activist with a group of people who were being hurt by another group. That activist "ghost role" made me realize that the group I was speaking with needed a model in taking a stand for themselves in dealing with outer conflicts.

I have found that a core reason why conflicts so rarely get resolved on the individual, relationship, and international level is that most people have too little relationship to the process of dreaming. I would say, in fact, that a big world problem is ignoring dreams. For example, we ignore that when we speak of someone else, we are dreaming. Without contact with dreams, you are an ordinary person trying to do well, avoid trouble, etc., but missing something deeper that could give you more intelligence, power, and ability to resolve personal, business, and world tensions.

There are many great therapists, psychologists, and shamans who can help you with dreams, but my favorite source is *your own dreaming body.* Whenever I get stuck, or before starting on a new adventure, I talk to Amy about my inner tensions. Then I ask my dreams, the nonlocal field, the universe itself, what *it* suggests about resolving the conflict.

What Are Dreams?

Since about the age of 10, after reading Freud's *Interpretation of Dreams,* I have made most of the decisions in my life after listening to my dreams. Usually we consider dreams to be those images you remember from the night, from your subconscious, your unconscious, etc. But dreams are also linked to the sensations you get from the field you live in, from your body feelings and fantasies. Because of the nonlocal or quantum aspects and dreamlike interconnections between us, dreams and dreaming are one of the main ways of connecting to ourselves and to others.

Dreaming in the form of dream images is part of the universal field that connects us. For example, as we walked down the street one night, Amy and I talked to a young woman who was sitting on the stairs of her house. She had her head down, studying her little iPhone—she did not look like a person who wanted to talk to us!

But even though she was ignoring us, there was a "field" around her to which we could actively connect. What is that field? There is, of course, the electromagnetic field that her iPhone connects to, but also a *feeling field* around her that we can sense, and that is part of what I call the dreaming. Connecting to that field can help you communicate better with people. I wondered, if I wanted to talk to her, what should I say?

Sensing that field, I said, "Beep! Beep!" like the iPhone. That was a great beginning! Then, while walking by her on the street with Amy, I said, "Do you get the same reception inside the house as outside where you are?" "Oh, yes," she said, "it's good," and that started a conversation that could have lasted longer but which Amy and I enjoyed just in passing.

My point is that if you want to communicate with people, connect with their reality and the dreaming *field or atmosphere.* Dreaming is all around us. Whether people look normal or in a more altered state of mind, there is a field around them, and you share it even if you don't want to.

What I want you to consider is that the dreaming field is a key to relationships. The deep democracy practice of relationship is to relate to people where they are in consensus reality, in dreaming, and from the essence level, to the dreaming field that connects us. Isn't that easy to say? Why is it that we don't do that very often?

"Commune-ication" is central in phases 3 and 4. We are trained to be *"phase-ist,"* that is, to marginalize dreaming. We stress phases 1 and 2, and marginalize phases 3 and 4. There is a consensus that reality is the reality of objective, measurable experiences. But there is also a shared field that can only be felt when you are in a dreamlike state. This shared field might be similar to what field physicists call an electromagnetic field or a gravity field. Relating to a person through the "field" is a form of "commune-ication," that is, communing with the field to relate to the person and all else in that field.

"Commune-ication" is a phase 3 and phase 4 practice of communing with the *"field" between and around us.* In commune-ication, I am here, *and* I am there. I will go more deeply into the concept and practice of *"Commune-ication"* in Part VIII, Communing for Conflict and Peace.

My fascination with dreaming began early in life when I became interested in science and psychology. My brother told me that I started a dream book when I was five years old! I would paint or write down my dreams. I don't know how I did that, because I did not know how to write yet! But that is what he said.

Why did I do that? I loved my parents but realized as a very young boy that you could never totally trust adults—trust kids and dreams first. Adults are OK, but dreams are more honest and creative. I was born at the beginning of World War II, so my parents tried to hide as much of that as possible from me. Perhaps that is a reason I began to look at my dreams. By the age of ten, I had finished reading Freud's *The Interpretation of Dreams.*[41] But I did not agree with Freud when he said that dreams were "wish fulfillments" or showed that I wanted to sleep with my mother (or father) . . . ! I thought that Freud could only think that because he had never met my parents. For me, dreams were simply mysterious!

My brother was interested in psychology, and at 14 was thinking of becoming a psychiatrist. So I guess I must have heard of that book from him. Yet, I don't really know how I got that book! I just wanted to read about what goes in my dreams. I liked Freud, but did not think he was completely right.

I understood that sex was a big problem for most adults, but at my young age, sex was not a central theme for me. So, I decided that if Freud was not talking to me, what he was saying was not as general as it could be. Still, I loved Freud for many ideas and especially for his brilliant idea of laying back on his couch and freely associating, letting your associations and "dreaming" flow.

My dream studies continued much later, when I found myself studying at the Jung Institute in Zurich. I have a deep thank you to my guru, C. G. Jung, whom I still feel in the back of me, and to my Jungian teachers who taught me about dreamwork. So many people that I knew in those days were wonderful, and I love them all. Marie-Louise Von Franz was brilliant at dreamwork, and the great woman she lived with, Barbara Hannah, was terrible at dreamwork, but fantastic at dreaming. She was the best! As I described in *Quantum Mind*,[42] it was Barbara Hannah who noticed, when I went to see her, that I was focusing on the lipstick that was on one of the cigarettes in her ashtray. She brilliantly asked, "But WHY ARE *YOU* interested in that lipstick?" It seems she guessed about a conflict I was just having in my first marriage. I was getting close to beginning new relationships and getting divorced. Today I would say that she was commune-icating with my dreaming field.

My point is that *dreaming* includes *all* the things that catch your attention. The little things that "flirt" with you belong to the dreaming, and they may sometimes be signals of nonlocal processes. I wonder if Miss Hannah was also thinking about her own relationships! These "flirts" are pointers to ways of resolving conflicts that we have not yet consciously recognized.

There are many ways that people have tried to talk about the dreaming from different perspectives.

For example, some people speak psychologically about the subconscious, or the unconscious, whereas indigenous shamans speak of the great spirit in the air, in the earth. All such shamans are dream teachers. The shamans we have met around the world believe that there is something in the air that can heal us and show us the way.

Modern neuroscience is finding ways to describe dreaming from the perspective of brain functioning. As many know, rapid eye motion (REM) at night is a sign that you are dreaming. What I call "flirts" are the experiences that create REM. They create the fluttering of our eyes at night, and also in the day. You can always tell when people are dreaming *through the eye flutters* that happen all day long.

In other words, dreaming is happening all the time, not just at night. I might be sitting at my computer, feeling, "I should write that paper!" But then something distracts me, a thought such as, "I'm stupid, why don't I just finish this?" Or, instead of writing, I open up social media to see what's happening. . . . That is all dreaming. To understand this dreaming, I might ask what is right about it? It is trying to teach me to relax while working at my computer.

The Deep Democracy of Dreaming

Dreaming happens at each of the deep democracy levels of our experience. You can see consensus reality aspects of dreaming in terms of REM or marginalized double signals in communication, or body symptoms with which the person does not identify. The dreamland aspects of dreams occur when you remember images or sounds and sensations from the night. The essence level of dreams, which I call the "pre-dreaming level," is where you feel moved by something, but no image, sounds, or "things" have yet occurred to your everyday mind. As this pre-dreaming rises up into dreamland, you might speak about angels, monsters, or whatever, but at the essence level it is a pre-dreaming sense that does not yet have a form. At the essence level, you just feel the field.

As we have been discussing, this "field" is a key to having a metaview, and therefore a key to conflict resolution and consciousness. So, we need to study dreaming to find paths through conflict.

Dreamwork Methods

There are many good dreamwork methods, though few of these methods were originally intended or designed to be helpful with conflict work. For example:

Associations: Remember Freud's free association methods or Jung's first quick association: "What is your association to that dream?" Surprising associations may reveal surprising and helpful stories.

Amplification: Jung's amplification method (and his "active imagination"), focused in part upon associations from mythology and folklore, was built on the belief that dreams may be related to history and the future.

Dream-figure role play: I am thankful to Fritz Perls for encouraging us to act out dreams; we owe a lot to the Gestalt community. Perls and his colleagues played with acting out people's dreams, but had not yet explored the unfolding of dreaming in groups. (See our book, *Riding the Horse Backwards*, which describes a seminar that Amy and I did at Esalen after Fritz Perls and Dick Price had died.)

You might be wondering which dreamwork method is best? I suggest that if someone feels that a particular dreamwork method "works" for her or him, then that method is the best. If the dreamwork method works for that person, it must be a form of processwork, because it is facilitating the person's process!

I recall many years ago a woman dreamed something about her mother and her father. The dreamer wanted to push her mother out of the bed so she could get into the bed with her father. I said to her, "Freud would say that you want to be closer to your father. I would say that you also have some problem with your mother." But she corrected me, saying, "No, I don't!" So I said, "OK, we will never talk about that mother again!" She responded, "You are very limited!" I amplified this dreaming and said, "Yes, I am very stiff and limited." She said, "You remind me of my mother"! So dreamwork was then easy. I suggested that she could be close to what her father was like, and not be only "stiff and limited." She laughed and laughed, and our work proceeded.

Dreamwork is a process. Follow a method if it works, and otherwise, pay attention, be fluid, and follow the process. *But my deeper question is, what are dreams?!*

A beginning definition is that dreams are images, sensations, sounds, or movements you remember arising out of a relaxed everyday state of mind, or a deeply altered essence-level sleeping state.

Dreams arising out of the essence level eventually appear in consensus reality in the many channels of our perception and experience. Remember proprioception, the visual channel, the movement channel (experiencing something in movement), or the auditory channel (what and how you hear things). Assuming that dreams are defined as dream images only, limits dreaming to only one-quarter of the world's population. Many people don't dream in nighttime images.

Asking what you dreamed is a good way to begin discovering the wisdom of dreams. But remember that you can see *the person's dreaming before she or he even tells you.* Everyone has solutions to their problems, they are just not conscious of those solutions in the moment.

Since dreams belong to nonlocal, shared fields, you can pick up dreams proprioceptively in *your body.* Things that happen in your body are pretty weird but very interesting. The experiential connection between our bodies and our dreams is where my concept of the *dreambody*[43] came from. If something tries to catch your attention through your body's proprioception, deal with it realistically as needed, but also consider it as a dream.

Dreaming is channel-oriented. If body feelings suddenly arise in a person you're working with, her or his dreaming is proprioceptive, so ask about the feeling and *use that energy* to discuss the person's dreams. If something catches someone's attention in movement or in relationship or the world, deal with it realistically, and also as a movement, relationship, or world situation.

Dreamwork that explores the dreaming in the perceptual channel in which it appears will usually be more effective than just intellectually discussing the dream content. Let's say there is a symptom that a person says feels like a burning poker. In this case, talking to that person in a normal tone of voice may not be as useful as relating to her or him with that dreaming *poker energy.* Model and use the dreaming process in your dreamwork.

Relationship dreaming. People hear things in the night or experience audible double signals in relationship during the day. For example, I modeled this in a seminar by answering the question, "How are you doing today, Arny?"

> *"Very well," I said, speaking with a clenched jaw and tight mouth. The participants giggled because they could see that my mouth was showing a double signal. That is dreaming.*

By careful observation, you should be able to guess what a person is dreaming from their double signals before she or he tells you the dream.

Another signal of relationship dreaming is when people talk about a person who is not present. From the perspective of dreaming, that person is right there in the moment as a ghost role. We need to all work on that "dream."

Dreaming Is a Nonlocal Shared Field

Dreams are shared. The dreamland field around you connects to people you know or have known. If you want to really communicate in the best possible way with others, gently mention your momentary dreaming, if appropriate. For example, sometimes when I am teaching, I feel that I am jumping up and down inside myself because I am so enthusiastic. Is that a shared dreaming? When I share that feeling with the class, I get excited feedback from the group. The perspective of dreaming reminds us that what we are experiencing is rarely only our own. This is an important point because isolation and loneliness are two of the most difficult aspects of life's problems.

Over the years, I have seen many people who have suffered terribly, and I have learned that some of that suffering is partly because of believing that their problems belong only to themselves. Just imagine having a therapist or a doctor who said, "Oh, my gosh, I have had the same pain as you!" I would go back to that person again, even if I had no pain!

Problems and conflicts and their dreamlike resolutions are often shared. One seminar participant shared a story of finding this connection with her knee surgeon: "I have had many knee surgeries, but recently I found a doctor who said, 'I have that, and I had this,' and what was interesting was when he did the surgery on me, the atmosphere was different than ever before, and waking up from surgery was better than ever."

As I said above, the essence level of dreams can be described as a "field." To understand fields, imagine a big tree moving slowly in the wind, in a grassy field. Notice that the little grass moves more rapidly in the same wind. In the same field, different motions occur according to our individual natures. In the same field, we may all act differently, yet we are in the same field. So notice the field; it is something you can always hear or see or sense. The field is an "atmosphere." Shared fields are, and can be, part of dreamwork. To connect to the dreaming, you might notice how the field moves you, as we were exploring in the chapters on meditation.

The concept of a field contains the characteristic of nonlocality, meaning that a field can support communication and effects over distance. We notice the effect of the moon's gravity field, which acts nonlocally to create the ocean tides.

I'll give you an example of nonlocality in dreamwork. The other night I went to sleep, feeling conflicted about dealing with so many problems in conscious reality, and I dreamed a solution. I dreamed that many of us belonged to the same church, and it had to do with nature and with the forest. I realized that to solve my conflicts, I had to share my processmind experiences with others.

The next day, Amy and I went hiking in the forest and we were talking about the trees moving around. When we got to the top of Washington Park, the forest was so wonderful, I said, "What a great church this is!" Then some voice in the distance yelled, *"Yeah! I am the reverend of the church of nature!"* I said, "Am I hearing things??" "No," the voice said, and a man appeared, calling himself a minister—a *real minister.* He said, "I get so excited whenever anybody talks about dreams in the air."

Jung would have called that experience a synchronicity: You dream something and then you bump into it in reality. But today I think he might not only use the word synchronicity, he might say, "Aha, you are in touch with the field; deep in yourself you connect to the dreams and experiences of others." That connection is what physics might refer to as nonlocality, as we have discussed earlier in this book.

A seminar participant who was studying Chinese medicine spoke about some of the ancient classical texts that described the dreaming experience of the classical physician: what the physician was dreaming about and how that physician was learning medicine that way. I appreciated being reminded that deep democracy and processwork might be seen as a relearning and possible updating of Chinese medicine and aspects of shamanism.

Fields are both spaceless and timeless at the essence level. At this level, you are just an "essence" beyond life and death. I have found that people feel conflicted and scared about the length of life partly because they are not close enough to this timeless metaview experience. When you are at this level, you experience a timelessness and often a kind of wellness.

Quantum Field Theory

As I have said, in quantum field theory, what we call a particle both is and isn't a particle in our normal sense of things. Before it is observed, the quantum particle behaves like an imaginary mathematical wave or wave field. But where is it, when I am not looking at it? The particle seems to sink back into the "field." It is only when I start to look and become aware that the *observer effect* happens. Then what was nothing appears as something.

At the quantum level, we cannot locate a particle exactly; it is not like a normal pea or even a grain of sand that is in one spot or another. The tiny particle is a wavy something and can appear as a "pea" or "grain" at one moment, and as a wave at another. In 1927, the physicist Heisenberg developed the "uncertainty principle," which states that we cannot know both the location and the momentum (the direction and speed) of an elemental particle at exactly the same moment. This principle suggests that the more we try to locate something, the less we know about it as a whole.

In psychology, we could say that the more we try to locate our dreams and dream field experience, the more they seem to be in and outside (non-locality) of us.[44]

This dreaming field can be described in Freud and Jung's language as the unconscious, as I said above. My point is that when you are deeply in yourself and connected to the dreaming field, then the outside and the inside are very close to being the same. The basic idea is that a dream is something you may identify with the nighttime, but that *dreaming field is going on day and night*, all the time, in and around you. The dreaming is a kind of inner vibrational experience even before it is an image or sound or movement. This dreaming is yours, but the power behind it belongs to everyone and everything.

Deep Democracy Dreamwork: Know the Dreamer!

Like conflict resolution work, dreamwork is an art and also a science. Dreamwork is a very strict science in trying to follow words and movements and flirts as best as possible, and it is also an art. Knowing the dream before you hear it is really important.

The empirical science of dreamwork includes the following tips when working with individuals or group participants.

- *Notice their main focus, and their channel preferences.* How do they express themselves? Intellectually? In terms of their feelings or sensations? Are they outer- or inner-focused? That is the way they need to be related to, at least initially. Notice if they are emotional and expressive, shy and quiet, direct or indirect, etc.
- *Notice their phase.* If somebody is in a conflict phase, you can speak as if illuminated by God, but they still might respond by saying, "That dreamwork does not help!"

- *Relate the dream to both "u" and "X" energies.* You should try to *relate the dream to both their "u" and "X" energies.*
- *Ask about their needs.* Ask people, "What were you experiencing before you went to sleep? What were your tensions, your needs?" People sometimes won't tell you, or won't even admit their needs to themselves. They may fear their own needs. But at least gently ask, "What were your feelings and your needs as you were going to sleep?" because the dream addresses those areas.
- *Remember that dreams do not only happen at night!* As I said before, many people do not experience nighttime dream images or cannot recall nighttime dreams. Worldwork and processwork are based on the idea that we are always dreaming. So, if a person cannot recall a dream image, ask about her or his dreaming body, or try saying, "Good that you don't remember a dream because it is here now. Stand up and look around the room. What visible thing or motion experience catches your attention first?"

By the time you have noted all the information about the dreamer—her or his conflicts, needs, various channel preferences, the experiences of the night, double signals, the "*mmmmm*" or field around you—you should know the theme of the dream before she or he tells you. If you are surprised by a person's dream, then you have not been paying attention to their problems, their dreaming, their double signals, and their "*mmmmmmmmm*" or dreaming field.

Know the dream solution before you hear it or the problems! Notice people's signals and the way they use their voices, and imagine they are singing. If you can relate to that particular sound, they will probably feel more understood.

Is what I am describing supernatural or mediumistic? One of my clients commented, "My experience working with you is that so often you say my dreams before I tell you my dreams, and I have always had the framework of you being mediumistic. But now the way you describe it, it's not about being mediumistic. You are saying it is really empirical."

Relating to a person or group means noticing their dreaming. Follow double signals. Doing that helps you to discern the background dream wisdom that people need.

Phases in Dreamwork (I repeat information about phases that you read in earlier chapters here, so that in the future, if needed, you can return to this chapter for your dreamwork, without having to read the entire book again.)

Phase 1: Happy days. "I don't want to hear any problems. I don't want to think about problems. I have been having a good time, so let me have this good time!" If the dream brings up a problem, *make it easy.* Or else, let's just relax and dream about something nice.

Phase 2: Tensions and conflict. Whatever the dream is about, don't forget to *use the dream experience* to address this phase 2 struggle.

Phase 3: Swapping sides. Dreamers may be rolling back and forth taking this side and that side, so relate to them in terms of the various polarities and their ability to take both sides. Go more deeply to the potential essence level experience of bringing all parts together.

Phase 4: Detachment. You can suggest, "Bring that illuminated feeling of yours into the dream," or "Bring the dream's detachment into reality." Use the temporary "enlightenment" to address the problems in their or others' lives.

Over the last years, I have made a habit of offering dream interpretations on my birthday, January 1, to anyone who wants to share a dream on Facebook. Hundreds of people write their New Year dreams, and I try to give them an interpretation. I have been working with people's dreams for more than 52 years, so that experience really helps! But what I do is get an impression of the field around the person by exploring how they show themselves on their Facebook picture. I try to sense what they are expressing and relate to that. For example, if you were going to interpret my dream, you might notice my

Facebook profile picture, which is an image of me looking at a flower. So if you want to interpret a dream of mine, remember that I need to commune with nature while in the world. Similarly, when someone comes to my office wearing their newest scarf, I talk to the scarf and to the one who loves and needs it. I try to relate the dream to her or his primary identity and to other, possibly less conscious, behavior.

Now, to explore the dreaming field for yourself, try the following dreamwork exercise with a friend (or alone).

Exercise: Dreamwork

I. Before hearing the dream, ask and note the client's conflicts and needs and which sensory-grounded channels she or he was in before going to sleep. Note the phase just before bed. Ask the client if she or he was recently in phase 1, happy and cruising; in phase 2, u + X tension; in phase 3, role switching; or in phase 4, close to the infinite? If uncertain, ask for a sound expressing the mood/phase. Feel the client's "*mmmm*," her or his mood.

II. Now both you and the dreamer pick up signals and flirts happening around you. Amplify those signals and then be *moved by universe*—be danced and get a tip.

III. Now hear the dream and its associations, and both of you *see the dream/night experience as containing signals, flirts, a dance, and the* "mmm" *of the field.*

IV. Ask the dreamer now what her or his dream meant. If the person needs help, suggest, "If that dream were mine, with those needs, channels, phases, flirts, and dance tips, it might mean . . . ." (Give the person a chance to say what the meaning is) and follow the feedback. If needed, ask the dreamer to relax into an altered blurry state, and in this dream state, to pick up a tip to complete the interpretation. Note insights and tips.

In one of my classes, a participant shared her dreamwork, and as I helped her go further, we could see how dream resolutions work by relating to the phase, the sounds, the "*woof*" and "*mmmm*" of each person.

N: When I was in Amsterdam recently, my father spoke to me for the first time in my life about my mother and her dying process, and how he was with her as she died. It was the first time he had spoken about it in 46 years. He was with her when she died, and he remarried afterwards.

Arny: So the other woman brought you up?

N: Yes, and he never talked about my mother, never mentioned her name, no photographs, never spoke about her. Now he spoke about it for the first time. He is 87. . . . I have no conscious memories of her. . . . And he cried, and spoke of how he stroked her when she was dying, and how he felt a sense of peace in that moment. And I could sense my mother's presence in the room, a joy, and her existence was acknowledged for the very first time.

So the question I asked myself before I worked on my dream was, "How could I have sensed her presence when I have no conscious memory of her?" And the answer that came out, which was a mystery to me, was . . . "luminous darkness." Suddenly all these vehement questions popped up in my head, like, how can darkness see itself?

Arny: (speaking with the same intensity as N) Who would believe in that essence-level dreamlike experience of "luminous darkness"? There is only one thing you need to learn, and that is, that luminous darkness is important!

N: (laughs) *I am thinking that you are returning something from my energy!?*

Arny: Yes! That is why you and I are laughing! You are a normal person in a phase 2 conflict, "Where is my mother, what is this dream stuff, this junk, this luminous darkness?" and I am saying (almost yelling), *You need that LUMINOUS DARKNESS for good health! Let the darkness speak! Turn all the lights off, and listen for the mothering in the universe. . . .* (noticing N's response) . . . *You understand that—it touches you.*

N: Mmmm (deeply touched). *Mmm . . . oh, thank you!!*

Arny: You touch many of us. . . . Your primary process is powerful and dramatic, as in phase 2. The sounds you make and your words, "Let's get realistic, come on! Don't give me this junk! Tell the truth!" sound like rational cognitive thinking, like the intelligent woman that you are. "I/we want to know the truth!"

And so I related to and used that phase 2 "mmmmm" *energy to relate in both a cognitive and dreamlike definitive way!*

N: (Nodding in agreement, smiling.)

Arny: The woof and power of the rational thinker helped explain that luminous darkness. But let me say again, "Remember (almost yelling as if with a Zen chop) *Luminous darkness!! When you turn the lights off at night, say good night to your Mama. . . . She is there!!"*

N: (Begins to cry)

Arny: Before we go further, let me just ask you about your mother. How did she die?

N: Colon cancer, I was three. She got ill after my birth in 1969 in Amsterdam.

Arny: Well, before this class ends, I want to say hi to your mother for just one second. (Walks to corner of the room, quiet). . . . *Was she in Amsterdam during the war?*

N: She was a German Jew, she was hidden during the war with her father, and her mother was in England.

Arny: Well, now she is free of that conflict, and free, like you, to explore "luminous darkness."

Several days after this dreamwork, N. shared the following with the class participants on the class email string:

Dearest Arny and all,
Just wanted to publicly thank you, Arny, for your most amazing and incredibly generous Dreamwork Intervention/Zen Slap you gave me—and I mean that in the most illuminating sense of the word. All those questions that were haunting me: "Is there something that continues after death that is still aware of change, even if there is no longer a space–time continuum? How can darkness see itself? Is there life inside a black hole?—the WAY that you answered me, not just the content but the surprising intensity of it and how you came right at me with the truth of my Dreaming ("luminous darkness is the answer"), literally blew me away, cut through my mind and all the cognitive answers my mind could have found. . . . This luminous no-mind zone is where I have no words because no words will ever satisfy when you're being haunted by a flying Zen Koan. . . . So thank you . . . for matching that and taking me into the Dream-Maker's Mind with your wondrous Zen Slap.

Things to Remember from Chapter 18

1. Notice dreams before you hear them, then hear them, and use the flirts and ghost roles and the "*mmmmm*" around the dreamer to understand the dreams.
2. Notice the dreamer's phases 1, 2, 3, or 4 to relate dreamwork to the dreamer.
3. Remember everyday phase 2 problems and conflicts to see how dreams resolve issues.
4. We are always dreaming, alone and with others, day and night, in all channels and in all levels.
5. Dreams are expressions of a nonlocal field and help resolve things we wonder about, including tensions and conflicts of all kinds.

CHAPTER 19

Dreamwork Without Nighttime Dreams!

• • •

NOT EVERYONE DREAMS IN NIGHTTIME images, but everyone can make *dreaming* a lifestyle practice. You can always *let go and dream* to help yourself and the world in all circumstances facilitate inner work, outer business, and world issues.

In this chapter, we focus on contacting the dream world in reality without nighttime dreams. I describe a new method that I call the *vacation effect.* It is a powerful dreamwork method to use when you are stuck.

Dreaming as a practice is important because the biggest planetary problem that I know about right now is the marginalization of dreaming. It seems that there is one main god on our planet: consensus reality in phases 1 and 2. In a way, I think that this problem is the world's one and only problem.

When it comes to dealing with government or dealing with yourself, a consensus reality approach is important. I love it, I use it, but it is rarely enough without connection to dreaming and what moves us.

Now, Jung considered dreams compensatory. He taught that dreams compensate for the limited viewpoint of our conscious mind. I agree that dreams balance our primary process. And, more than that, dreams also bring up new processes that can offer resolutions to tensions that the dreamer is not always aware of. So, when looking at a dream, please value the everyday mind and its problems, and then bring out the genius of the dream as well to resolve issues.

The problem, in my view, is that our everyday mind, our primary process, often neglects the power of dreaming. Dreams and reality need to flow into one another as phases. Be conflicted in phase 2, find a solution in phase 3 or 4, and swing between tensions and detachment.

Remember, you have a primary process because nature wants that too. Without that stubborn primary process and the conflicts it gets into, we might not perceive dreams and dreaming at all!

Our overall process zigzags. Now this way, now that way—now uptight, now relaxed and resolved. Processwork's deeply democratic approach says: Help yourself or your clients to flow with who they are, with their primary process, with "Now, I am uptight about this conflict," and with the detachment of dreaming, "Now, I am relaxed with a solution for the moment."

Help groups and organizations appreciate their normal identity and also the dreaming that is trying to make itself known. A good way to do that is to be fluid with momentary directions; swing with things. Working with the dreaming process in phases 3 and 4 simply makes life more fluid and rapid.

Dreamwork

In the last chapter, we discussed an overall method for deep democracy dreamwork. Before introducing the new "vacation" method, let's briefly summarize.

Remember, when you work with someone's dreams, recall the person the dream is speaking to—her or his needs, channels, and phases—and don't miss the hum of the field around them, the "*mmmm.*" Remember N.'s strong "*mmmm*" at the end of the last chapter? Using that field and her sounds and communication style helped me to connect with her.

Remember, try to know the dream before you hear it. Don't be surprised by the dream. For example, somebody came into my office recently and saw a mask on the wall. "Wow, look at that big face!" the person exclaimed. This was the face of a Haida Gwaii totem pole spirit. "Wow, that face is really big and out there," she said. I said, "Isn't that amazing?!" She said, "Yeah." I said, "OK. Now I am ready to hear the dream." What was it about? *Know your deepest and most powerful face; make it bigger and put it out there!* She loved that.

All of us can learn to be better at the skills of dreamwork. Yet being a great dream interpreter can marginalize your own, and the dreamer's, *capacity to dream.* If you are not careful, trying to resolve problems or trying to interpret dreams can marginalize the dreaming that is trying to arise. This next method of "vacating" will help you connect to the dreaming directly.

The Vacation Effect!

Now, let's turn to a new way of getting to the dream's power, a method I call, "vacation." Vacating the everyday mind works well in everyone, including folks who say they don't have much contact with their dreams or the dreaming process. It works great with organizations, even large ones, including governments. After having wondered for a long time how to assist ardent realists to dream, this "vacation" method appeared.

The *vacation effect means simply vacating* your everyday mind. When we are stuck, or missing contact with dreaming in the day, and don't dream at night, this vacation method can help dreaming happen.

Vacate means *quit.* It means *annul. Leave. Set aside. Empty.* Let go momentarily of your everyday consensus reality focus. Vacate! Another way of saying it is simply, be a Buddhist. Remember the Zen Master, Fukushima Roshi, who said, "Zen's empty mind is creative mind." *To "vacate" means to allow your mind to be empty and creative.* In "empty mind" we experience the creativity of phase 4 experiences.

The "empty mind" is a universal human potential, which means that everyone is equally gifted in dreaming and shamanism. Many people say, "Others might be shamans, but I am not." This means that some people identify more with being a shaman than others. Yet, we are all potential healers when we are empty and open to the universe.

The vacation effect requires *almost no learning.* Anyone can do it. That is why I say it works with almost anybody. The vacation effect is like Zen's empty mind, opening up to the dreaming and letting the dreaming pop up in a given moment.

I suggest that you practice the vacation effect whenever you are tired; vacate things temporarily—and take a quick nap if needed.

Vacation Channels

The method you will use for vacating depends upon the channel you are in. In the rest of this chapter, I explain various vacation methods.

For example, right now I might notice that I am in movement channel. To vacate, I stand up, let myself relax, and allow my body to wiggle. I allow my body to make spontaneous movements, and suddenly I find that it seems my body is dancing! How did I do that? Then I notice that I can hear a song coming up inside me . . . it is a 1950s popular song, "You Gotta Dance with Me, Henry!" I sing it to myself and feel the atmosphere it creates: "You gotta dance with me, Henry—alright baby . . . dance with me, Hennn-ry!" etc. By vacating myself and opening up to the universe, I realized I was being invited to dance more. This was the dreaming in the moment. I suspect that many of us are like Henry, who needs to be invited to dance, invited to dream.

Visual "Vacates"

Vacating the visual channel of the everyday mind can help you find your (inner) guidance and resolutions to consensus reality issues. The following method to vacate the visual channel was inspired by Amy.

Take a piece of paper, or simply use your hand, and put it in front of your face for a moment. Take a breath or two and relax for a minute. Now, while the piece of paper or your hand is in front of your face, imagine what face would like to emerge through this paper out into the world. You have a very nice face, but there is another face in the back—a dream face that is trying to emerge, and can emerge, when you vacate the visual space.

What face do you imagine coming forwards? Even if it is weird, believe it. Catch the dreaming that emerges from the vacated visual of your normal face. Then try to transform your actual face now a little bit to represent that dreaming, until you know what is trying to emerge. What is it trying to do? What is its viewpoint? Who is it? What does that face say? What does it imply? Make a note to yourself about what that face is saying.

This practice allows the dreaming to emerge in the visual channel. Sometimes you may find that your ordinary mind does not like the dreaming that emerges:

> *Q: What if you can't connect with what it wants?*
> *Arny: What face did you notice?*
> *Q: Grrraaaawwwww!*
> *Arny: I love that sound, it makes you laugh—how come? It looks a little different from your normal face.*
> *Q: It is gnarly—it is not very pleasing to the eye.*
> *Arny: Is it a monster face? Yes? OK! Then you need to be more of a monster to resolve all your issues.*
> *Q:* (laughs)
> *Arny: You are very powerful and probably very shy about it.*
> *Q: (Nods yes.)*

In this example, I helped Q. to understand and befriend what was underneath her visual channel dreaming. When she vacated herself, a monster came out. It looked like a monster to her ordinary self because she is a wonderful person, but there is a bigger power underneath.

Another way to visually "vacate" is to imagine it is nighttime. Look into the darkness, and ask yourself, "What do I imagine I see there?"

A third method to visually vacate is to look into a mirror and imagine what face looks back from the mirror other than your own. Look into the mirror, or imagine looking into a mirror, and instead of seeing yourself there, who or what do you see looking back at you? It might be a dream solution to problems you and your world are working on. This method works especially well with teenagers.

Bodily "Vacates"

Dreambody work comes from noticing what you are experiencing in your body. Vacate your normal body experience right now, and feel sensations inside of you trying to arise. Are they fatigue or excitement, pressure, nervousness, etc.? Now go further with those experiences. Try to see them as piece of nature or as a person or being. Vacate your body and follow your experiences! Body dreaming is very informative; it is helpful in understanding who in you is wanting to emerge, and what the world needs from you just now.

Movement "Vacates"

As I described above, you can vacate your movement channel by standing up and relaxing and allowing spontaneous movements to arise, a practice I called *space–time dreaming* in my book *Dance of the Ancient One*. Space–time dreaming is a way of vacating your normal movement. In my example, I was excited about the invitation to "Dance with Me, Henry," because my primary process was in a teaching mood, not a dancing mood.

When you are stuck with a problem and need a vacation, just try asking yourself, "What movement would my body like to make if it could?" This can be very helpful. Try to accept whatever it wants to do. Then try that movement and wonder, what is it trying to say?

A seminar participant shared an example of using movement vacation in working with people with Parkinson's disease or epileptic seizures. Often these conditions scare people, and they want to make sure that they don't move. Yet by encouraging the epileptic person to move more freely, they were able to come out of those seizures. Similarly in a case with very severe, uncontrollable Parkinson's: When the woman let herself move freely and spontaneously, all her shaking just stopped.

RELATIONSHIP "VACATES"

If you get stuck in relationship with an individual or organization, and are asking yourself, "How should I deal with a certain person?," try vacating the relationship channel yourself. Simply imagine someone, or some figure, or some imaginary thing, entering into that relationship with the person or group.

All you need to do is relax and imagine another being—human, animal, or otherwise—coming in right now. Do this when you are in a stuck moment in relationship with an individual or in group work. You may be very surprised at all the potential to be found in your "vacations"!

For example, I used a relationship vacation with a couple having a relationship problem. This man and woman had sexual problems—each had her or his reason, each said the other one was not doing it the right way, etc. So, I said, "Now, let's vacate the relationship channel. Let's get out of that relationship for a moment, and imagine someone or something else coming in and relating to the other person who is a problem for you." The man saw a "slimy animal, slipping along." That was just what the woman needed. He was too "pushy" and not "sliding" around enough!

Try thinking about a relationship right now. Is there a relationship you want to deepen or are having some tension with? Take a moment and imagine some other being, or imaginary figure, or person entering into that relationship who is *not you*. What does that figure do to help?

Sometimes the figure you imagine might be scary, or seem like it will behave badly, or hurt the other person or group. This is a dreaming practice, so remember that you do not have to "really" become that figure or identify with it completely. You are on vacation! You can bring in just a little bit of that dreaming—"This is not me, but . . . "—as it might give you a new way to deal with the difficult relationship.

For example, one of my class participants asked,

Q: What if what I just imagined is scary and seems bad?
Arny: What did you imagine? Don't tell us the relationship, just tell us the figure.

Q: My figure was floating and screaming in rage. I am not sure what to do with it.

Arny: You can say, "This is not me" to the person in relationship, because it is not you—you are on vacation. But something in the air wants to scream! "You stupid ass! Won't you change right away!" Then you can say, "OK, now let's talk and have dinner."

Bring it in as if it is only partly you. Because it is. Bring it in a little bit, say "Woof! I don't want to be in phase 2 fighting with you, in a rage. I am not someone who rages a lot, but there is something that wants to strangle you—please change!"

Q: (Bursts out laughing)

You might be wondering if you can use the vacation effect in organizations or government work. I have helped people at the top of large organizations do this when they don't dream. You can suggest, for example,

> *Imagine a "not-you" in your organization and role. Vacate your position, go on vacation, and imagine some amazing new kind of person or figure that enters into that organization instead. What does the new kind of person or figure do??*

Leaders often become stiff because of responsibility, but this process can help them and everyone. For example, one of my leaders had a "vacation figure" that was a firm believer in a given religion. The leader himself said that he hated religion! When this leader got into conflict with other people, I suggested he say, "Take a minute, we have talked a lot, so I want to relax for a moment." Then I suggested the leader tell me what figure he imagined might appear instead of himself. The leader said to me, "I saw a figure, but I don't like it! It was Jesus! You won't believe this, but Jesus just said to me that he loves people." This was the exact opposite of what that leader was normally feeling, but it was what was needed. The figure of Jesus relaxed the whole inner and outer situation and helped everyone feel better.

Sometimes the vacation figure may be similar to the person's normal identity, but in an amplified or a more extreme form. This can mean that the person needs to go further in the direction she or he is already going. Or the person may need more support to do what she or he is doing, so say, "Don't be shy to be yourself." That's vacation!

Phase "Vacates"

Finally, you can try *vacating the phase* you are in. Remember that in phase 1, people are enjoying themselves, "I don't want to hear about problems!"; in phase 2, "I'm in conflict, I have problems!!" is normal; in phase 3, the person feels, "I'm on this side and I can fluidly move to the other side"; and in phase 4, "I'm blissed out and detached." A person, relationship, or group may be blocked or stuck in one phase and vacating that phase itself can be very helpful.

Whatever phase you are in, if you feel stuck in a given situation, say to yourself, "This is the phase I am in now . . . how about vacating that phase temporarily, and consciously choosing to explore another phase?" A common example is choosing to meditate—in other words, deliberately choosing to drop out of the current phase by accessing phase 4. Mindfulness and meditation have been so important historically, and growing recently, because people are trying to vacate and drop out of phases 1 and 2 of ordinary life.

On the other hand, some people occasionally feel stuck in phase 4 and sense that they are avoiding life. "I am enlightened, feeling really cool and relaxed. It's a great feeling, but something is missing here, and I don't know what." Try another phase!

My point is to *learn to vacate your everyday mind and dream. Let go temporarily and check out the results.* Try this out for yourself by exploring the following "vacation guide" now.

This exercise is best done with a friend/helper, but you can also attempt it by yourself; simply omit the final step.

Exercise: The Inner Wisdom Vacation Guide

1. Helper: Discuss the dreamer's everyday life and problems and consensus reality questions on the dreamer's mind. Note the mood, main channels, and phases.
2. Ask about recent problems and dreams, associations, and/or experiences from last night's "sleep."
3. Vacate conversation, follow double signals, and explore "flirts"—that is, things that catch the dreamer's momentary attention—and make notes.
4. Vacate visually: Put a paper in front of face and see what face emerges.
5. Vacate sound: Relax and make "snoring" noises to see what sound experience emerges from inner wisdom guide. Then compare these sound experiences with recent dream/or nighttime experiences and perhaps interpret those experiences.
6. Notice what phase you have been in and vacate it for another phase that pops up.
7. Helper: Vacate yourself and explore the common dream field with the "dreamer," with your phase 4 dance being moved by the space between you, and notice if it helps you as a shaman to help the dreamer with her or his dream and "calling."

Vacation Examples

This chapter has explained how you can "vacate yourself" occasionally to know the way of dreaming in the midst of tense situations. In my classes, participants have reported some of the following delightful and surprisingly productive results of taking a vacation!

> *A: After finishing my PhD dissertation, I gave myself a vacation and then what came out was to give myself a little more free time. Now, in this present "vacating" exercise, a monster appeared who needs a bigger project! The monster needs a bone!*

Arny: That sounds healthy. Everybody says, "Take it easy, you are too tense," and that is OK, but you also need to vacate so monsters can live.

A: I thought I would feel better vacationing, but I became bored!

Arny: And if the monster did what the monster wanted to do, what would it do?

A: Bite somebody or write a book, something really chewy! Something about conflict and how to work with it!

Arny: I thought so. So listen! Either you write that book or everybody will "Growl!" I see your wonderful strong feedback! That is so amazing! Great feedback. . . . Monsters live in phase 2! Get out there and fight! Wake up the public! Thank you, woof for you!

Q: I was surprised when I vacated. An entity said it was Native American. . . . I personally was having all this turbulence in my life and I was hesitant and did not know what to do next, and the Native American said, "We were never hesitant, we had to do things all the time! We had to get food, we had to move, we were 100% present, we lived on the land, we were married to the land!" I thought, wow, I am normally not any of those things and need to change!

B: I am shy to ask about the image that came up in me. I actually witnessed a snake!

Arny: When you vacated yourself, a snake came up ?

B: Yes. I got married 13 days ago, and I had dinner with in-laws a few nights ago, and they got into a fight, and the mother was nasty to her partner. I witnessed it, and it was hard. I feel like I don't want to see them again . . . so the snake came up when I was thinking about this encounter today. So I was trying to play with that snake energy, but I did not know what it meant.

Arny: I don't either. I would not "play" with the snake, I would rather "vacate" yourself so you can be the snake.

B: Ssssssssss (slithers toward Arny and pretends to bite his stomach).

Arny: Yes! That's good, HISSSS! Now, let's say your in-laws were there and you were going to be a snake. What would you have done?

B: As the snake I would have said, "Stop talking with a mean tone of voice. Be more human!"

Arny: That's right! That's all you need to say in that conflict! "I am a snake, hisssss! Stop talking like that! Otherwise I will bite you!" It is so simple.

Things to Remember from Chapter 19

1. "Vacating," dropping your momentary identity, uses the dreaming process to facilitate easing any tensions with yourself, relationships, businesses, and the world.
2. To contact your deepest self when you can't remember dreams, try "vacating" yourself visually, in movement, in sound, etc., and/or vacate your present phase, and notice dreams emerging to resolve problems—at least temporarily.

CHAPTER 20

721 Dreamwork: To Whom Your Dreams Belong

• • •

YOUR DREAMS BELONG TO A universal, nonlocal field that might be what the Taoists called "the Tao that cannot be said." In the last few chapters, I've explained how dreamwork and dreaming as a lifestyle practice mean connecting to the universal field to which your dreams belong, in order to get help with the problems of ordinary reality.

In this chapter, I describe how to use the 721 feedback method (presented in Section VI) for dreamwork and dreaming. 721 provides another method to enrich our consensus reality approach to problems by connecting us with the nonlocal universal field that moves us.

Before we explore 721 dreamwork, let us briefly review the approach to dreamwork that I have presented so far, and consider some of the ideas behind this approach. In this approach, we need dreams to resolve inner and outer problems.

Dreamwork in Brief

Remember that you can notice dreams and the dreaming process even before a person tells a dream, as I suggested in Chapter 18. Notice double signals and ghost roles. Somebody says to me, for example, "I am so excited about things," as she sits down and lets out her breath. Can you identify the double signal? She actually dreamed that she was relaxing, meditating on a mountain. This is what I mean when I say, "See the dream, watch the body signals." Dreamwork with a person starts the moment the door opens and she or he walks in.

Remember or discover the questions, tensions, and conflicts the dreamer was experiencing before dreaming. Most often, dreams speak to these natural and personal tensions.

My updated meaning for the term *dream* is that *dreaming* happens all the time, day and night. It is a manifestation of the essence level, and a reaction or counterbalance to our everyday, often polarized, consensus reality thinking. This is a new attitude towards dreamwork. If you don't dream in the night, vacate during the day. Vacation—there is nothing to it. Notice double signals, ghost roles, symptoms, etc. We are always dreaming; it is a process that helps us to flow more easily with the tensions and questions of consensus reality.

What about dream interpretation? When working on the dream, we always wonder, "What does this dream *mean*?" But be careful, *in the process of pondering the meaning of the content, don't marginalize the dreaming process* in the moment—for example, the spontaneous motions of the body that can, themselves, be interpretations. If you are close to dreaming, you can guess your nighttime dreams and help yourself and the world more effectively.

Each of us has an inner wisdom and conflict resolution dream guide. I have been stressing that point throughout this book. If somebody or some group does not know what to do, just have them stand up and let their bodies relax and move as in phase 4. I stress paying attention while moving to *repetitive* motions, for they are close to showing how the essence level arises in the form of dream motions, images, and ideas.

In the last chapter, I presented the *vacation effect* in which you can vacate channels and phases when you are stuck and need a dream. If you don't know how to deal with an individual or group situation, you can always vacate your everyday mind, and perhaps some dreaming will pop up. Most of the time, you can see that dream in body signals as well as nighttime dreams.

The Universal Wisdom Field

Historically, dreams were thought to be due to spirits or gods of various names and domains. As I have said, more recently Freud's subconscious or Jung's unconscious were seen as the source of dreams. I think all these terms refer to a *universal wisdom field and the experience of being moved.* The word *field* means, as I have been saying, a powerful space around us that tends to move us. We are pulled and moved, turned and twisted as Einstein's space–time suggests.

The reason I call it a "universal" wisdom field is because anybody at any time can tap into being moved, and often resolving experiences arise.

Physics, Taoism, and the Universal Wisdom Field

Previously, I have mentioned the connections that I see between modern physics, Taoist ideas, and processwork. Here, I show how these links relate to a process-oriented, phase-aware dreamwork approach.

Part of MIT's physics department works in combination with other departments to do research with DNA, the stuff in our bodies that carries our genetic predispositions. They are discovering how quantum theory helps us better understand DNA and life.[45] Quantum theory implies that particles of given systems are nonlocally entangled. Perhaps, not only are our body parts entangled with one another, but in principle, also our lives with the lives of others.

Whether we are elementary particles, friends, potential friends, or momentary enemies, our lives are entangled—interconnected, intertwined. What you feel and work on also changes me *without either of us knowing how.* As I have been saying, dreams seem to be nonlocal; therefore your resolution to tensions will probably connect you to others working on the same tense issues and fields.

A class participant commented on how this entanglement effect known in physics is almost part of mainstream psychological knowledge. For example, this effect can be seen when a supervisor helps a therapist work with a client with whom she or he is having difficulty. Sometimes when the therapist crosses her or his own edge, the client seems to change magically. Thus, when the therapist works with the client in a later session, the initial problem is sometimes no longer there.

As I've said, Taoists called the wisdom field "the Tao that can't be said." Chuang Tzu, one of the earliest Taoists, woke up one morning with a dream. He apparently said, "Did Chuang Tzu dream of the butterfly or did the butterfly dream of Chuang Tzu?"

Today, I would say that Chuang Tzu is himself in consensus reality and also in dreamland, so that he realizes he is not a butterfly, but also senses that both he and the butterfly are dreams of a powerful field. As part of that field, he senses that both he and the butterfly are dreams. At the essence level, he is the Tao that can't be said, the field that moves all things.

In other words, in dreamland and the essence level, we are both real people and—like everything else—descriptions of a universal field.

What is the name of this "field?" For the Taoists, it is called the "Tao that cannot be said." This is identified by the *I Ching* as the power moving a coin flying through the air. Apparently the ancient Chinese believed in the Tao as a field, as a universal wisdom field. The field expresses itself in terms of opposites, such as yin then yang, which form the different trigrams and hexagrams of the *I Ching.*

It was Lao Tse, who came hundreds of years later than the *I Ching*, who named the field as "the Tao that can't and can be said." In another words, the opposing energies of yin and yang and the hexagrams are only the Tao that can be said. The subtlest aspect of the field moves the coins flipping in the air!

Today we can suspect that the "Tao that can't be said" is the immeasurable quantum wave description of objects. *Lao Tse was basically saying, don't just stick with what you can see and marginalize the power of dreaming behind what we see.*

If you are tense, or want to help others with conflicts, then follow the Tao and let it "dream up" solutions. You don't have to wait until sleep to dream. Connect with the "field" right now and let it move you.

This reminds me of Richard Feynman's quantum theories, wherein he imagined a background field. He suggested that perhaps an elementary particle *tries all the possible directions before it knows where to go—or I would say, follows its "Tao."* Physicists have also had the intuition—connect with the field to know what's next.

This wisdom can be translated into our work as, "Relax and try all paths forward and backwards in time, to know where it feels best to go next." Rumi, the 13th-century Persian poet who was also a jurist, an Islamic scholar, theologian, and Sufi mystic said,

"Stop acting so small and insignificant, you are the universe in motion!"

One of our class participants commented on how this idea of the field appears in Eastern physical practices.

> *Different movement traditions have that field sense as well. As you get more advanced in Yoga and Aikido, you are always studying this dreamlike thing. As you get more advanced, my teachers are now teaching us just to be empty and just be moved.*

Another participant commented, "Part of the problem that humans have is the tendency to go against the Tao."

I would say that CONFLICT with "the TAO that can't be said" is perhaps our central conflict. We remain in consensus reality, where there is yin and yang, this and that, good and bad. Conflict is natural. But then conflict typically marginalizes one person/ group/ country/ species over another, and because of all that marginalization, we desperately need "the Tao that can't be said." We desperately need diversity consciousness, to recognize and respect tensions of all kinds, and to see these problems as a call for more field consciousness. Connecting to the field consciousness can often happen through connecting with nature, as was shared:

> *I just went out into nature and paddled on a lake last weekend. I went to get my head straight. I was doing some vacationing—vacating the mind, as you were talking about—and I was trying to get some answers*

to these problems, and the wind came and the kayak started moving. It just started to completely change directions, and I heard a voice say, "That is how to make change."

Process advice is: Follow change, notice, and follow directions as they change.

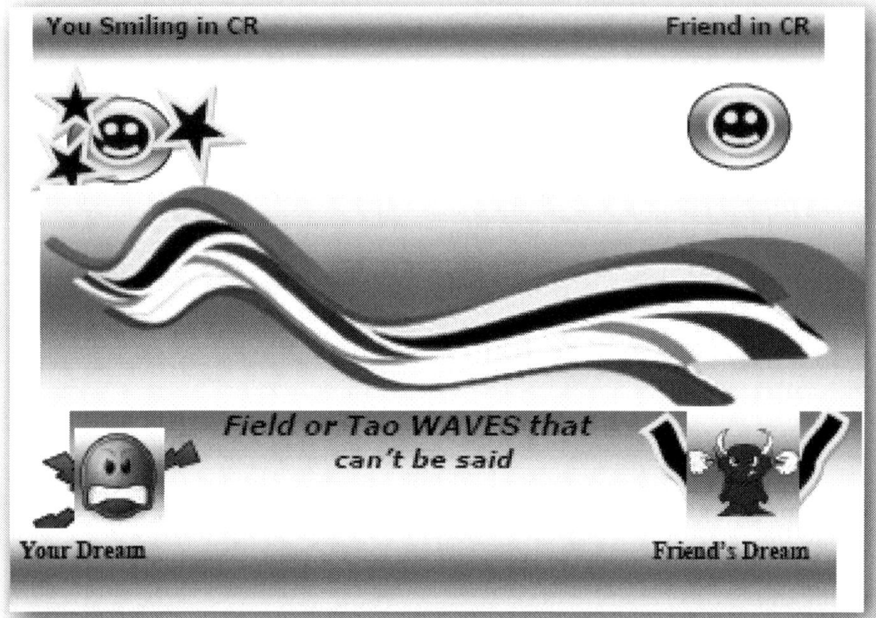

***24.* Dreams.**

In order to imagine and illustrate the universal wisdom field and how it connects us to others and their dreams, I created the preceding illustration.

It represents you as the smiling figure at the top left. The black wiggly lines are the "nonlocal field" or "the Tao that can't be said." When you interact with that field, you might get a particular dream; for example, say you need more power, and below you a "Grrr figure" appears in that field. That "Grrrr" balances your CR sweetness and gives you the power to deal with the problems you might have in life.

Your friend, represented in the top right of the picture, has another dream image of devilish power, which is different from yours even though you are both sensing the same field. See the difference between your image and your friend's.

You both sense the same field, but because of your personal consensus reality natures and the particular tensions you must face, your dreams are different. My point is that you can try to stay close to your dream and to the dreaming in the background which is moving you both, and all of us.

It's the field that allows you to "commune" with nature and with the essence of people in the field. If you are in touch with the field that moves you and your momentary dream, you will know, "Oh, I can do this or that" and also feel closer to others and the world around you. I introduced the idea of "commune-ication" earlier, and I come back to the practice of communing in Part VIII, Communing for Conflict and Peace.

In dreamwork's first training, we learn how to notice the dream in dream images and in dreamlike signals (double signals, ghosts) in consensus reality, and how to work with the dream to help resolve the often subtle questions of everyday reality. The second training in dreamwork includes the skills learned in the first training, but also how to "commune" with that dreaming background field. Here, we try to understand the dreamer's world as a part of your own, a world that may need similar solutions.

Perhaps this is related to what is reported in near-death experiences. Life and death are mainly CR descriptions of who we are. Often when people are dying, they are just going on with "life." For the deepest part of you, death may not exist and you will be simply following the field—and in a way, there is nothing new in that! I like thinking about such things but cannot prove details about that universal field in consensus reality other than it is universal; you see aspects of Taoism and mysterious fields in quantum physics, dream experiences, and various religions.

Remember, the dream is like a trigram that comes from the Tao that cannot be said. Follow the dream, and don't forget the Tao that can't be said.

Now, let's go further in both practical and experiential terms. I want to show how the method of 721 feedback (introduced in Section VI) can be applied to dreamwork. The dreaming field that I described in Chapter 18, a nonlocal universal field that connects us, is at the basis of 721 feedback, and is the reason that 721 can be useful in dreamwork.

721 Dreamwork

Let us use the 721 feedback method, presented in Chapter 16, to work on dreams. Recall that in business, 360 feedback means getting feedback from people above and below you, feedback from your peers, and your own feedback. That is consensus reality 360. In the following figure, you can see this represented by the top circle.

In individual work, as in group work, you get a lot of feedback. Some comes from your own conscious considerations, some from "X"-like critics. You often don't like these "X" feelings and ideas very much. "X" may be feelings you notice but don't like thinking about, or they may be body problems or a problem you had before bedtime. 360 CR means remembering all the wonders and problems of reality, its supporters and critics.

721 Dreamwork *includes*

360—Consensus Reality Forums. Bring in your own and all the CR voices you love and dislike in your dreamwork. This means, for example, there may be a critic saying, "You stupid idiot, you are the same jackass you always were!" Then, let's say you have a person inside yourself who says, "I love you." And you have a real body problem "X." In addition, you may have a reality situation you are trying to solve. In 721, deal with the CR 360 first before you go deeper. Get into the forum and play with parts of reality.

+ *360 Dreamland.* Then bring into the forum the feelings and "voices" of your double signals and dream figures. Bring in ghost roles of things you were talking about that were not present. Also notice gossip or fantasies about some person in your thoughts. Role-play ghost roles and the dream figures from the dream. Remember, you are in an open forum, open to dialogue. This is a kind of worldwork for dreamers.

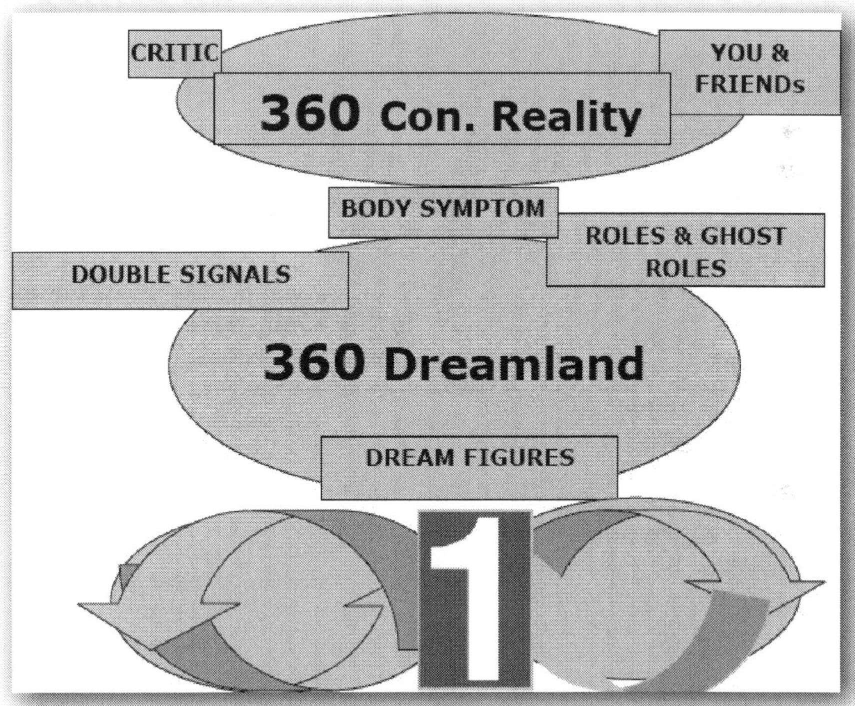

25. 721 Dreamwork.

+ *1 Essence level.* Then in the "1" of 721, let your body be moved by the Tao that can't be said. Both you as an interpreter *and* you as the dreamer can take part in this dance. After talking about lots of things, encourage the dreamer to simply stand and let her- or himself be moved and watch for little repetitive motions. You can do it too, as the interpreter.

I have been doing 721 dreamwork for years, though I don't often identify it as such for dreamers. I just do it, and they will jump in, correct things, and things flow. It's a lot of fun.

721 can also be done by "jamming" or improvising with the dreamer as if you were both musicians, playing off each other's words, movements, sounds, and rhythms of each other. Pick up the rhythm and tone of the situation, follow the field—each has her or his own creative and unpredictable style. Some people do it gently, some people are wilder when they "jam" with you. Whatever you call it, don't forget to give room and time for *just being moved.* Allowing yourself to be moved can give you an insight that goes beyond what you have just done and can be very helpful. 721 dream interpretation can be used in part or as a whole in any context.

How does the 721 practice relate to the psychoanalytic idea of transference? When I first studied dreamwork, people talked about transference a lot—transferring some person or situation from the past, (often feelings about parents) onto the present situation. For example, I might say, "I hate you! You look like my father!" That is negative transference. A positive transference, might be, "Mmmm, I like being with you . . . you remind me of my mom." 721 relaxes transference work because much of the so-called "transference" is based on the fact that the dreamer is not aware of the shared field, or the possibility of an open forum for dream figures. Most transference conflict problems are due to a lack of interaction between CR and dreamland figures.

Now you can learn 721 dreamwork yourself by practicing the following exercise. It can be done alone or with a helper. If the dreamer wants to do 721 all alone, all the better.

Exercise: "721 Dreamwork"
360 CR

1. The dreamer speaks about CR tensions and problems, and tells a nighttime dream/or dream experience and any associations to it.

2. The helper asks about and explores the dreamer's needs, notes CR channels and phases, and watches for flirts and ghost roles.
3. The helper then enacts the dreamer's CR situation, her or his needs and phase(s), and begins to dialogue with reality figures. The dreamer is encouraged to correct the helper and to enter into the dialogue. When the dialogue stops for whatever reason, go to the next step.

360 Dreamland

4. Helper: Make note of dream figures, ghost roles, flirts, etc., and do 360 with all dreamlike figures; dialogue and play them out.
   Dreamer: At any point, enter into the 721 process. JAM with your helper, enter into the 360 CR parts and dialogue, and go deeper to 360 dreamland dialogue (with role switching).

1 Essence Level

5. Both dreamer and "interpreter" be a little shamanistic. Drop out and go to phase 4; just let yourselves be moved by the universe with phase 4's "super-vision." Notice if a dream tip or an interpretation arises from just being *moved by the universe. Get feedback from the universe.*
6. Helper and dreamer: Note what was helpful in 721.

Notice that 721 dreamwork is like worldwork in its ability to bring conflicting parts together and get FEEDBACK FROM THE UNIVERSE.

One of our participants shared the following discovery after completing the exercise.

> *Oh! Big discovery! For the first time all the elements of my childhood dream fell into place and it all made sense, and I feel very moved (big feelings; cries). Finally, I don't feel so polarized any more. I could feel everything, and all dream parts in my body.*

What a wonderful insight and a reminder to everyone. Remember, appreciate the dream—it is a miracle by itself! Then try 721 to integrate all levels of reality. Emphasize the last step: Let yourself be dreamed. This process needs awareness, and that awareness is your second training in dreamwork.

Things to Remember from Chapter 20

1. Notice dreams before you hear them.
2. Use 721 to explore that mysterious phase 4 power that moves you (and all of us).
3. As the interpreter, remember, you are not the point.
4. The main point is the dreamer's experience of her or his own dream teacher: the Tao that can't be said and the forums it produces.

CHAPTER 21

Your 721 "Cellphone" for Feedback from Your Body and Our Universe

• • •

As I HAVE BEEN SAYING, the dreaming process can be seen in nighttime dreams but also in the many dreamlike experiences that occur during your everyday life. In the final three chapters of Part VII, I integrate the 721 feedback practice into the tense world of internal body conflicts and symptoms. To complete this book, I bring bodywork back to worldwork for a healthier life for all.

In Chapters 4, 5, and 6, I stressed the changing phases of body experience. Now, I shall integrate those body phase experiences with 721 to work on conflicts not just in the world, in relationships, and in dreams, but in your body as well.

Many people experience how symptoms sometimes isolate them. But now, in the context of the perspective of nonlocality, much of your "personal experience," including body symptoms, appears to be not only yours, but also shares nonlocal interconnections with the world around you and beyond you.

I named this chapter *Your 721 Cellphone for Feedback from Your Body and Our Universe* to stress that body symptoms are part of worldwork and a universal issue. Like all your experiences, body symptoms are yours and they can also be nonlocal—your problems may be connected to others in your neighborhood and world.

We know from conflict work, that many people you don't like, the "X people," are often like symptoms that you would like to make more pleasant or get rid of entirely. But with awareness, we can often connect to and use those "X" energies.

When I walk down the street, I often see people carrying and talking/texting on their phones. Given the chance, it seems as if human beings always tend to converse and communicate. This communicating, when made conscious, can become an open forum, or even a "721 cellphone" forum, through which to talk with all our parts and symptoms.

The idea is simple. Realize that if you do open forums in the world, *you can continue to change the world by doing those forums inside yourself.* There are always all sorts of voices and body symptoms buzzing inside of us, trying to say "Hello!" We just need to pick up our "721 cellphone" and work with them.

***26.* "X" in the sky over Mt. Bachelor.**

When I thought of bringing out the 721 idea of talking with your "X" and other parts, I saw a remarkable piece of feedback from the universe. Amy and I looked up in the sky near Mt. Bachelor, where we were skiing, and I saw a huge "X" in the sky. I thought, "Oh, the universe is into viewing and talking with 'X!'"

As you know, the medical attitude is very important—it's good but very different. Medicine wants to kill or reduce phase 2. "Something is wrong! What? A symptom?!" However, from a larger, more process-oriented perspective, symptoms are not only something to take care of, but an expression of your diversity issues, of tensions between the "X" and the "u" in yourself.

With awareness, your genetics and physical condition may no longer be deterministic. Who you are and how long you live can be connected statistically to physical things but may also be connected with awareness. This idea of mine about the healthy aspects of awareness has not been proven statistically; it is mostly an observation from having worked with thousands of people.

The Beans!

Let me give you a personal example. I went into a restaurant with Amy recently and immediately entered into a somatic conflict, phase 2. I ate a lot of beans—and conflict began! Those beans wanted to come out of me more quickly than I expected!! The beans were telling my rear end something but I was not yet ready to hear. The beans were saying, "Let go! Let it flow!" Phase 2! Beans began to come out and sent me running home to get Pepto-Bismol®, medicine for those beans.

While sitting in the bathroom, I finally asked in phase 3, "Why are these beans coming out so quickly?" I began dreaming. I got interested in dreaming. *What dreaming and meaning does that flow of beans have?* I realized that I was uptight about a specific meeting I was part of, and the flow of beans helped to remind me to flow with the situation! Beans reminded me to flow and get to phase 4. Phase 4 came from exaggerating the symptom, as the beans led to emptiness! In phase 4, I was more detached, relaxed, and happy with everything.

How did I shift from phase 2 to phase 3 and 4? My second training helped. I am usually in phase 2, like all of us. We are usually against the body problems we have, hoping to take medicines or get something to get rid of those problems. Can I, can you, sometimes feel compassion for myself/yourself even when problems appear or return? Can you find your devotion to phase 4? Can you access your second training, even when you eat the wrong beans? Can you still say, "*Mmmmm*, maybe I can learn something from this." That is a phase 4 act of compassion. In phase 4, you can say to yourself, "I am a mess, and I also want to appreciate the possible significance of what is happening."

The second training stresses what I have been calling phase 4, the essence level in 721 open forums. I'll show how to use this training with my example of the beans.

Demonstration: 721 with the Beans

360 CR. When we went into the restaurant, the cook said, "Hi! Nice to see you guys again. I can cook you up a real *healthy* dinner!" I know that cook and noticed it was the first time he'd used *healthy* when describing his food. Also, part of the consensus reality situation was the fact that the stomach virus was going around Portland.

So here in CR, there is the figure of the cook saying that things are healthy (even when they are possibly not) and my own self, ignoring the cook's signals. Also in CR is the medicine, Pepto-Bismol. I ignored some of the signals in consensus reality! In addition, in CR beans were coming out quickly. So I ran for the Pepto to STOP the FLOW. That was the beginning of a 360 CR forum.

360 Dreamland. In dreamland, I role switched. Now I supported the flow, now I stopped it. I was Arny, then I was "flowing" with the beans. 360 dreamland helped me realize that I was flowing as the beans and this "flow" needed to connect with the part of me that was "uptight" about outer world problems. So, I brought those problems into my dream forum and learned to flow with them, moving back and forth between the different roles.

1 Essence Level. Finally, my 721 forum went to the processmind level, and just moved spontaneously. From phase 4 came the idea that I should be realistic in my work *and* flow much more as well.

That was my 721 practice with beans; it helped me with outer world problems and also with my health. The dreamland roles were: I am the flowing beans, saying, "Just let this whole thing flow." The normal me asked in dreamland, "Where do I need to let things flow?" The beans explained, "You are really uptight about this thing you are going to facilitate. Relax!" I responded with, "But I can't relax!" However, switching to the role of the beans, I started to flow more with my reality problems.

My essence-level experience resolved my problem. My dreambody dance was to be tight and then relax. That was my process, but it was also needed by that particular restaurant. The staff are very flowing and related, but not TIGHT ENOUGH, not careful with CLEANLINESS and GERMS. Both I and the restaurant need to flow, *and* need to be careful about reality. After my 721 inner work, an outer action was to give the restaurant that feedback.

Multi-dimensional 721 forum updates dreambody work, it updates medicine, worldwork, and psychology. To get the most out of symptoms, take the energy of the symptom, feel your way into it, be the symptom, and be its opposite. Then follow the universe.

If you are the helper, and your client cannot do it, "shamanize" and do 721 for her or him. Don't worry about taking symptoms on yourself, that does not seem to happen (unless you are in need of that problem). When the client sees you doing 721, she or he will give you feedback and might begin "jamming" with you until the next steps appear.

You might be wondering about genetics, like someone in our class. She asked,

> *With genetics, what about the dreaming process in which a therapist is working something through for a family system. Is an ancestral system being carried through you?*

This question about genetics connects to the question about nonlocality. For some reason we were born into a particular family system, gender, culture, race, and nationality. That is part of the CR situation. But in dreamland and at the essence level, our phase 4 experience may go beyond personal problems and provide advice that may touch upon family history. Perhaps you have a symptom in order to help resolve problems from which you and your family system have suffered. Similarly, in principle, it is possible that working with 721 on environmental poisons in the body could positively impact the poison in the earth.

Now you can try this 721 symptom work yourself with the following exercise. Use it to help you become deeply democratic with all the parts of yourself and the world.

Exercise: 721 Dreambody Work and the Second Training

1. What's your normal "u" energy like? Feel it, see it, and show it. Show it in movement. What is your worst real or feared body symptom? Show the "X" energy in movement. What phase are you in with "X" (phase 1, ignore it; phase 2, upset/fight "X"; phase 3, play with "X"; phase 4, detached and flowing with "X")?
2. Feel-see-move the troublesome symptom "X" energy and *follow and unfold* its process until you sense the possible significance of "X" and its "feedback" for you.
3. Now do a 721 *open forum*. Helper, play too, if needed. First in 360 CR, speak for "u" and then "X" and bring in medical views as well. Next drop into a 360 dreamland forum, and let u + X and possible dream figures and flirts interact and switch roles. When there is a relaxed or quiet moment, go to the next step.
4. Go to the processmind level and feel and hear the universe's feedback by letting the universe move you until your movements repeat. While "dancing," notice if "universe feedback" or tips arise for your health and life and imagine how to realize these tips. Note possible learning.

In one of my classes, the following discussion arose after participants tried the exercise for themselves.

P: Why are my "X" and "u" not the same, but always changing?

Arny: That happens normally as you become more fluid. My "X" also changes, as my "u" changes. In this exercise, the important thing is the momentary "u" experience as well as the energy of your body symptom, "X."

H: I did coma work in Japan and when the client came back from the comatose state, I interviewed her, asking, "What were you experiencing during the coma?" She said she had a long dream, the same dream she had when she was a child. When she was a child she was chased by a black shadow, and when she was in the coma she was chased by the same thing.

Arny: That supports my hypothesis that the biggest, most difficult, or wonderful events in life are aspects of the dream we are carrying. In a way, we are dreams trying to reach consciousness.

A: It seems as if we have a lot more to work on, the older we get, right?

Arny: Symptoms get intense in aging, not just because we get older, but also perhaps in part to make us more conscious of our multidimensional 721 nature. We are real, we are dreamers, and we are something infinite.

Things to Remember from Chapter 21

1. Your *721 "cellphone"* is your tendency to talk with yourself as you walk down the street. We are all walking open forums.
2. Use worldwork's 721 with body symptoms, and be deeply democratic with all the parts of yourself and the world.

CHAPTER 22

"Not-Doing" Symptom Work

• • •

WORLD CONFLICT FACILITATION WORK HAPPENS best if you work on your own conflicts first, inside and then outside. Conflict is personal, psychological, medical, and a world diversity issue. If you can learn to work on your body problems, you can help yourself, and others as well, to go deeper when you are home alone and in public.

The second training in dreambody work is phase 4's "not-doing," the experience of being moved by the universe. It seems to be good for everyone, as it is beyond life and death. In this chapter, I focus on the attitude of not-doing in order to bring phase 4, or the essence level, closer to everyday reality. We have previously explored not-doing in Chapter 5, on symptoms and relationships, and in Chapter 8, on recurring problems. Not-doing is also related to the vacation effect that we explored in Chapter 19.

I believe that 721 feedback belongs to the evolution of bodywork and medicine. Medicine began long ago in the form of Aboriginal spiritual traditions, and shamanism; now we have modern medicine, but we lost shamanism. We need to bring the shamanistic, medical, social, and psychological worlds closer together.

I remember when I first started to work with body issues at the Jung Institute in Zurich, Switzerland in the 1970s. A leading Jungian from another country said, "Dreambody work might be dangerous. If you start to ask people to feel into their body, they may go psychotic!" Modern Western mainstream people are always nervous about dreaming into symptoms, relationship problems, and world issues.

Actually, over the last 40 years of my career, no such psychotic moments ever occurred. But that negative opinion of my colleague shows that bringing psychology and medicine and worldwork together is a social and psychological issue. Imagine if you went to a typical doctor today and said, "I need to express the dreams that are in my body." You would probably be shy to do that. Perhaps not in the future?

Times change, and people are now doing meditation and bodywork everywhere. Dreambody work evolved into coma work by not assuming that people were only comatose. Processwork helps people in so-called psychotic states by not assuming there is something sick or wrong about them, but by taking a more natural science attitude that all people are in a process. Let's study it. Remaining open to people is a huge social issue. Not only diagnosing things as sick or healthy is a huge diversity issue. It is similar to saying, "If you do not act and look and believe the things that the average person does in this country, then you are 'sick.'"

In one class, as I was teaching about these topics, I noticed that I was dancing. I stopped and did a little public inner work to find out why. I realized I must be like one of the teenagers I have seen in the street dancing. Perhaps I am now an open-minded teenager who has not yet bought into the "adult way" of thinking that marginalizes dreaming.

Near death? Dreaming with the body reminds me of when I worked with someone who was diagnosed with stage 4 cancer, which means the medical community no longer knew how to help. Death was her expected next step. But when I began to work with her, she immediately started to sing and dance around. I asked her about the experience of the symptoms, and she said that her symptoms felt like children playing in the water, and then she started to play! She even took my hat off and started to play with it.

Why, if you are supposed to be dying, might you want to dance and play around as if life were just beginning? You don't have to answer that question, I just like asking it. My answer is that our bodies dream. In consensus reality, we come and go as Newtonian machines. But in dreamland, we are free to have many forms; we are free from the diagnosis and opinions of others. Freedom to dream is healing.

I heard afterwards from the person's doctor that she felt better than she had felt in a long time and could not stop talking about the experience. She was no longer interested in talking about the next chemotherapy.

As I spoke about being moved beyond life and death, a class participant shared a biblical quote that came to his mind, a statement from the apostle Paul, who said, "I die daily." The participant reflected that perhaps some of the crisis points that we go through in our lives can be like an underworld experience, and are preparations for the ability to let go into death.

In my practice over decades, I see people getting into trouble over fearing death. Everybody over the age of 30 starts to think about death. I think of death as a preparation to live completely. I am not against death. Death in a sense is a preparation for life. If you think about death, let go and live—see what happens next. Death is one of the healthiest things to think about.

Process thinking focuses on flow and process, not only on the CR concepts of life and death. Dying in this sense is part of the second training. It is a phase; it is phase 4. Remember in phase 1, "I don't want to think about things." In phase 2, body symptoms, heal them! In phase 3 switch roles with the X, and in phase 4, detach from it all, let go, *die out of your normal identity* and be moved by the universe.

One of our participants asked a question shared by many.

> *Suppose that you really do want to detach, but you feel really stuck and you feel like whatever it is you want to let go of is really hanging on. I imagine there is not just one thing to do. But what is your perspective on that?*

My answer is that if you want to really hang onto something, then hang onto it as much as possible until you are exhausted—then you will have to let go. Phases change by themselves in time. When you are stuck, you might remember the techniques we explored in Chapter 8 about burning the "X" energy as a way to transition from phase 2 to phase 4, or in Chapter 19, try vacating the channel or phase you are in.

A first training attitude is "We are a 'thing' that lives and dies." A second training attitude is, "We are a not-doing dance." In Chinese, the term *not-doing* is *wu-wei*. There is nothing wrong with "doing" things when you have to do them, but if you can wait for the energy inside you to do the things you have to do, you are close to the Taoists' *wu-wei*. From this viewpoint, we *have a life to live, and at the same time, it is not ours to live.*

I love the attitude of Lao Tse as it appears in his *Tao Te Ching*. There he says, "Beings or phenomena that are completely in harmony with the Tao, behave in a natural, uncontrived way." He goes on to say,

> *"The goal of spiritual practice for the human being is the attainment of this natural way of behaving as when the planets revolve around the sun."*

Being a planet moving around the sun? He sounds like a scientist as well as a Taoist! It is as if he were telling us to follow the gravity field as it moves us about. Today, he might say, devote yourself to phase 4 compassion for yourself and all beings. Because phase 4 *is* a phase and not a permanent state, the compassion you find for yourself will probably need to be found again and again.

The threat of death or serious illness is, in this sense, a kind of gift to find this phase 4 experience of compassion, and with it to begin a 721 feedback process to connect with the field that moves us.

Demonstration: Not-Doing with Amy's Symptom

To demonstrate this not-doing approach to working with symptoms, I asked Amy if I could work with her during one of my classes.

Arny: What would you like to work on?

Amy: I would work on trouble sleeping. My whole life I've had the experience of almost falling asleep and then something like a "Grrrr" shakes me—my "X" says, "Grrrr! Think about this! Worry about that! Don't go to sleep!" My "X" says, "There is so much to think about!"

Arny: What is your normal "u" energy like?

Amy: Over time, I am a sort of wave motion (makes a wave motion with her arm).

Arny: That "X" disturbing your sleep is different. It goes "Grrrr!" and is different from the way you identify yourself.

Amy: Yes, but I can pick it up and be tough too. Not often, but I can.

Arny: (to the class) *OK, so she has a "u" and an "X" and is sometimes fluid.* (to Amy) *Now, Amy, just relax for a moment and let yourself be moved around spontaneously and carefully, and notice any repetitive movements. Take your time.*

Amy: (moving, turning, spinning) *I notice something repeating. I drop and then spin* (shows head moving backwards in a spin).

Arny: Now continue your dance and as you are doing it, let a fantasy arise about what you are doing.

Amy: If I exaggerate it . . . more repetitive movements occur. . . . It feels like diving into a pool of water (amplifies the movement and dives downwards). . . . *It is a fantastic feeling—I am not doing anything . . .* (floating back up) *. . . just diving in and then I just float up . . . plunging in and then something moves me up.*

Arny: Now, while doing that dance, what would you suggest to me if I was somebody trying to go to sleep?

Amy: I would say, "Go really deep. . . . You are up here on the surface, so completely let go. Go deep down to the bottom of the water, and then it will bring you back up. It says, 'You can afford to let go' because it will bring you back to what you need. Don't think so much!'"

Arny: You can let go?

Amy: Yes, and then really new things will come up. Don't try to figure it all out with your mind. . . . Thanks, Arny, that's great, thanks!

After this work, Amy remembered a poem that she wrote in 2003, more than a decade previously. Here it is:

I Want to be Nothing (by Amy Mindell)
(Recited by No One)

Oh to be nothing,
To just roam all around
Without any form
Through rivers
Through towns.

To let go of my thinking
To drop my willful head
To be open and empty
Like when I'm dead.

"It" will start to move me
Make me dance, leap, and fall
I won't "do" anything
Because "It" does it all.

The Not-Doing Dance

I hope that Amy's dreambody work helps to illustrate the basic idea of this exercise. By letting go into that "not-doing" processmind dance, Amy's process showed her how to let go of her everyday consensus reality attachment. When she let go and followed her dreaming processmind, she was not integrating one energy or another, as we have been doing. Instead she was integrating the processmind process, the *not-doing dance.*

We have often focused on integrating different energies. But in this exercise, the point is to bring the entire essence level closer to everyday reality to let it do "not-doing."

Not-Doing and Getting Stuff Done

Often people ask how to balance not-doing with doing and being organized in life with clear tasks to do every day. My answer is that *if you really are doing not-doing, you can do more doing and be even better organized.* Amy explained how she sees me modeling this.

> *When things come up, usually I say, "Oh, I will do that later" and if things come up for you, your "not-doing" is to just do the thing, and it is just done. Then you have extra time—you get so much done, I cannot fathom it. I procrastinate, and it takes me triple time.*

It is quite a mystery, yet somehow "not-doing" can do more things than "doing." For me, Arny, not-doing means that if something pops up in my mind, I don't plan to do it, rather I do it with "not-doing." Doing is connected with the thought, "I have to do this," and that is OK, but if you do not-doing, then the first time something comes up in your mind, you let it happen.

Then you will have done it before the thought was completed. It is the same with body tensions, relationships, and even international conflict. Follow the not-doing of your processmind; it will give you an overview, a metaview, that brings polarities together and works things out.

Now, try this for yourself with the following "not-doing" exercise. You can do this on your own or with a helper. The helper may find that your "not-doing" will have a nonlocal connection to her or his own process.

Exercise: Shamanism's Not-Doing Symptom Work

Reflect on these questions for yourself, or have the helper ask you as the client.

1. What's your normal energy "u" like and what real or imaginary worst symptom "X" energy bothers you the most these days? Show and move with both the "u" and "X" energies.
2. What phase are you in with "X" (phase 1, peaceful; phase 2, conflicted and tense; phase 3, role switching; phase 4, detached)? Sense and amplify the symptom's "X" energy to guess its possible meaning.
3. Now do "not-doing." Let go and let the universe move or dance you, and wait for repetitive motions. Note if u + X are in the dance. Note also any fantasy arising from the repetitive dance experience.
4. Is there a metaview of how u + X are possibly both needed in the dance? Feel this phase 4 "not-doing" dance, until it implies how u + X are both parts of same movement process. Catch insights and consider how to actualize them, how to live the not-doing part of your nature that combines both "u" and "X."
5. Helper, also do a not-doing phase 4 dance. Are insights from your dance useful for you *and* the "client" as well? Discuss possible shared insights with one another and make NOTES!

After participants in our seminar tried this exercise, they shared the following learnings and reflections.

> *T: What I discovered in my "not-doing" dance was the fluid energy of Kokopelli, the goddess of fertility and revelry.*
>
> *I have to perform in public. But the goddess told me in that phase 4 experience that, "the audience will forgive you for not being technically excellent, but they will never forgive you for not having a good time."*
>
> *G: I know her insight is totally true, because if you are not playing and enjoying, you are not giving the best thing to the audience. The best thing is to have fun on stage because that is really how audiences are transformed by your pleasure, by your play.*

T: Yes, that fits for me.

Arny: Yes, not-doing gets you in touch with the goddess of creativity and having a good time.

N: The fantasy that came up for me in my "not-doing" dance was totally unexpected. It was about a Bushman. I think their dance was called . . . "dancing the ropes." These South African people believe that when they dance, they connect to the divine by dancing, and by shaking they bring down the ropes connecting to the spirit world!

Arny: Wonderful! Can you show me how you wiggled to bring down those ropes?

N: It was like this (wildly wiggles her hair, opens her eyes wide, and comes very close to Arny's face, with a wild *hissssssss*).

Arny: You sent me into an altered state!

N: That is the point! . . . I am shocked—I did not expect I was going to come so close to your face! Are you OK?

Arny: I am completely changed! I loved it! If I let go into what you just did, I notice there is no me, there is just nature.

N: Yes.

Arny: (Suddenly rain pours down on the ceiling very loudly) Wow, perhaps your dance brought down the "ropes from Heaven" which the Bushman spoke about. This not-doing body work may connect to the universal field we live in, the moment in time in our environment . . . the rain.

Those are not just rain drops from heaven, perhaps they are also the "ropes from the skies"!? Perhaps this not-doing body movement dance is a way to know what Einstein called "the mind of god"?

As these reflections illustrate, you can use your body experience to connect to our world with "not-doing." My point is to show how your symptoms may be yours, but may also connect you to the whole world. In the next chapter, I show how they connect you to history that is still alive today.

Things to Remember from Chapter 22

1. Conflict work works best if it is a lifestyle of working deeply with all issues, including your own symptoms and the conflicts they create.
2. Your phase 4 dance is a shamanistic "not-doing" dance that's good for your health and connects you to the world, the earth, and the skies.

CHAPTER 23

How Symptoms Point to Your Worldwork

• • •

***27.* Gravitational waves generated by binary neutron stars.**

IN FEBRUARY 2016, THE GRAVITATIONAL waves predicted by Einstein in 1916, one hundred years ago, in his theory of general relativity were empirically verified. My friends at MIT were very excited. (Thanks, NASA, for the picture of such waves generated by two neutron stars orbiting one another.)

I connected with Professor Edwin Taylor at MIT, a world expert on relativity theory. He wrote to me that "everyone is smiling at MIT—they are all walking around smiling." That is because MIT, together with Cal Tech, developed the particular instruments that made it possible to measure the subtle gravitational background waves to our consensus reality.

What are gravitational waves? I have been saying for a long time that people feel the universe in ways that are hardly measureable. Mediumistic shamans have always sensed things "buzzing" around them. Part of processwork is to imagine and experience something we have been calling "the universe" moving you, especially when you need new information. The information you receive can be healing.

Einstein's gravitational waves add a physical analogy to "vibes" that many people have always sensed "in the air." I am thinking for the moment of the South African Aboriginal people who sense the universe shake and dance for healing, community, and spiritual reasons. Perhaps they, like many indigenous cultures, have known about gravitational waves since the beginning of time. Physics, in a way, is just catching up.

In any case, when two big planets, or any two massive material objects, come close to one another, they move and vibrate the space around them. Einstein realized that something like a rocket ship over the earth measures speed and distance differently than we do on earth—not just because of its speed but because our measure of the space between us depends upon our speed relative to one another. Space–time curves according to the energy and momentum of whatever is present.

When two massive objects are near each other, they make one another dance a little; they create waves in space–time. The waves that go out make the space between them vibrate. Every psychic "knows" that people send waves out from birth forward.

Gravitational waves, however, are very special—they can go through things. They go through chairs in this room, they go through dust in the universe. They are gravitational radiation. In contrast, light waves get stuck and can't get to us if there is too much dust. But dust and other objects do not bother gravitational waves! So because gravitational waves can go through things, we may eventually be able to view the beginnings of our universe. Then we will know more about when and where we came from and what happened at the beginning of our universe.[46] It is very moving for me to consider that we might eventually look back almost to the beginnings of time.

You might be wondering how we can "see" to the beginning of time. Let's pretend the "Big Bang" made a lot of sound, like a loud clap I might make in a room. Now, if I can hear this sound on the other side of the room, I can imagine what kinds of things could have made that sound. Though I cannot see the beginning, I can take a guess about what happened by listening to the sound. It is an emotional, touching experience to imagine back to the beginning of something infinite.

As we have been exploring in the previous few chapters, *721 dreambody work requires essence level and phase 4 experience.* As you know, I have stressed the importance of bringing the medical view, your own view, and different consensus reality views together with dreamland's role switching. Remember to play out and make conscious ghost roles such as aging, social views of your body and death, other people, and any other things catching your attention.

Remember in 721 to bring in cultural views in the body symptom work, as well as consensus reality views of your body in your open forums. CR viewpoints may criticize you and can make you feel sick.

As a little boy I remember my first grade teacher sending me to the school nurse. Why? I was feeling well and having fun! But my teacher sent me to see the nurse because she thought I looked upset or nervous about something.

I said, "I feel well!" The nurse said, "Don't be shy, tell me what's wrong! I see that *your eyes are slanted*." I had never realized that my eyes were slanted or different than anyone else's. Later, when I asked my mother if my eyes were slanted, she said that people from Mongolia (Asia) were in our genetic history.

This is a painful story about the governing CR unconsciousness at that time! According to that CR view, if you look a certain way, there has got to be something wrong with you! This was an anti-Asian or anti-African or anti-Semitic view. Instead of saying, how interesting, kids come in all various types and colors, these teachers had little diversity consciousness.

My point is that a given consensus reality viewpoint about you, especially a racist viewpoint, is enough to make you feel unwell. It is extremely important to bring that CR view into your 721 CR forum work, as many body feelings may be connected with social issues.

Some of your "symptoms" are not symptoms but reactions to social beliefs and the atmosphere around those beliefs. Some symptoms are not meant to be healed; they are not indicators of physical illness. Symptom work needs CR awareness. When you look in the mirror and say, "Oh, I have a spot here and here, I should wear that and not this," you are probably *not* seeing yourself as you are, but are looking at yourself from a CR viewpoint about what is acceptable.

In worldwork, processwork sees you in CR; it sees how you look, and what your critics think. In dreamland and the essence level, you are full of dreaming figures and vibrations. What hum or music is coming out of you? You are not just a person but also a hum and a dance. Quantum physics would agree. We may look like "things," like particles, but we are also "waves."

In speaking about the wave–particle duality, Einstein said,

> *"We have two contradictory pictures of reality; separately neither of them fully explains the phenomena of light, but together they do."47*

The uncertainty principle, applied to process-oriented psychology and dreambody work, is this: We are people and waves; we need both medical and dream-dance views. We are certainly people, but we also need a dreambody uncertainty principle.

In physics, this principle says that the location and the momentum of a particle cannot be known at the same time. Here stands Arny Mindell. You locate me as being here, but you cannot know to where, and with what speed, I will next move. We cannot totally know ourselves or others without dreaming.

For example, when I went to Zurich years ago to study physics, I did not know that there would be a huge momentum when I got there to go into psychology as well. You know where you are now, but exactly where you will be going and what you will be doing months from now are governed by psychological and physical uncertainty principles. People may say, "I know you," and then be surprised when suddenly you are doing something new. We need this uncertainty principle to remain open, to appreciate and work with ourselves and others.

Try answering the following inner-oriented questions:

- Think of the most difficult body symptom that you have. What symptom bothers you the most?
- Now feel the potential movement or energy behind that "X" symptom, act it out a little with your body, show "X" with your hands.

- Ask yourself now, "Does this hand motion remind me of somebody I know?"

I would suggest that your symptoms may have a nonlocal connection to that person.

This way of thinking about dreams and body experiences raises the question: Who are you? The dreambody concept is that you are a dream trying to happen in a body. Symptoms, troublesome as they may be, are dreams trying to be realized in this world.

In phase 2, we are in conflict with that symptom—we don't like it. We are a war zone, so we need an open forum! In phase 3, we can switch roles, and in phase 4, we are dancing our dreamlike energies. Without this view, you might get stuck in CR, thinking that you look good or bad, believing that you are healthy or sick.

To illustrate and explore the connection between dreambody work and worldwork, I'll share Amy's inner-work exercise as an example, and then present work that I did with someone suffering from loud sounds in their ears. This person found a teacher figure who wanted to make sure that certain painful world history events are not forgotten.

After these examples, you will find the exercise instructions so you can try this for yourself.

Example: Amy's Body Symptom Inner Work

Amy: I worked on my acid stomach and constant throat irritation symptoms. The "X" energy tears up my throat and makes it difficult to speak. My normal self is more wavey.

When I did the processmind dance and you asked me who was moving me, it was something like the hunchback of Notre Dame. This felt really good, very freeing from having to be something more socially acceptable!!

And the message was, "Bring out the rejected dreaming of the night." That feels so right to me, so mythic for me. . . . I had forgotten the hunchback's story. The hunchback was a rejected figure that tried to save the person he loved and finally died with her. She and he would bring out the dreaming of the night that is needed for me now.

Arny: Thank you, thank you for introducing yourself.

Amy: It is a pleasure.

Demonstration: Who Are You? Dreambody Symptoms and Worldwork

I share this example of working with someone on her experience of loud sounds in her ears especially because of the synchronicities that came up.

W: I have noise in my ears, and I've had it for some years now. I've had my hearing checked, and I have 15% less hearing than an average person. It is not that much, but a little bit.

Arny: What do you experience in your ear, what sounds?

W: It is like "shhhhh" and a high-pitched note.

Arny: Hearing sounds is very common. Sometimes in the morning when I wake up, I can hear my heart beat in my ear. Now how could you give me your sounds? How can I feel, hear, and see them?

W: It is like "mmmmmmmmmm" (hums) *and then it has "nnnnnnnnnn"* (higher-pitched sound) *constantly. . . . Part of my sadness is that I don't have silence or quietness; it has been there for years . . . except when I sleep, I don't remember, of course.*

Arny: Your eyes got a little sad when you said that. I wanted to put my arm around you—can I do that for a minute? I am sorry, it is hard.

W: Yes . . . I love silence. . . .

Arny: (After a few minutes) . . . *Now let's go deeper. Try to make those sounds in my head.* (Tilts his head toward her) *You can do almost anything you want with it. Go ahead. . . . I love silence.*

W: (Makes high-pitch sound, with hand coming towards his head)

Arny: Go away! Waaaahh!

W: (Continues with motion and sound) *It sounds like mosquito now! . . . But I have more diverse sounds, this is just one.*

Arny: Let's say I am now going to join you while you make that "X" symptom. You and I as the "X" now really want to make this sound to her!! "Do-de-do-de-do. . . ."

W: It is difficult to do it to someone else. But . . . (makes a huge, extended sound, with arms outstretched) *Wwweeeooooowwwwww!!*

Arny: (playing W) *What the hell is that? That is a lot more noise than I have heard in a long time! Get some medicine, five tranquilizers, get my ears checked, check my blood pressure, too much aspirin! Do you ever have any of those things?*

W: (Laughs as "X" makes a high-pitched sound with arms outstretched)

Arny: (turning to the class) *Everybody, let's make that sound together!* (Group joins in and makes huge sounds!)

W: (grinning and laughing) *It's weird to hear and to see so many people yelling and smiling. . . . I suddenly saw people, because I was focused on you, and then you moved away and I suddenly saw the whole room . . . I am shy* (hunches her shoulders inside her scarf, takes a big breath). *It is nice, more gentle in here. . . .*

Arny: OK, now let's go further. Allow yourself to be moved spontaneously.

W: Alright. (Shyly rises up on her toes, then slumps over, swings and sways, steps forward and down, back and forth.)

Arny: Continue to explore your movements until something repetitive appears.

W: Something like this happens in my dance (makes a jerking motion, with arms rising up, then relaxes).

Arny: We see the quiet part of you and the more expressive side! Do you have a fantasy of who you are or what could be doing these movements—a piece of nature or human-like being?

W: (Amplifies her motion, swings her whole body about.) *I have something in my arms and I am letting it go out . . . it is very pleasant.*

Arny: And where do you see that motion in nature or in people, a person who might do something like that? An imaginary figure who would do something like that?

W: I imagine a wind that goes like this, and then there is some kind of a cliff. It goes like this to the edge and then swoops down . . . like wind over a sand dune.

Arny: Ah, in your basic dances, you are like a cliff or sand dune. One part of you is quiet and the other just flows. Does that seem right for you?

W: Yes, I prepare and . . . then suddenly something just goes and does things.

Arny: You prepare, check it out, then let it go. So be that cliff or dune for a moment, and I am going to ask you a question.

W: (Goes back into the movement)

Arny: I am going to be a person now with a very big ear problem. I have a sound in my head that goes like "zzzz!" all the time. I asking you, dear wise dune figure, to give me a tip about this terrible problem.

W: What I discover is not about my ears, but it is about being more careless—*take care of yourself less!*

Arny: But what happens if I am shy, how can I be careless? Show me how.

W: (Puts arms around Arny) *You don't have to do anything. . . . You don't have to push yourself to be brave or anything . . .* (makes a little dance or balletic leap).

Arny: Yes, don't push—be careless and let leaps happen! The ears are trying to encourage you to sometimes be careless.

W: Thank you!

Arny: (As she goes back to her seat, Arny follows her.) *I'm following my processmind to do something on your behalf. "Shamanizing." Let me see what my body is saying.* (Wiggles around and a pointed finger pops up.) *Hmm, I don't know you well enough to know if this could be useful for you, but what comes up right now is that you are a teacher and you want to make a point. . . .*

W: There are some points that are important to me. . . . I think of my city, Warsaw, and the history of that place. There are many points to be said, things that should not be forgotten. . . . Warsaw, Russia, history, Germany, World War II, . . . everything is there.

N: (A class participant began crying said) World War II! I wanted to say that when I made your sound, W. I remembered somebody who died in Auschwitz. She was called the "Mystic of the Holocaust." That thought came out of nowhere and that is why I was crying.

W: Thank you, N, you bring tears to my eyes here, thank you.

In this work, we found that loud sounds in the ears are the wind blowing and perhaps teaching or speaking about history that wants to be remembered. Making the sound of your "teacher" can change the world.

Now try this exploration of dreambody worldwork for yourself with the following exercise. You can do this on your own (skip point D) or with a helper.

Exercise: Symptom "Vacating"

A. Client, choose, explore, and make motions for your worst symptom energy, and then do the same for your normal "u" energies. How do the characteristics of "X" appear in one or more people whom you know? Can fighting/opposing "X" medically and/or as those people help? (Do so if needed.)

B. Do 721. This means, do 360 open forum process in CR with the "u," "X," and medical opinions. Then do the 360 dreamland forum; switch roles between the "u," the "X," ghost roles, and flirts. Feel deeply into the "X," letting it move your body and letting it change your facial expression! Finally, in phase 4 explore the essence level and let yourself be moved by the universe (carefully). Note repetitive "dance" movements and possible insights into how "u" and "X" might be part of one (dance) process.

C. Vacate yourself while dancing and hear/ imagine/ explore/ create a human-like figure moving around in a way that mirrors your dance. Note, name, and sketch that figure. Have you dreamed about this figure of your timeless self? Be this figure, and listen to and record its advice about your body and your life's task.

D. Helper, quietly do a phase 4 dance and *together,* shamanize with each other, that is connect with your eyes open or shut, sensing nonlocal connections for possible insights about body, relationship problems, and life tasks. Share these insights.

Seminar participants who completed this exercise shared the following comments and insights.

A: My symptom was cancer. What did I discover? The energy in me needs to be released. . . . It is quiet and still. Yes, quiet, unobtrusive, just sitting there . . . but this "quietness" wants to come out and be quite verbal.

R: There was a tightness in my pelvic area. Playing the tightness symptom maker, sort of relieved it and brought out a powerful body dance that relieved the symptom!

N: I have had a tension in my heart, not like a heart attack—really tight, clamping down—so doing that in my exercise I saw an image of an Asian woman who said, "Do compassion and spiritual service from the heart." She was a woman who acted from her heart, and I tend to act more from my head.

S: I had this lovely experience of coming in with a migraine and . . . was so moved by the movement that emerged that my symptom went away. I have had this migraine for four days, so to say that it went away is a pretty significant thing. But the medicine was in my partner's movement as well, it was the exact medicine that I needed! (Shows the motions of turbulent boiling.) *Isn't that beautiful!*

Arny: Oh, my gosh, the symptom energy and your partner showing you that energy was healing.

S: It was so beautiful.

I was very touched by all these body experiences resulting from conflict with the "X" symptom energy. In particular, I recall W.'s loud ear noise that, together with my "dance," brought out her teacher, who spoke about World War II in Warsaw, Poland.

After this class was completed, S. mentioned on the class internet string that her father had been imprisoned in the Warsaw ghetto during World War II. Another student listening to the class from Israel told about relatives who had also lived and died in that ghetto. Then a third student listening in to the class from Warsaw told us she now shops across the street from where S.'s father had been imprisoned in that Warsaw ghetto.

In a way, the sounds in W.'s ear were louder than could be imagined. They spoke to people around the world. Remember history, remember conflict. W.'s and my inner teacher say, "Speak out about history, about marginalization. Let's reduce pain and war and make a better world."

My message to you, dear reader, is this: 721 dreambody work should become a lifestyle, a way of resolving conflict, in your body and in the world.

Things to remember from Chapter 23

1. Work on your symptom energy and the conflict with the "u" that comes from that "X."
2. Notice the processmind dance that results; that dance may not only be part of your bodywork but also your and everyone's worldwork, attempting to bring opposing energies together.
3. Symptoms are nonlocally connected to world history and potential world solutions.
4. Make dream and dreambody work a lifestyle, so that what you do inside to feel well also helps with worldwork.

PART VIII

Communing for Conflict and Peace

• • •

To work best, working at dreams and symptoms, inner problems, and organizational and world issues should become a lifestyle. Use the dreaming process to help with real conflicts every day, if possible.

In this part of the book, I bring together many of the ideas and practices we have been exploring to remind you of earlier work, and to show how working with yourself and others requires familiarity with "your own" nonlocal, sacred, and creative space.

Why? This space allows you to relate more deeply, *to "commune" and facilitate* problem resolutions and flow, in yourself and with all those around you.

CHAPTER 24

Communing in Relationships

• • •

IN CHAPTER 18, I INTRODUCED the concept of "commune-ication" and how it is connected to the dreaming process. Communing can be a key to resolving conflicts and creating good relationships. I have stressed that "communing" is a phase 3 and phase 4 experience. Here, I talk about commune-icating in our processwork theory and summarizing deep democracy in terms of levels, phases, and forums. I show how communing is part of a *sacred creative space* that holds friendship, peace, and even conflict.

Sacred and *creative* are rarely used adjectives in connection with conflict and war! Yet, such a space still exists near the essence level, waiting for facilitators to access it. Without "dreamland" and "essence level" experiences, our world remains blocked and stuck in consensus reality with all of its polarizations. This is especially true when it comes to historically rooted conflicts. As you know, we need a practice that works as well for inner experience as it does for everyday reality.

As I was teaching about this topic on the Oregon coast, in the winter of 2016, a huge storm suddenly brought thunder roaring over the roof of the seminar space. We were all delighted with this outer world sound, and I wondered aloud to the group, "Perhaps I should make more noise, or all of us must roar for world change!" Everyone "rooaarrrred" with the thunder in agreement!

One of my basic questions is, "Can we flow with tense, uncomfortable situations?" Usually the answer is *no*! We get stuck in consensus reality's polarizations. But with more dreaming (and roaring), we can say *yes*—we can flow with the storm and with tense scenes better.

By understanding process phases, we can recall that conflict usually appears as a tense, phase 2 phenomenon, even though, like the weather in general, it is part of a universal cycle of big bangs. So expect thunder in the skies and on earth! Remember that phase 2 is a part of nature. It belongs to everyone, to every group, every relationship, every country, and to day and night. Conflict is a phase that reminds us of our diversity. Go deeper into other phases to process conflict and create better relationships. In phases 3 and 4, commune.

***28.* Dervish Dancers.**
Wikipedia

I have included an image of Dervish dancers[48] to help show what I mean. They are "communing" with the universe, with "God," with nature. You commune when you sense some intelligence in space and let it move you. In the same way, you "commune" with a tree when you let the space of a tree move you, when you feel into flowers, grass, or the sea. You enter a slightly altered state, in which you can feel and move with nature and communicate best.

By "communing," I mean to be in touch with the universe and to use that experience to "sense it," to "commune-icate" with yourself and others.

As I have said, your first training methods in relationship and conflict work are important, but often, when you are under tension, or when your own trauma has been re-constellated—when history is bothering you—your ability to commune-icate becomes disturbed.

We can now add commune-icating to our theory and practice. Let me summarize again, deep democracy in terms of levels, phases, and forums.

Deep Democracy Levels, Phases, and Forums

You will recall that deep democracy is associated with:

- *Levels*: In consensus reality we are separate parts: You are you, and I am me. In dreamland that separation is not clear anymore because of nonlocality, and at the essence level, you and I merge as powers in a field.
- *Phases*: In phase 1 and phase 2, "u" and "X" are the energies that you identify with and have trouble with. In dreamland, phase 3, 360 role switching can happen. At the essence level, phase 4, you can commune with the world, the universe. Here you can meet your deepest altered state of consciousness, and with practice, you can bring it into the other phases of reality.
- *Forums*: Deep democracy appears as the practice of forums, as I showed with 721 feedback. In Chapter 16, I explained how 721 developed as an extension and deepening of the business concept of 360 feedback. In 360 feedback, your peers, superiors, and subordinates give you feedback in the hope that this will change you for the better: for example, "You did that stupidly" or "I like you, you are a great person." However, recent studies have found that 360 feedback does not work so well, and costs more in time and energy because it is so disturbing. It seems that the person receiving feedback is so rattled that she or he then spends a lot of extra time working on relationship problems.

So in 721, we turned 360 CR feedback into an open forum that you can do within yourself and also outside, with all the people and parts liking or disliking you. From this viewpoint, you can only meet parts of yourself in life. So whoever likes you or doesn't like you is also part of you. This means that you need their energies! 360 dreamland enables you to go deeper and role switch and feel those energies. Finally, contact with the "1," the essence level, helps you to commune in the midst of conflicts.

The first training is about learning to work at the CR and dreamland levels of deep democracy. It is about phases 1, 2, and 3.

The second training is devoted to phase 4, which is behind these other phases. Because we are so attached to consensus reality in conflict, we often forget phase 4. Yet, it is a key to worldwork of all sorts.

Phase 4 is a deep, pre-dreaming experience. When you are in your deepest sleep at night, you are in a pre-dream phase 4, where there is a sense of peacefulness and creativity. Phase 4 is also present in the day, we just rarely notice it.

The following diagram presents Deep Democracy in terms of 721 levels, phases, and forums.

DEEP DEMOCRACY in terms of		
Awareness ***LEVELS***	***Process*** ***PHASES***	***Universal*** ***721 FORUMS***
Consensus Reality	**Phase 1, u ☺** **Phase 2, u + X ☹**	**360**
Dreamland ***~Commune***	**"u"~ ☻ ~ "X** **~Phase 3**	**360 Dreamlike** **~role switch~**
Essence	**Phase 4 ☺**	**+"1"**

***29.* Levels, phases, and 721 forums of Deep Democracy.**

721, Communing, and a Sacred, Creative Space

721 feedback and commune-ication are closely linked. Let's say somebody verbally attacks you, saying, "I don't think you are doing this right! You are not the right kind of person! You are stupid!" or "You should have done . . . differently!" These are some of the typical things people hear all the time. Or, "You are stupid, a mess, you are not perfect, you don't look right—look in the mirror again!" Every morning before work you might hear a voice inside yourself saying, "Look at that wrinkle,

look at that hair, how about that rear end of yours, is that in the right position?"

To work with that feedback using 721, communing begins in phase 3, as you switch roles in 360 dreamland. Switching roles while feeling/sensing phase 4 deep in the background allows you to get deeply into the "X." Make its face, its eyebrows, its brow. You may find that "X" in your family or in personal, historical abuse issues. That is one of the reasons it is on your mind; it may be asking not only for your personal consciousness, but perhaps for your historical and global awareness as well. So, please, feel your way into that "X" that bothers you; even if it is a small thing, it is unusual and important.

If you feel put down, it's hard to work on yourself or with others, and so you need phase 4's detachment in phase 3. To some extent, your body itself can teach you how best to "commune." Communing is an aspect of the shamanistic part of you. Phase 4 is the state of not knowing and just being moved at first, without images or specific feelings associated with it yet. This state of mind allows insights and images and dreams to rise up into consciousness.

Phase 4 is a pre-dream state that occurs at night when you are snoring. That state happens in everyday life too; it is a meditative state needed for good health. In phase 4, "you can let go and dream" and dance.

Our job is to feel that phase *in the middle of the mess*, to feel into and "commune" with others, to feel and understand what they are feeling, in part because you, too, sometimes feel that way but have forgotten it.

I call the phase 4 aspect of communing a "sacred space." Sometimes the word *sacred* sounds like more religious rules and regulations. For me, phase 4 is "sacred" in the sense of being open to spontaneous flow prior to any of your ideas, rules, or regulation. It is "sacred" in the sense of being in touch with "something" that is moving you.

I call phase 4 the pre-dreaming "sacred" essence of communing, which is prior to god concepts. It is more like the Tao that can't be said. It is like the Buddhist concept of "empty mind." When you are really open, "empty" becomes "creative" mind as the emptiness emerges in terms of images in phase 3.

Devotion to phase 4 means *appreciating it as the center of all the phases.* From phase 4, you can accept and expect people to be in phase 1, in the mindset that says, "I am happy, and I don't want to look at any problems." Likewise, it is natural for conflict and lightning to happen in phase 2.

As I presented this idea in our seminar, the thunder rattled the roof again, reminding us of the flow of nature's phases. "Thank you," I said, delighted, and our participants celebrated the synchronicity. I felt that nature was reminding us: Learn to work with the whole system . . . and expect similar problems to happen again. Like the storm, good weather also comes and goes. Similarly, peace is not sustainable—it comes and goes!

One phase 4 idea is that peace is not sustainable. Everybody loves peace, but peace is not a fixed state, it is a process. *Peaceful resolutions are not sustainable. What is sustainable is learning how to relate.*

From the phase 4 viewpoint, thunder happens, then rain, then sun, and then thunder again. Everything changes. Having that attitude every now and then will allow you to work in conflict areas without getting burned out.

Our training is to notice when troublesome things start to happen. Then take care of yourself, fight, scream, and yell, work at it, leave, and at the same time don't be surprised that it is happening. All the phases are important. If you don't do what I am saying (and most of us don't!), you get depressed and go into phases 1 and 2 yourself.

Who is your BEST teacher of all this? I love teaching, and I act like a teacher, *but the true teacher is your own body.* Other people can be helpful, but your own body in phase 4 is the greatest and most trustworthy teacher of all this. All I can really do is just remind you of that.

You may be wondering how to use communing with the other side when, for example, in a workplace you may end up having to fire that person.

My point is that if you are in phase 3, you can feel into the person you must fire and appreciate who she or he truly is. *Communing means reading into others, discerning why they behave the way they do.* When you enter the sacred space, phase 4, communing goes further and something unpredictable will appear! In the workplace, for example, you might say, "You don't do some things well here at work, but I know what that feels like too. I don't fit in everywhere in part because *you and I may have other true gifts meant for other things! Those gifts may not be seen or used here.*" Communing with the person you have to fire can allow you to support the person's creativity to find the best place for her or his nature.

Meeting Yourself

From a phase 3 viewpoint, you can only ever meet yourself. *You cannot run into a problem in the outer world that you don't have inside you.* For your own well-being, you need to dance with the energy of what is bothering you. In phase 3 dreamland the idea is to switch roles *and commune.* Then go deeper to the unpredictable and spontaneous phase 4. Communing in phase 3 and phase 4 will give rise to a metaview, as I discussed in Chapter 15. It gives rise to your true leadership.

For example, let's say you meet a person who is disturbing to you; this person is an "X" for you. Let's say the "X" person's movements are stomping, and your normal "u" movements are soft and flowing. When you let go and are moved, you will notice that the movements you identify with are there, and the other person's "X" movements are in your dance as well. In a way, *you need that person's particular energies for your whole dance.* There is never a conflict from the viewpoint of the deepest level.

As one participant exclaimed, "I just got it! Every time we can't step in and take the other side, we are turning against ourselves, we are closing down a part of ourselves, closing down a part of our hearts. . . . Turning only against this person, you cut off that part of yourself and shutting your heart down." Another participant commented, "I have always heard that it is 'you' out there, yet it is not so easy to see the other as yourself."

This idea of meeting yourself is both simple to understand and very difficult in practice. I also feel that I am just getting it. Hating someone eventually becomes disliking yourself! Yet, it is not always easy to love the other, especially if the other has hurt you.

So, you have to start where you are. First take a stand against the other and protect yourself. Wake up the other side if you can. Then share her or his state of mind. If the other person is one-sided and rank unconscious, consider how you might be one-sided, thinking you are better than others.

When I was a child and people wanted to kill me because I was in the wrong religion, I said, "I don't know anything about religion, I never heard about it! Who is god anyhow? I do not know about god!" Then they said, "Your god is bad!"

In order to create a sacred, creative space, I have to commune and find out how I might need those guys, and how/where they are in me. They forced me to learn to protect myself and to take a stand. They had a power that I was not yet aware of in myself. But I developed power and eventually fought back. Today I love those people. Today I understand and can feel into them. They were also poor. They wanted a free and open world that would not hinder them, and were told that I was part of a system that was in their way. I came from a financially poor scene as well, so I totally understand their fear and resulting aggression.

Everyone has had abusive experiences in their life. People hurt you in an unconscious way. Just being rejected by a parent or pushed out can be abusive. Most of us carry such events in our personal history. Over time, we need to pick up their energy to protect ourselves in phase 2, and also to commune in phase 3 and phase 4 to understand our abusers as part of ourselves.

You may be wondering, if peace is not sustainable, does that mean that we are condemned to suffer through wars? As one participant remarked,

> *Since I was a young child, I have thought that war was a choice that human beings make. The first evidence of mass graves that showed evidence of human-against-human violence was 14,000 years ago. Before that there was evidence of small violence but not large group violence. And, so I thought that my life purpose is to be one of those people who help end war as we know it. But as you say, we need to get educated. With the process and phase concepts you just described, life is a flow*

cycle, including conflict, reconciliation, peace. But do we need to be physically killing each other? I don't think so.

I agree. We don't need to do as much killing as we are doing now. I can see the meaning of taking a stand and protecting yourself. I see the meaning of some violence, but 99.99% of it can be avoided. We do need to say "stop!" But then we cannot stop there: We need to "commune." It is the practice of relating that is sustainable.

Another participant shared an unusual example of maintaining relationship while taking action. In a story from a teacher in Thailand, the police arrested some people and before they took them to prison, they took them to dinner together. This is commune-ication-based policing, a phase 3 and phase 4 way of relating to the apparent "criminals" and not just treating them as "other."

Exercise: Communing Inner Work

You can explore the practice of communing with the following inner-work exercise. In this exercise, the point is to experience space as a palpable substance—something with power, perhaps like a lake or the sea, something surrounding you that can move you. If you cannot stand easily, you can do this on your chair. You can have very powerful experiences even in sitting. Just allow yourself to be moved in your chair.

Second Training Relationship Inner Work: Be Real, Dream, and Commune

A. Feel, move, and show your normal "u" energy with your hands. Make a little sketch of it and name it. Choose a difficult relationship and act out the strongest negative "X" energy or feedback from that person. Express this energy with your hands. Give it a name and sketch it on your paper.

B. Do 721: That is, stand (if possible) and create a 360 CR open forum where u + X speak about their viewpoints and dialogue.
   - Now 360 in DREAMLAND: Still standing, switch roles. That is, go back and forth between the "u" and "X" sides, *feeling deeply into and speaking* for each side. Notice and express any double signals that arise, quick flirts that catch your attention, or any other figures that you imagine are present. Then when you are ready, go deeper.
   - Now "1," the ESSENCE LEVEL: Still standing, carefully let your mind drift toward emptiness and sleepiness, and in a pre-dream state, notice how your body begins to move. *Carefully let go even more as you begin to sense and feel the sacred, creative space around you,* whatever that means to you, and *let the space begin to move and dance you about spontaneously.* That is, let IT move YOU. Be careful of yourself and others!

C. While moving, sense the "*mmmm*" and commune with the awesomeness of that "sacred" dance. Focus on the feeling, movement, breath, sounds, and imagery of that sacred space process and let that dance space name itself.

D. Continue dancing and note how u + X energies may be parts of that dance experience. Express or emphasize the u + X a bit more while moving. As you continue to dance and commune, melt into that creative, sacred space until it brings you a tip about dealing with that relationship problem.

E. Finally, still feeling and being moved by that *sacred space,* imagine living it more in reality and with that "X" person by sensing her or him as a part of you, whether that "X" is a personal, business, or world situation. Write down insights and the name of your dance-space experience. Make a little sketch of that sacred dance space and share it with someone near you.

Demonstration: Communing (Arny, with Amy facilitating)

Amy: Let's work with you, Arny, to model this. What would you say is your normal "u" energy?

Arny: It changes, of course, but today it is sort of rolling along like that (shows wave-like pattern with hands and sketches it on the board) . . . *rolling along, rolling water* (draws waves).

Amy: And do you have a difficult relationship, hopefully not with me! It could be me, but any difficult relationship that is bothering you?

Arny: I get a lot of communication from different people and places in the world, and frequently people say, "Help me!" Sometimes I think I am too present on the internet and Facebook. That would not be so bad, but what is hard for me is dealing with people's needs and pain. They often say, "Help me!" or "My organization is in the middle of a disaster!" Government people expect you to answer immediately, as in, "We need your help right now—we need it today."

I know how to say, "No, I don't have time," and all of that, but often their pain remains with me. I can say, "No," but it is not always satisfactory for me.

Amy: Is there a particular relationship or do you want to focus more generally?

Arny: Yes, I cannot say the details, but remind you about that "somebody" who said last night, "I need your help, and I need it right now. We need your help! Please help us in the next couple of days!"

Amy: What is the most disturbing "X" energy for you in that person?

Arny: (Makes a grasping movement with hand) *This energy says "Help me!" and tries to grab me. I understand they are desperate, but still. "Help me!" pulls on my heart strings. The "X" is a pushy, punch-like energy.*

Amy: Can you make a little sketch of that "X" energy and give it a name?

Arny: (Draws sharp-edged squiggle and writes "Pushy.")

Amy: So now let's explore the 721 open forum. In 360 consensus reality, maybe you can just speak for one side of this conflict and then speak for the other side. Let their viewpoints come out and hold a dialogue.

Arny: (Taking the "u" side) I don't have the time!

"X": You have to do something! You can do it! I have read one of your books! Please! Please! Help!

Arny: I would like to, I hear that particular problem, but I can't do it, not right now, I am in a seminar.

Amy: Now let's go into 360 dreamland, and switch sides and deepen them. Feel behind them. Also, see if you notice any double signals in yourself or the other.

Arny: On my side there is a double signal that I did not yet bring in, a kind of desperateness. I notice my hand double signal implying, "I can't. I need help!" This is something I've never said. "I NEED HELP!"

"X": So now I, Arny, will go on their side, and will come back to mine and try to commune: "You have gotta help us! Now! Please! We know others who've worked with you and they told us you could help!"

Arny: I will try to "commune." Let me feel into them and speak for them. (Now, as the "X") "Do it! Do it for God's sake. . . . " Oh! I got it! If I commune and feel deeply into them, I can recognize the desperate feeling of needing something from someone! I know exactly what that is like. I have not felt that way for many years, but when I was younger I could feel that desperate sense.

"X": (Arny, switching roles to be "X") *Help us, please, it is agonizing! We look pushy, but you are not understanding where we are coming from. You don't know!!!*

Arny: That touches me—because I do know that desperate feeling. I am feeling it now. . . . I sense the desperate situation your group is in. There are people who want to kill. . . .

I can commune with them and say to "X," "You remind me of myself and groups I have helped, where I could do something, but though I want to, in the moment, I just don't have the time just now."

Amy: Now to the essence level: Find this pre-dream state, where your mind is empty; let go a bit more to sense and feel the sacred, creative spaces around you. Notice how you move and commune with nature and space. Let the dance name itself.

Arny: It is the ocean splashing on the rocks. The "u" energy is rolling along, and the "X" splashes out. . . . My dance gives me a tip: "I know where you, dear person in need, are. I feel what you feel, I have been there myself and with others. I know about that, and I know you are capable of caring for yourself!! Don't put yourselves down, you can do it! Your dreams know the way. You have what is needed, not just I!" I realize that they, the "X," look at me as the teacher, and they do not see their own inner teacher and power in themselves. I will press them to believe in themselves and not put themselves down.

Nonlocality and Dream Ships

The point is, we are both real and mythical beings as individuals and as relationships. Relationships are relation or "*dream ships*." The background stories and first relationship experiences and dreams imply that relationships are "carried" and organized in part by those dreams, those "dream ships." You experience this if you "commune" with the other person. When you start to commune, you enter the nonlocal quantum level. There we dream together; every relationship is a dream trying to become conscious.

In communing, we are exploring that dream ship. Whenever possible, share your dreaming and communing publicly. Do 721 in front of the "X." Have your so-called internal dialogue out in front of the other person while he or she is observing you.

Communing, feeling into the other, is a key to working with all people. It is something I learned years ago about working with extreme states of consciousness. An *extreme state* refers to conditions that are usually considered ill by the medical community. If you can pick up the nature of the other person, however you describe that nature, and if you can act some of it out, go back and forth between your view, and your experience of the other, you can then ask the real person for feedback. Doing such role play can have an incredibly helpful effect on everyone involved.

Do it in relationship; do it for someone you like who feels stuck or with anyone. I strongly suggest doing this work in front of the real person, or with a friend who can imagine being that "real problem" person, and as that person, give you feedback. Dear reader, if there is no one near you to practice with in the moment, you can skip to the discussion after the following exercise.

You can use this exercise for working on conflicts in relationship as well as intimacy and sexuality issues.

Exercise: Communing in Relationship

Second Training: Commune as a Realist and a Dreamer in Relationship (Dyads)

A. Dreamer, choose a most difficult relationship on which to work. This can be the same person as you used in the earlier exercise, or another person. *(No need to mention names, if you don't want to.)* Describe the situation to your partner. Remember being with that difficult person and act out the strongest negative "X" energy (coming from you *or* the other person) with your hands and body. (*Dyad Partner, please take note of the "X" energy so you can play it later on.)* Dreamer, draw and name this "X" energy in some way on your paper. What's your typical "u" energy like? Act it out with your hands and body. Sketch and name that "u" on your paper as well.

B. Now do 721 as inner work led by your Dyad Partner.

- *CR 360*: Dreamer, stand (if you can) and create a CR 360 forum for u + X to communicate. That is, let each side state their position and dialogue a bit.
- *Dreamland 360*: Still standing, Dreamer, create a forum for u + X where you switch roles. That is, go back and forth, feeling and speaking deeply for each side. Bring in and represent any ghost roles that are mentioned, double signals in you or that you imagine in the other, flirts arising spontaneously, or dream figures you sense "in the air." *When you feel it's enough, go deeper. . . .*
- *Essence 1*: Still standing, Dreamer, let your mind drift toward an empty and sleepy place, that is, in a pre-dream-like state, and notice how your body begins to move. Carefully, let go a bit more as you begin to sense and feel the sacred, creative space around you, and let it begin to move and dance you about spontaneously. Continue moving until your motions become repetitive or the meaning of them becomes clear. Be careful of yourself and others! Sense the *"mmmm," that is, the* awesomeness of your sacred dance as you *commune with nature's space* and let the dance-space name itself.

  Continue dancing and note how the u + X energies may be parts of that dance experience; express them more strongly in movement. As you continue to dance and commune, wait until your dance brings you a tip about dealing with that relationship. Make a note.

  Now, feel that dance again and note the feeling, the movement, breath, sounds, imagery you are using to live that sacred space and *imagine using it to commune with "X."* Make notes about insights, write down the name of the dance-space experience, and make a drawing of it.

C. *(Read all of this first.)* Dyad Partner, remember the difficult behavior of "X" and play out the difficult "X" person. Then watch the Dreamer doing 721 in front of you. That is, Dreamer, do CR 360 feedback between the "u" and "X." Next do Dreamland 360 by switching and deepening roles. *Then express* the essence 1 sacred space by moving and communing, at first subtly, then in relationship to your Dyad Partner playing "X." Finally, Dyad Partner, notice and speak about any EFFECT this whole process had on you as the "X." Dreamer, note what you learned.

D. Dyad Partner, please give honest feedback about how the dreamer's work affected you. The best feedback means reporting that certain things moved you and some didn't.

The sacred, creative space created by communing could transform our individual, relationship, and world problems. The world suffers terribly from racism, sexism, homophobia, and all the anti-religious "-isms." But the most central "-ism" of all, I call *phase-ism*. We get stuck on phases 1 and 2—"*I am me! You are you!*" So, commune, bring in phase 3, and remember, "*I am a little like you.*" Being phase-ist and ignoring the dreamland and the essence levels is a world problem that we *can* reverse.

Things to Remember from Chapter 24

1. To facilitate for yourself and others in the best possible way, commune deeply with "X" while doing 721 open forums. Feel deeply into phases 3 and 4, sometimes experiencing "X" as yourself and sometimes as a sacred and shared space.
2. Communing is a key to personal psychology and relationship problems. Commune with others and, when possible, act out 721 for the benefit of all.
3. Often the people we like the least are in our dreams. Why? Perhaps to remind us of our incredible diversity and potential for unity.

CHAPTER 25

World Conflict and Quantum Nonlocality

• • •

In this chapter, I continue to stress the idea of communing with the "other" to access a sacred, creative space and get to know yourself as well as the other. I return to the idea of nonlocality that I introduced in Chapter 5 and have been exploring throughout the book, and describe the implications for personal interactions, group life, and our relationship to death.

I share an exercise that prepares you for facilitating conflict in groups by helping you connect to the sacred, creative space so you can commune with all sides while you facilitate. Finally, I demonstrate the practice with an example of an open forum that occurred in one of our seminars.

But first, let me share Amy's experience of using 721 feedback on a situation in ordinary life.

Example: Using 721 in a Business Deal

> *Amy: To make it really short, something happened with my computer. I was upset and decided to call the computer people, the "support-tech." "You can't get through," I heard. Finally they let me "chat" in a "chat" session. I heard, "You are the 109th person in line. We will be with you shortly, don't worry." So I got really worried, and my disturbance was escalating. Finally*

a message appeared, "Can I help you? What is your problem?" So I had to write it all again. "I need your help . . . ." It turned out that my computer needed a part. The chat person said, "My organizational rules state that the part will take six months to get." So I was sitting there chatting, and my blood pressure was going up, and I thought to myself, "Oh, we are studying 721—I will try 721!"

CR: I decided to go into consensus reality and do 721 online with him. I took my side, "You guys are driving me nuts!" His side said, "Sorry, but I have to follow the rules." Then I decided to go into dreamland, thinking, "Why not try taking his side?"

Dreamland: I communed and said, "You know, you must have so much pressure, and it must be hard dealing with people like me all day. And of course you need to follow rules or your company won't function. You are trying to support your company and that is important." Then I took my side, "I am pulling my hair out, I am going crazy"—and I went back and forth between sides in dreamland—and then . . .

He said, "Yes, Ma'am, I am also a customer when I get off work, and I know exactly how you feel right now."

Amy: I was so happy, I did not care about my computer any more. I thanked him and it was just a beautiful moment, we both felt so heard. Since I still did not get the computer part, and since he could not see me visually, I went to the essence level and experienced a wild sacred space dance in our office while he waited for me. Then my dance relaxed and I was able to open up to him and say, "I know you will follow what is right for you and that is going to be OK for me too."

And he thanked me, and I could tell he was really relieved, and I was very happy. I felt in that moment that I had improved this relationship and had changed the world a tiny bit. My missing computer part came earlier than expected, but that did not make me as happy as the relationship scene!

Arny: Thanks, Amy, for modeling how you can "commune" in business. You did that crazy dance during an internet conflict! We all need to do the same!

Amy: Yes, our dance comes from a sense of creative space. Van Gogh's painting of Starry Night *(Wikipedia) shows how space is creative and can move us. I think it is amazing how Van Gogh could depict this swirling aliveness of space.*

30.* Van Gogh's *Starry Night.

Arny: What looks like a thing or a person to begin with are spaces filled with powers and roles.

In conflict, focusing only on the people can miss the fact that we are all roles in the midst of the spaces in which we live. So remember, in phase 3 dreamland, don't just switch roles but feel really deeply into this side, even more deeply than is reasonable. The results may surprise you.

You might recall, from Chapter 24, the inner work I shared about people asking a lot of me on Facebook. It was such a surprise but the very next day after that work, and the first time in my whole life, after I went home and opened my email, six different people had joined together in one email thanking me for stuff I have done for them via Facebook and email!! Nonlocal connections. The people who wrote said specifically, "We don't understand how you answer people so fast when they ask you for something! How do you do that?!" Can you believe that?

Nonlocality!! What amazed me out was not just the fact they were thankful, but how the they knew to write the day after my inner work! They sent their emails about the same time that I was working on that problem. SPACE IS FULL OF POWER. The Tao is nonlocal and touches all who are connected with you. In other words, your Tao is also the Tao that is needed not just for you, but for all. One of our participants commented,

> *It astounds me how prolific you are with books you publish, the seminars you put on, the classes you do, it blows my mind! Are you going to tell us your secret?*

My secret is that *you have the secret.* My secret is to admit that the wisdom is inside of you!

Communing, Nonlocality, and Synchronicity

This idea of communing is based on the sense of nonlocality: that is, being next to and inside the other. As you may know, quantum nonlocality in physics is the apparent ability of one photon, when measured, to instantly determine the up or down state of its "twin" regardless of the distance between them. I know physics can be intimidating to some, but I like to bring in science because psychology marginalizes science—just like physics marginalizes psychology—and yet the two fields are trying to come together.

How does nonlocality work? As I mentioned in Chapter 5, Einstein thought nonlocality was "spooky action at a distance." Jung talked about such interconnections in terms of synchronicity, that is, "acausal" connection through similar meaning. Physics does not have an explanation; it simply formulates nonlocality as a fact for particles in the same system. In psychology, we can say that as you change, others with whom you are emotionally connected, even at a distance, may also change as well.

David Bohm was one of my favorite physicists; he died while I was studying. He suggested that a tiny elementary particle is guided by its quantum waves.[49] When I transfer that notion to human beings, it means that we don't know what we are doing when we are being moved by these universal experiences, call them physics or spirituality or shamanism. We don't know what moves us, but we can feel it, and it has practical, everyday consequences. For me, nonlocality is the sense of how space moves me.

Nonlocality is a social issue. We need to re-think, "What is reality?" Reality is measurable, but "reality" requires not only imaginary quantum waves to understand it, but dreamlike Aboriginal traditions as well. Our consensus reality concepts can be marginalizing and very racist. In consensus reality, parts can be measured and separated, "I am me and you are you." But in dreamland, "*You are a part of me*, even though I marginalize you outside and inside."

Two of our participants shared the following comments about their experience of nonlocality.

> *L: If I go deeper into phases 3 and 4, I can sometimes feel, "I am me and I am you," I am not just one person. You are not a locus; you are not one thing in one spot. You are loci—loci means several places at once. That is in dreamland.*
>
> *In reality, I am here and you are there, but another aspect of reality that is supported by quantum thinking is, "I am in several places at the same time." So when I work with myself, when I feel and work with my body, I don't forget this deeper level of nonlocality that spiritual traditions have always spoken about.*
>
> *T: I studied for several years with a shaman, and in his tradition people would speak telepathically. When new people appeared in their village, the village people would say, "Oh, yes, we knew you were coming even though we have no telephone." We were taught that all of us are one.*

Total reality exists in parts, as measurable Western consensus reality, and it also exists in quantum and dreamland thinking as you/me, and at the essence level, as IT. Don't be surprised if you can connect at a distance in these other levels of reality.

However, nonlocality does not mean that I can work on myself to change people at a distance. What I am saying is different. Conscious hopeful thinking is "causal" thinking. Consciously organizing telepathy has not been proven. Trying to influence things with your everyday mind for better or worse is doubtful. But I will leave that topic open for the future to explore. Rather, nonlocality is a phase 4, deepest art experience. It is why we can experience a sacred, creative space through commune-ication.

For certain, if you go deeply enough into yourself and what looks like a polarized state, you find that, from a deeper level, *you and the other person represent different movements in one dance.* You and the other are BOTH needed for that dance. You and I are like two sounds of one musical. *I am, because you are,* as the South African Ubuntu people say, and as I have said in Chapter 17.[50]

In group process, what this boils down to is this: *As a facilitator, if you share what your groups might be experiencing, your work will go more easily.* Practice this and find out for yourself. There are many different diversity issues. As an activist, fight. As a facilitator, fight in CR *and* feel into the different parts of an organization or group. There is a non-polarized dance to be found. I am me, and I am us.

A Question about Communing with an Abuser and Death

> *E: I am not quite sure I can find the words for my question, but if I am a person from a very obviously oppressed group, it may be more challenging for me to dream into the ground of someone in a group that is oppressive to me and my people. I could die before the other side wakes up. So, do I need to learn to do this?*

As I have mentioned previously, this is one of the most challenging aspects of commune-ication. Phase awareness helps. It is almost impossible to dream into a group that has hurt you with their unconsciousness of rank and power. As always, the first step is simply to shout, "Dammit! Wake up!" That is phase 2, and that is very important.

After protecting yourself as much as possible, if you still feel that you could die before the oppressive side wakes up, which is something many of us who have felt marginalized for one reason or another have felt, "I could die" might be an indication of letting go and dropping out of consensus reality into other dimensions. As a participant explained, this does not mean dying, psychologically or physically, but, "dying out of my identity." My advice is: Every time you think of dying, please do—not physically—but let go and drop into the deepest part of yourself.

This identity of "death" happens on both sides, as the participant explained: "I also know that, when you are part of a mainstream group, it is also sometimes difficult to wake up to a rank you did nothing to earn but must somehow be responsible for in the role. Thank you for making dying really attractive."

Dying might be terrible for those around the dying person, but symbolically speaking, it is one of the "best" things that can happen to us as facilitators. If you ever think about dying—and everybody does at one time or another—let go.

The point I am making with your deepest art and the second training is that facilitation needs to be an everyday lifestyle and spiritual practice. In the first training, role switching is a method. The second training is about communing, going so deeply into the other side that you understand them better than they understand themselves. It is about the capacity to access a sacred, creative space where you feel: Yes, "I am me and I am not the other person," *and . . .* YES! *"I am the other."*

Some of our seminar participants shared the following reflections.

G: I remember seeing you do that, Arny, in a workshop on LGBT issues. There was a minister being extremely brutal, and you connected to him where he was put down as a child—then he transformed. Is that what you are talking about? Feeling it on the inside, relating it to your own life experience?

Q: I started studying "shapeshifting" with Stanislavski, the great Russian director on Method Acting. The teaching is about really going into a character as an actor prepares for a role, from within your body. The book An Actor Prepares *has been very helpful in my private practice for shapeshifting.*

R: I wanted to put this into the context of the development of processwork and about feeling into the role of the mean, brutal guy. It is a metaskill that you have had, that Amy has studied and written her metaskill book on, and it is the deepening of that. That has always been one of the magical parts of processwork . . . and I feel like you are teaching us how we can develop that now as a conscious skill.

Thanks. Let me illustrate with an example from our life in Portland. Amy and I were in a local park, Washington Park, and there were young men skateboarding down the stairs. Then the police arrived and a cop got out of his car and said, "Get the hell out of here." He was really angry at the young people. He was the "security" for the park. Tension started to escalate. As we came closer, we saw a diverse group of young people, and the cop was a white older man. So we came in and facilitated for the young people. We spoke for the police while supporting the young people, by communing with both sides: "We understand you are trying to take care of the park and are frustrated. It must be a horrible job; you are constantly pulling your hair out. These young people want the best for the park and city as well." The young men were quiet. The whole thing relaxed.

The cops had their guns and weapons right there, but they got back in their car and drove away after we said, "We thank you very much for trying to keep the world in order." By communing, we were able to make them feel proud of themselves and then they could be more open to others.

The sacred, creative space I am describing is a source of nourishment. You can see this in a quote from Lao Tse about the essence level. He said[51]:

Others have more than they need, I alone have nothing. I am a fool, oh yes, I am confused. Other people are clear and bright but I alone am dim and weak. Other people are sharp and clever, but I alone am dull and stupid. I drift like the waves of the sea, without direction, like the restless wind.

He goes on to say, "Everyone else is busy. But I alone am aimless and depressed. I am different. I am nourished by the great mother."

Lao Tse reminds us that his nourishment comes from the great mother, the universe, from the waves. He is moved like the sea. Perhaps he knows the "1" from 721, where 360 is in reality, 360 in dreamland, and the 1 is the essence level. Perhaps Lao Tse was the first quantum physicist and realized that his psychology and the whole world are organized by the "the waves of the sea."

The next exercise prepares you for facilitating conflict in groups by giving you more access to that nourishment. It will help you to connect to the sacred, creative space so you can commune with all sides while you facilitate. Following the exercise, I illustrate the practice by sharing an example of an open forum from one of our seminars.

Exercise: World Process Inner-Work Commune-ication Dance for You + All

This second training inner-work exercise allows you to apply this sacred, creative space experience and 721 feedback to an organization or group or to a national or international issue on which you would like to focus. It is intended to be done before participating or facilitating a group process. However, you can practice it at any time to gain insights into the issue.

In this inner work, try identifying your experiences with a spot on earth. Why? One of the reasons is that many people around the world have always identified themselves as coming to birth from a particular spot, not just from parents, but from a particular spot or piece of earth that has given birth to them. My view is that you are a piece of nature, a piece of the earth and universe.

A. Think of a group, organizational problem, or national or international problem on which you'd like to focus. Imagine the issue and the person, subgroup, or group you dislike most in that issue and their most difficult "X" energy. Stand, if you can, and feel that energy and act it out with your hands and body. Name and sketch this "X" on your paper. Now, feel and act out your normal "u" energy. Sketch and name the "u" on your paper.

B. Use your second training and do 721 with devotion to phase 4.
   - *360 CR*: Imagine both the u + X sides of the issue in a forum. That is, stand (if you can) and speak for one side, then the other, and next let them dialogue for a moment.
   - *360 Dreamland*: Still standing, switch roles by moving to one side and speaking for it, and then the other. Intensify each role even more deeply than you might normally and bring in any ghost roles mentioned, double signals, or any other dream figures that you imagine in the field. *Try to "commune," that is, try to connect to the spirit and ideas of those manifesting that "X" energy.* Then, when you feel it's enough or you're ready to go even deeper, go to the essence level.
   - *1 Essence*: Still standing, let your mind drift toward empty and sleepy, that is, in a pre-dream state, and notice how your body begins to move. Carefully, let go a bit more as you begin to sense and feel the sacred, creative space around you, and let it begin to dance you about spontaneously as you commune with nature. That is, feel and let nature move YOU. Be careful of yourself and others! As you move and dream with the space around you, let sounds emerge from that dreaming space-dance. Be careful of yourself and others, and imagine what aspect of nature moves and sounds like your dance. That is, what part of nature are you that is dancing in this way?

C. As you continue to dance—as you continue to dream, move, breathe, feel, and commune—*notice how the u + X "belong" and connect in the dance experience. Now, bring the u + X out strongly as you continue to move.* Then let that dance give you a tip to help resolve the u + X CR tensions. Notice quick, flickering insights, images, and/or feelings that may arise to facilitate the situation. Make notes about your insights. Also, write down the name of the piece of nature you were dancing and draw it in some way.

In the final part of this chapter, I share an example of a large group open forum on a social issue chosen by the group. The participants completed the preceding inner work, and then we asked them to try and remember their insights and to use this deep aspect of themselves during the group process.

Open Forum Example

WORLDWORK update. For learning purposes we asked the group to try the following group process:

Whole Group Assembles for a 721 Process. Reader/Facilitator, read all of this before beginning.

- Each recall (and try to use) your 721 commune-ication insights.

Facilitator, share your 721 experience and guide the group:

- *360 CR*: Set up roles and let them dialogue.
- *360 Dreamland*: Deepen the role play and explore role switching. Notice and bring in any ghost roles mentioned. Slow down at hot (very intense moments) and cool spots (moments of relaxation).
- *1 Essence*: Facilitator, if needed, stop to *recall and use your dance (and in this practice session), tell others to do so too*, to deepen the process. Continue until solutions emerge and/or the time is up.

  Discussion: Finally *(after 10 minutes)*, all discuss if and how the 721 and communing processes were used and how they helped.

The open forum commenced with participants sharing issues on which they wanted to work.

A: I want to work on what is happening with police violence towards African American men, in particular, but also all African American people, and how I can work on that is by working on my and our unconsciousness as white people, exploring the way we can come to the table as allies.

D: I am thinking about exclusion, working on Donald Trump-ism—where Trump is against everybody, and it sounds like racism, but it is Trump-ism.

T: I want to work on what I call the Muslim dilemma: *Muslims living in community and having to deal with ISIS or "Daesh." I really hate the mullahs (a Muslim man or sometimes a woman) educated in Islamic theology and sacred law); these are the people today who are driving the dogmatic aspect in Islam.*

B: I want to work on hate groups, all the groups identified by the Southern Poverty Law Center. The KKK, the Nazi groups. All of them.

J: Global Warming: How we work with people, how we motivate them to deal with this issue constructively. How to work with people around this issue.

P: The refugee issue in Portland itself.

At first the group worked with the Trump issues, then on problems in the Islamic community. Here, I give a brief description of the work on the Muslim community, as it is less familiar to the general public.

Worldwork on the "Muslim Dilemma"

T: Within the Muslim community, especially in the U.S., there are a lot of people who feel . . . that the movement called, "Not in My Name" is a fundamentalist sickness in the Muslim community. The rest of us Muslims don't want to associate with them. Yet at the same time we also feel responsible for it. How do we handle this fundamentalist problem that is starting to take over in the U.S. and Europe, making devastating changes in the Muslim community?

It is beyond Isis. The fundamentalist Islamic world movement is pushing towards Sharia law, the law of Islam that dogmatically pushes people, especially women, down. Muslim communities in Europe and America are feeling as if they are dying. Recently, because of the refugee crisis in Syria, the fundamentalists killed 300 children for going to school in Pakistan—all of this happening because of fundamentalism. It is very hard to be Muslim right now.

Arny: It is agonizing.

T: I really wanted to step in, but it is very hard for me to step into the role of the mullahs, that is, the fundamentalist teachers and what they are doing right now to our communities. I want to understand it. How do I communicate with those people so they can listen?

Arny: Yes, let's work on the fundamentalists.

Amy leads the whole group through inner work, after which the following 721 process occurred.

"X" (the fundamentalists): *We want to stop the Western energy!*

"u" (U.S. Muslims): *We just want to be Muslim and lead our lives in the world.*

"X": You are corrupted already by the West! You are no longer civilized. Follow the Koran and its important details. You are becoming Westernized, losing the essence of Islam. We fear the destruction of our people . . . so we must kill you. Otherwise, all that we have will be destroyed—everything we believe in will be destroyed—we can no longer see God. If this goes on, we must kill you.

"u" (T, now playing the Western Muslims): *We are being killed, we are dying.* (People playing the Western Muslims fall, as their leaders weep for the dead.)

Arny: Here is an edge and hot spot: Dying and going deeper. (With encouragement, the group acting out the Western Muslim side "died" in the sense of going into the state of "letting go" to explore being killed, or "dead.")

"u" (the dead Muslims): *Now we can connect with the spirit and energy of the universe, Allah, who can help to cure the madness on the fundamentalist side. We, the "dead," say that we are feeling moved by the universe, and COME BACK TO CARE FOR THE EXTREMISTS. (The dead now move towards the "X" (*the fundamentalists) *and, communing, bless the fundamentalists, saying) We give you our apology, and did not realize we had become Western in the sense of having forgotten our essence and connections to the infinite.*

"X" (being blessed by the "dead"): *Now we can feel again . . . your dance of the dead is what we needed and were missing.*

T (as the dead wave their hands over the fundamentalists): *This waving is what my grandmother used to do to heal me.*

"X": Yes, when we see that waving, we too feel loved, like children again.

The various parts of the group all came together as everyone was touched. The resolution to this process occurred as those playing the Western "dead" Muslims picked up the spirit (and ghost role) of Allah that was moving them. The "dead" were moved by the universe (a kind of processmind experience) that helped everyone in the group recall the missing Muslim foundation of spirituality: Allah. People realized that identifying as a normal everyday (Western) person dreams up fundamentalist reactions because the God connection was lost. There were many tears as people came together.

This open forum was an amazing and dramatic process. The key was getting closer to Allah, a ghost role. To do that the Western Muslim role had to die (out of the present identity)—that is, to detach from consensus reality. Why? Otherwise, the everyday mind over-adapts to the consensus reality of today's world too much. At some point many of us have the feeling, "Oh, by acting like a realistic everyday 'normal' person, I am losing something!" So, this aspect of the Muslim community conflict is, in some ways, a universal issue, a world issue.

Afterwards, we asked the facilitator, who identifies as Muslim, "How was it for you trying to facilitate when you were so emotionally involved?"

T: It was really hard. I think I noticed at one point that I stopped facilitating, and then Arny stepped in, and I remembered to commune and get a little more of that detached meta-position. Arny, you said, "Go in deeper," and that made me realize that I wanted to see what would happen if we went into the experience of death.

Our world dreams up fundamentalism, perhaps in part, because most of us get cut off from our deepest selves.

After the large group experience, participants in our seminar formed into smaller groups to experiment with the communing inner work and facilitation practice. Afterwards they shared the following learnings.

R: In our process, it was so easy to get involved in the back and forth of the polarity and to sort of lose our awareness and to forget to go down to the communing. . . . You helped us detach from the polarity and remember.

Arny: Aha, practice! Communing could happen once you found the missing elder, she who can hold the pot and commune with all.

R: It is so radical to hold the pot, to feel into and love everybody.

Arny: Yes, in a way, it is a dying of the CR identity; it is a second training issue to value all the people, roles, and phases.

E: I felt my learning was to stop everybody for moments to explore the "cool spots," and then to go further into the hesitation for a moment, and then wisdom appeared! And from this point, there was the learning.

M: Yes, I want to say cool spots were a huge learning for me because in the pause, there is a moment of peace. The cool spot was a very wonderful teaching for me, and I felt it helped the group.

Things to Remember from Chapter 25

1. Remember deep democracy's phases: phase 1, relax and forget problems; phase 2, fight for your view, protect yourself, try to educate the other side; phase 3, switch roles and commune; phase 4, drop out, find detachment or get depressed, sense death, and find phase 4 to help CR.
2. Communing is a second training practice, sensing "X" in phases 3 and 4. Communing can appear in quantum physics *as nonlocality.*
3. If you are in a conflict with somebody or with a group or organization, first take a stand. Then recall your second training and feel deeply to commune and know "X" as yourself.

CHAPTER 26

Buddha in Conflict Scenes

• • •

COMMUNING FOR CONFLICT AND PEACE is a challenging practice but very practical and accessible when using the exercises and techniques of 721 and your deepest art. To conclude learning from previous chapters, we can say that to "*commune*" means to *commune*-icate, to sense your own and the other's buzz or "*mmmm.*" *Commune* means being in touch with nature and the "*–icate*" means using that while being in everyday reality with others. The word *commune* is the essence of the term *community* and means "coming together."

Commune-ication is a central skill and metaskill in the second training. The best time and place to learn the second training is when you don't like someone. So, fight in phase 2. From a phase 3 and phase 4 view, *you can only meet yourself on the road.* You may need this viewpoint if you do a lot of conflict work, and if you must work with killing and awful things. If you work with groups and organizations that want to kill one another then—"commune-icating" to know their energy in yourself can help.

The most amazing, impossible, and helpful aspect of the second training is to be able to look at the other person and know that, *"I am looking at me, at an aspect of myself."* Then, you will be able to commune with them so they can understand and feel this shared understanding. Separating from them is important, but it is only a phase.

With this practice you may find that the *essence of whatever is bothering you is also connected with nonlocal historical world issues.* The people and issues that bother you are a personal problem, but they may also be the *world communing with you*, and an inspiration for you to help the world.

I have previously shared questions from seminar participants about the difficulty of communing with another person or group that has been hurtful, oppressive, or abusive. This is perhaps the biggest second training challenge.

I remember an example of working with a conflict in Germany between the liberal left wing and the neo-Nazis who did not want refugees in the country. It was difficult for me to commune with the neo-Nazis, because many of my family were killed by them during the World War II. Still, I tried.

I felt into them and realized . . . everyone, most of the time, wants their home for themselves. "Keep the foreigners out; all those religions, colors, and sexual orientations are foreign to us." I am not like that, but I do appreciate not having too many extra people trying to live in my bedroom with Amy and me. That feeling helped me commune. I won't go into further detail here. My point is that just communing, only a little (hard as this was), enabled conversation, and the potential for better communication and a better possible future for at least some of the "foreigners."

For the normal part of you to get in touch with that part of yourself that could be violent is horrible. But occasionally you can do it; there is a little part of you that can do that, even if normally you are not violent or hateful. As someone commented,

> *Yes, if we can accept that fact that every one of has those outer parts in ourselves, if we have all possibilities within us . . . then we won't be so surprised first of all when trouble comes up.*

Remember Ubuntu!

Communing reminds me of Nelson Mandela, whom I speak about more in the next few chapters. Recall the South African Zulu tradition of Ubuntu—"I am, because you are"—which I am now using as if we are all part of a one-world community. I am moving with that ancient Aboriginal communing concept in part by saying, "I am here, in part, perhaps because of the world issues, and I am—in fact, we all are—because of one another."

I am encouraging you to appreciate the consensus reality idea that says *we are separate*, and *also* the second training concept of communing. Remember the example in Chapter 23 of someone who worked deeply on the loud sounds in her ears. She was normally very quiet, and yet the "sounds" spoke to her about social and historical issues that were usually not spoken about much in her part of the world. She then connected locally and nonlocally to others, in class and online around the world, on that issue.

My point is that the *essence of whatever is bothering you may be connected with nonlocal historical world issues.* What is bothering you is a personal problem, but may also be *the world communing with you*, and an inspiration for you to help the world.

Phase and level consciousness creates the most sustainable relationships. First say, "Stop!" Then recall phase 1 and just forget the problem. Then in phase 2, fight. Eventually phase 3 will remind you to "feel into the other side." Phase 4 will help you detach all together and see what the universe suggests.

To learn all this, trust your body. It, or you, are the best teacher of this work. 721 communing is a form of meditation and reminds me of something the Vietnamese Zen teacher, Thich Nhat Hanh, said in his book, *The Sun, My Heart*[52]:

> *Prince Siddhartha retired to the forest to sit beside a stream for many years before returning to the world of people.*

***31.* Buddha in the Forest.**

Today we can say, commune with nature and bring its wisdom and movements back to our world. Be Buddha in the forest, and bring a bit of Buddha into conflict scenes.

Now you can explore this for yourself with the following inner-work exercise.

Exercise: In Tension? Commune with Nature

1. What are your present roles in the world (e.g., being at home as a family person, meditating, helping others, conducting a business, working in psychology, participating in helping groups, working in organizations or governments, participating in social action work)?
2. Stand (if you can), relax, and temporarily vacate yourself of the roles you were just talking about and commune with the universe. That is, see if you can have an empty and pre-dream sleepy mind. Carefully notice how you are moved by the space and field around you.
3. Follow body motions, sounds, and images *until they are apparent and possibly repeat themselves.* (Be careful of yourself and others if they are around!) Where in nature might you find these sounds and images? Go to that piece of nature and meditate there; commune with nature as you move, make sounds, and see images.
4. Finally, as you continue to dance and make sounds, communing with nature, recall a conflict you must deal with and notice how nature communes with and helps you with that tense situation.

One participant shared the following comment after completing the inner work.

> *I was strong wind moving* through *the forest. It wanted to support me and other people to move around more in their positions, and flow more with life as a whole. I was a kind of Buddha figure, emerging from nature, to help world conflict and world ecology.*

Things to Remember from Chapter 26

1. Commune and rediscover yourself as a timeless NONLOCAL piece of nature. Be that piece of nature in action to communicate best with yourself and others.

PART IX

Education for New Government

• • •

Chapter 27. How Education Creates World Change through Creative Relationships
Chapter 28. The "BIGWAY" for Organizations and Government

IN THIS FINAL SECTION OF the book, Chapters 27 and 28, I suggest how education can change governments and how world governments reflect a basic worldwide need for better education.

Educational systems today are often inadequate in teaching us how to deal with relationship and world diversity issues in both a general and a face-to-face sustainable, systematic way.

32. Nelson Mandela on Education.

We need teachers and leaders who teach students or win people's support to be able to model not only strength *but also relationship ability.*

I believe the world will change—in part, through your and my examples—from the bottom of the ladder of power, upwards . . . and not only from the top down! So, let's try!

CHAPTER 27

Education Creates World Change through Creative Relationships

• • •

Nelson Mandela, former president of South Africa and 1993 Nobel Peace Prize laureate, spoke not only of Ubuntu, "I am, becaujse you are," but also about many things, including education. He said, "*Education is the most powerful weapon which you can use to change the world.*"53

Education as a weapon to change the world? Why not more armies and more war? I show in this chapter how education can become more powerful in world change, through the practice of what I have been calling *721 feedback*.

In this chapter, I share some of the general principles of an education system based on 721, and an inner-work process specifically focused on how to commune with one of your worst teachers. By using 721 to commune, you may find a deeper teaching as well as possibly relieving hurt that happened in that part of your personal educational history.

Today most educational systems recommend "fighting" laziness, getting stronger, passing tests, etc. I realize that despite alternative schools that stress the process of relationship, mainstream educational systems around the world usually do not. They ask instead, "Can you pass a test? Can you learn A, B, and C?" Because if you can't learn that, *you flunk*. Teachers are paid to make you strong in the sense of performing in a given way, when asked to do so on a test.

This attitude about getting stronger is needed. We all need to get our life together and do things in a consensus reality way. But although, "Get it together and answer me when I ask you a question!" has good things about it, it also ignores dreaming and relationship. After you pass an educational system, it usually means you have passed what we are calling the first training; that is, you have only passed the cognitive material. You have usually still not learned about the second training, about feeling your way into other people's experience.

I believe that learning to commune should be part of education too. Communing with your partner, when you are having a problem with the world around you, needs to be part of our mainstream educational systems around the world.

Education's Future

In psychological training and in all education, *wonder* needs to be part of our educational system. Not just facts but encouraging people to wonder and to be inquisitive. Where did we come from? Who are we? Why are we here? Why is there so much conflict?

From the biggest perspective, you and I are all parts of the universe looking at itself. As parts of the universe looking at itself, we may raise its consciousness! As I have been saying, recall, learn, and teach others that what you think *here* may be connected over *there*. My buzz is connected to yours. I say *buzzzzz* because in physics, we are quantum waves as well as people.

In January, 2013, the Dalai Lama said, "Broadly speaking, although there are some differences, I think Buddhist philosophy and Quantum Mechanics can shake hands on their view of the world."[54] What you do, and the movements you make, even if you are by yourself, may influence other people at a distance. We are coupled processes.

Awareness includes the parameters of consensus reality, with its disciplined attitudes, and also the expansiveness of nonlocality, with its limitlessness. In reality I talk *to* you, but in dreamland I *am* you. This CR and dreamland combination is a most marginalized aspect of our world. This marginalization, as I have said, is one of the biggest social issues.

School systems can reverse this problem by teaching about diversity issues and also about *diversity in the levels of consciousness.* Schools can teach deep democracy.

I want to emphasize three elements to bring deep democracy into education: transparency, phase awareness, and using 721 feedback to commune even when you must be critical.

Transparency

As an educator, just as a business person, therapist, or government person, one of the most impactful interventions is to be *transparent.* That means, notice and show your dreaming, your double signals, etc. Show your rank consciousness and unconsciousness. Talk about it!

Being a white, heterosexual, U.S. man, I often have more social rank than others, so I have to be very conscious about it. Each of us has power and rank in some place. Be transparent; please, talk about rank—make it part of the conversation everywhere. Talk about how your rank can make you ignore others.

Talk about what is inside of you to people, talk about your lack of rank consciousness in certain situations. As teachers, discuss signals and model consciousness. If we were all more transparent, there would be far less conflict. You might not like who you are, but at least show it! Show your debates with an "X."

Part of education is being transparent about how, "I am also you!" If people bother you, remember that they are part of the dance you do. If you let go and relax entirely, you will see your various energies in your movement, and one of the energies might be like the person you don't like. This is psychology A-B-C. *Remember that the people you can't stand have energies that are in you as well.* You might need their energy!

This is a controversial idea for some, so it is something to consider, not to insist upon. Some of our participants grappled with it.

E: Why do I, as an individual, need that "X" energy of Trump to be alive? I am doing OK without it, thank you!

Arny: I would say if you can't stand him, let go and discover that his energy is part of your nature.

E: It is true, I do have some Trump energy.

Arny: You are the most honest person I have met in a long time!

D: In working with kids, one concept that they absolutely love is to steal the energy of the bully—they love that.

Arny: Oh, beautiful, great work! Steal the energy of the bully!

Commune and Criticize

Criticizing is a part of our educational systems and a source of trouble in relationships and group life. How do we, as teachers and students, criticize others? Everybody has their own way of doing it, but here is one way of doing it.

First: I don't like what you are doing! I think it is disgusting, and you need to change!

Then: You know, I am a little bit like you, and in fact, I totally understand where you are coming from. I still want you to change, but I understand where you are coming from.

If you have to criticize somebody, do it, but also tell her or him, "I have been there before." To get your criticism across without only traumatizing somebody, say, "I have been there before, so keep your eye on me as well, so I don't fall into the same thing I am criticizing you for." I guarantee the person will remember that.

As an activist, hoping to make change in the world, the people whom you are trying to awaken are you. If you remember that, and tell them that, I guarantee your relationship with them will be better, and they will be able to listen to you.

As activists, we all need to remember that the people we want to awaken are "ghost roles," problems that we too may have without realizing it, powers we have that we may be using unconsciously against others. A conscious activist knows that she or he is the "other" and can use the "X" energy more consciously to create better relationships and succeed in the work even more.

When you support someone, you support yourself. When you criticize someone, remember how you, too, are growing or have grown in that area. If the student needs the teacher to be elevated, then be elevated as the teacher, thank the person for raising you up, and also remember to raise up the student as well!

Teach about Phases

- Phase 1: Have a good time!
- Phase 2: Be conflicted! It is important to take a stand: "*Woof!* I don't agree with something! Wake up!" Phase 2 is a wakeup period. Have the energy and the strength to put your foot down and say, "Let's wake up about this or that."
- Phase 3: "I am the person I am trying to wake up!" It is a process, not one or the other.
- Phase 4: Let go, drop into detachment and compassion for all parts.

All the phases are important. I am stressing now phase 3 because it is often marginal, but phase 2—taking a stand for diversity issues—also gets marginalized. Recall that if you focus only on reality, you will marginalize something infinite about and around you, and then you can get depressed.

Please teach about depression; it is a core issue in our world.

Amy: It is natural to be depressed.
Arny: Some people are smiling about that, how come you are smiling?
P: It is great to hear it! Depression happens, it is not an emergency.

Arny: Not at all, in fact it could be a gift.
R: What is a quick way to talk with a friend who is getting depressed?
Arny: A quick way is to commune, and say, "Oh, I am so sorry! I sometimes feel down too, when I am struggling too much. So, I need to give up sometimes. Let's give up together, let's temporarily give up."

Often people near death get afraid of the future. You can help by revealing how you sometimes need to let go and give up to go beyond the here and now. My point is, you can reduce their struggle and conflict by "communing."

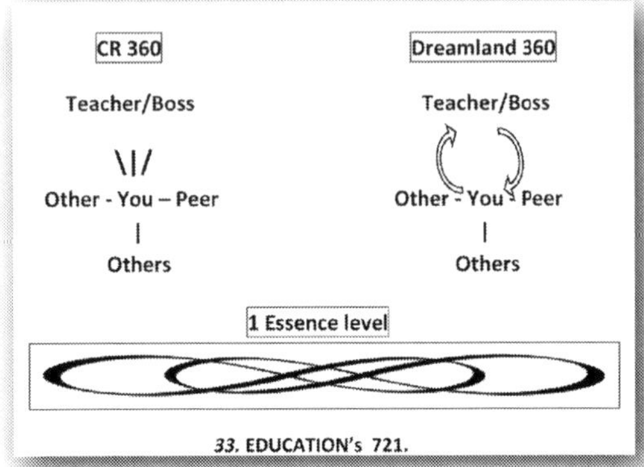

33. EDUCATION's 721.

Introduce 721 Feedback in Education

721 is about awareness, discipline, and creative mind. See my diagram, which models 721 in education. 721 is a key to worldwork as well as inner work, and especially education.

360 CR in education (from the "student's" point of view) means acknowledging all roles, all the different parts of your educational system, including your teacher (as if she or he were your business boss). You are at the center of that 360 CR getting feedback from, let's say, the worst teacher you ever had. Here is where a possible forum with that teacher or those teachers can happen. Get all their feedback and speak about your ideas as well.

360 dreamland in education means teachers and students switching roles. I don't mean just role switching—which we know already is a key in worldwork—but taking it even deeper to the practice of *communing.* I want you to go so deeply into the critical role that you can almost feel how you might be *like that experience.* Go back and forth as in open forums.

Finally, study how to get feedback from the essence level, from the universe. This essence level is a pre-dreaming experience that you have before images, ideas, and dreams appear.

Demonstration: 721 with Your Worst Teacher

I am going to model the practice of 721 in education with my worst teacher, Miss G. Let me introduce you to Miss G. and what happened in consensus reality.

She was the teacher I liked least of all. She was my ninth-grade teacher and always poked her boney finger at people and pushed it into their bellies. She said, "I want everybody here to do 15 little exercises tonight and hand them in tomorrow morning." She was teaching algebra. "You have to do these 15 algebra exercises, and if you don't do these 15 exercises tonight, you'll have to do 15 more the next night!" She was not good at communing! This was consensus reality. I was 13 or 14 years of age. She said to me and others, "I insist upon this! Either you do it or you will flunk the class!" I said, "But this is only one assignment! How can you flunk us for the whole class?" She said, "Be quiet and do those exercises!"

A friend of mine and I decided to create a stink bomb and put it under her house. She had a white-walled house, and we put the stink bomb right under the wall and set it off. "Pssswwfffff!" After the bomb went off, nothing happened to her house, so she stuck her head out the window.

That view of her was one of the high points in my young life. My friend and I hid behind a tree, watching her. I remember seeing her disturbed face all upset, in the window, and the smoke on the side of her house. I remember the next day I was really scared to go to school, but at least there was no homework for a week! I should not have done it; I don't know why I was not punished—we got away with it for some reason. In any case, when we came back to school she was a bit nicer! Social action! The stink bomb was not as successful as I hoped, but it had the right effect.

Now, I'll present my inner work to illustrate the practice of communing and using 721 with a difficult educational relationship. Remember that 721 includes 360 feedback from consensus reality, which was in the story above, then 360 from dreamland, and 1 from the essence level.

> *Miss G* (Arny is playing this role): *I am the teacher, and I want you to do that homework, and if you don't, I will fail you!*
>
> *Arny* (as himself)*: I hear you.* (Hoping for the moment to get back at her.)
>
> Now going deeper into dreamland, I will switch roles and feel into Miss G.
>
> *Miss G: I want you to do that homework as soon as possible. Do these exercises right away, and if you don't do them, then I am going to get really upset.*
>
> *Arny: Now, I am going to commune.*
>
> *Miss G: Students, you have to do these things exactly right and quickly.*
>
> *Arny: As I commune with Miss G, I sense her exactness as part of myself: "You have got to do this, and it has got to be right! You will work in different cultures, not just one. It has to work for all ages! Does it work with babies, with people near death, with the old and the young, with people of every skin color and sexual orientation?! It has got to do that, and only then will I be happier!" These thoughts are part of my own self-demand for exactness and are sometimes, a big part of me.*

After my inner work, I imagined meeting Miss G again and saying, "I totally understand where you are coming from. You have a different style than I do, but I agree with the essence of what you are doing." I am not just picking up a projection onto her; I am feeling deeply into that person to help resolve past and/or present conflicts.

Communing already helped me a lot, but now I want to experience feedback from the essence level. Here, I let my body be moved spontaneously; my hips do a little wiggle, my hand flies up and then drops gently back down. I notice a thought, "Yes, be exact and then relax."

The essence level added more details to my educational relationship conflict:

"The point is to be accurate and then to relax."

My inner work prompted the following reflection about racism in schools from a class participant.

> *J: Your story of Miss G. triggered a memory of being in the third grade, growing up in India. A teacher separated the children who looked fair-skinned from the children who were darker-skinned, who had to sit in the back. Now, trying to get to the essence level of this teacher, what I touch is . . . ohhh . . . a deep yearning for beauty.*
>
> *Arny: A deep yearning for beauty—my god . . . amazing. . . . How were you able to do that just sitting in your chair? Real beauty is beyond looks.*
>
> *J: I have felt such things for many years.*
>
> *Arny: There is something about you, J., that allows you to do that. What is it that allows you to commune and puts you in the front of the class? Have you always been like that? Have you always been able to feel into people and stuff like that?*
>
> *J: Yes.*
>
> *Arny: Lucky you. Thank you for telling us.*

Communing is a way of feeling deeply into the other person, and then any social action that needs to happen can happen in a way that is easier and more sustainable. The key to sustainability and sustainable activism is getting the other side to be a little bit on your side by feeling into its nature.

It can be important to cognitively understand the other person's personal history and social context, as well as different kinds of rank and social marginalization. For example, my worst teacher was a woman. Especially at the time I was in school, sexism was quite prevalent and women possessed no rank or power, so they often had to be stronger and better to show that they could do something.

Communing is really a practice of connecting with the feeling and essence of the other person and with what she or he may be unable to say. You cannot know the other person's history, but you may be able to connect with her or his deepest nature.

You might be wondering whether once you have done this kind of communing inner work, is the relationship situation finished? My answer is NO, relationship is a process, and problems will probably come back again. Solutions are interesting, but the *process* of relating is a bigger point. Remember, it is also important to take a stand, to say, "*Woof!*" Then, to go further.

One of our participants reminded me that, "It is challenging for mainstream people who are not religious, process-oriented, or New Age-y to get to the essence level." Indeed, getting to the essence level is a very big thing. That is why I sometimes say to motivate people, "Getting to the essence level will make you money or more popular!"

When Amy and I worked with the American Chamber of Commerce recently, we shared a story of one of my early clients, who had been the vice-president of one of the largest automobile companies. He came to see me in Switzerland, where I was working. He wanted to know, how do you sell certain cars in given cities?

How could I know? I was a Jungian analyst just beginning to develop processwork! I was 34 at that time. I knew about movement and I did what I am suggesting now. I said, this will make you money; it is the most marginalized part of your life. Stand up and let yourself wander around a little bit . . . and you can figure things out. So, I did just that myself for him. Suddenly an idea came to me: "Take the Cadillac out of the showroom, drive it to the biggest intersection in cities where you hope to sell Cadillac cars, open the windows widely, turn on music, and blast it out into the streets." He said, "Are you crazy?" I said, "Yes!"

In any case, that helped his company sell their car, it became the best-selling car in particular cities. I was happy and he paid me my fee of 45

SFr for his session! (That was about $20 at that time). He was happy, and I was very happy too. My point is that you can get good ideas for CR by following the essence level.

When Amy and I shared this story with the business people at the American Chamber of Commerce, we did not use any flowery language but only encouraged everyone to, "Just relax sometimes. Your brain can be over-taxed, so you cannot think of everything partly because you are under so much stress. If you relax and let go, something intuitive might come up." They did it!

The following exercise will lead you through the inner work I demonstrated above, to help you commune with your worst teacher and to find the deepest essence of that educational interaction. You can do this on your own or with a helper as a dyad.

Exercise: 721 and Your Worst Teacher

A. Recall your worst teacher and her or his most disturbing "X" energy. (Helper: Note the teacher's "X" to sense it later.) Student: What's your normal "u" energy? In what phase are you now with that teacher's "X" energy? Peaceful, phase 1; angry, phase 2; communing, phase 3; detached, phase 4?

B. Now explore 721. In 360 CR, go back and forth between "u" and the teacher's critical "X" energy. Then in 360 dreamland, do an open forum, that is, play and *switch roles*; *feel deeply* and commune into "X" until things begin to resolve.

C. "1." Let go and let your body be moved by a universe dance. Be moved by space until repetitive motions occur, and then notice what insight occurs from those repetitive motions about the teacher–student relationship. Speak about your insights.

D. Helper: Imagine being the "worst" teacher and as that teacher, share your reaction with the student who was just trying to commune to improve the relationship. Student, make notes about your learning.

After completing the exercise, class participants shared the following learnings.

S: I found that behind my most difficult teacher was her love of teaching. That love of teaching was in the background of her neglect of me as a difficult learner. . . . She loved teaching so much that what she did neglected me. In this work, I also came to loving teaching . . . myself! With more metaskills, more awareness, more second training, I realized that in the background that teacher's neglect of me was her love of teaching excellence. . . . I realized that I could also love teaching but find my own way by using my own skills and a different style.

J: I worked with the same teacher who told me and other darker-colored people to sit in the back. One of the things that I got from the "X" energy of the teacher was, "Stay there! Stay there at the back!" The word that came to me when I got into that altered state was, "Stay!" When I dreamt into the energy of the universe, I heard, "I need you, stay!" I felt the universe telling me, "I need you, stay . . . and SPEAK!"

Arny: Yes, we need you, I need you! Stay and speak out. Speak. You are needed to stay and speak.

J: . . . and witness.

Arny: I need you to stay, speak, and witness. Thanks for making things more conscious for all of us: Stay, speak, and witness. I feel like bowing down to that wisdom in you asking you to, "Stay, speak, and witness."

Things to Remember from Chapter 27

1. Recall Nelson Mandela's comment, that "*Education is the most powerful weapon which you can use to change the world.*"
2. Update education with 721's open forums in schools.
3. Model transparency, commune with your opponents and with your worst teachers and students to be a great educator and a great learner.

CHAPTER 28

The "BIGWAY" for Organizations and Governments

• • •

Nelson Mandela said,

. . . in every human heart there is mercy and generosity. No one is born hating another person because of the color of his skin or his background or religion. People must learn to hate, and if they can learn to hate, they can be taught to love, for love comes more naturally to the human heart than its opposite.

—*Mandela's autobiography.55*

IN A WAY, WE LIVE on a planet without parents. Very few of us had parents who were able to show us how to negotiate conflict. Most parents were not very good at conflict themselves. Many of us are therefore "orphans" in the sense of being on a planet without an elder, without someone who can show us how to live and work with tensions. Our ecology is not in good shape, pollution is increasing, glaciers are melting, and weather patterns are increasingly challenging.

Today, some people in some nations are beginning to recycle their paper, plastic, glass, rubber products, etc., but very, very few people recycle conflict. As a result, we go to war, and blow up people and buildings, and the pollution gets worse. Depending upon the calculation, in about 150 years our planet will have so much pollution, that most of our illnesses will come from food, air, and water. We already have too many such problems.

Thus, in my view, one of our biggest needs is learning how to elder people in helpful ways of handling tension and conflict. Since global issues are connected to personal problems, if I complain about unresolved global issues, I must, and we all must, work on this personally as well in our own lives.

Let me be less theoretical and more practical. Last night Amy and I went out to eat at a restaurant. Our waitress was in a bad, one-sided mood. She did not listen to our wishes and brought the wrong food! Of course, we said, "Well, this is not what we ordered!"

"What do you want?" she said, abruptly.

"What we ordered," I said.

She left, got the right food, and threw it in front of us and quickly left in a mood. I needed to commune before I could eat the food. So I communed with her at the table! I got into her energy and played her out. "Plonk!" Quick! Bad mood! Though this is far from my ordinary self, I began to really understand her better. She had *so* much to do, she felt she must protect herself against the public. This communing reminded me of my own problems. In any case, Amy and I started to like her again, and we could eat and enjoy our food. Later we offered the restaurant help with their problems.

I must remind myself to commune because we all need to be reminded. Communing is connected to dreaming and role switching—something most people rarely do. So, set your alarm clock daily to commune with your worst monsters! I know you will love doing that, because it saves time from otherwise fixating on someone or something you don't like!

How Do We Elder Governments?

Living and working around the world, I have met numerous world leaders. In this last chapter, I want to offer you a new and relatively simple method for leading, or for advising others, in leadership positions. You can use the following divination procedure to find the directions organizations and countries need to take. This divination practice builds on all the second training skills, metaskills, and ideas that I have been sharing in this book.

We turn to divination in order to find eldership because it gives us access to phase 4, to that bigger field that moves us.

Divination is the practice of seeking knowledge of the future or the unknown by what is called "supernatural means," by means of laws beyond our present scientific explanations. I recently became fascinated with the earliest known Chinese diviners (before Taoism and Lao Tse). They heated up bones until they cracked in order to find the way forward by studying what the cracks indicated.[56] These diviners believed that the cracks in a shell when heated showed the "way."

***34.* Divination Scapula. Inscribed from the Shang Dynasty (reign of King Wu Ding).** Wikipedia
Below, see *35.* The BIGWAY direction that is open to the "u" + "X"

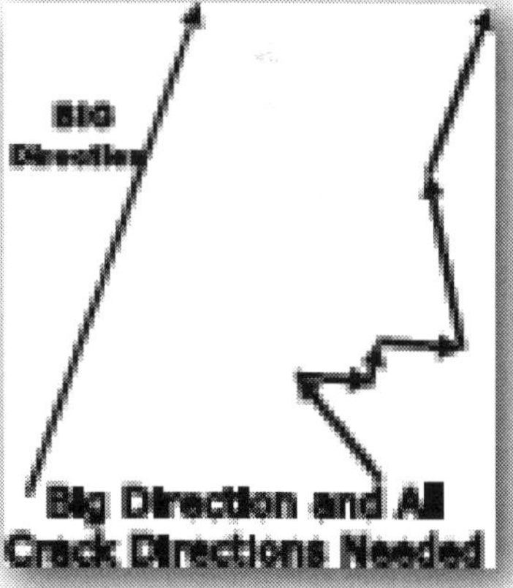

That was 3,000 years ago. Why on earth would I be interested in something that old? Isn't that too old! Shouldn't we forget it? No! We need to learn more about *cracking through consensus reality.* We have computers, but we don't have bone cracking, and *cracking could help us dream to find the way, the "BIGWAY!"*

What do I mean by cracking? Cracking is needed when we are too rigid and stiff. We need to *crack,* smash, and let go of our "bone-y" consensus reality mind. If we don't loosen up, we risk doing so unconsciously by "cracking up" in an accident or with "crack" (cocaine, etc.). I am using "cracking" in the sense of cracking through your own rigid everyday mind. Crack your "head open" so you can have an "open mind."

Open Mind, Bone-Cracking Divination

Such divination was present around 1660–1046 BC, even before Taoism and the *I Ching*. The ancient Chinese felt they needed something that was really spontaneous and unpredictable to find the right directions. So they decided to heat up and crack turtle shells or the shoulder blades (scapulae) of an ox or other animal. They believed that the resulting cracks showed the path, the way they needed to go. See picture 34 of a Divination Scapula.[57]

Leaders of the time would ask the diviners questions about their personal health, about going to war, about the economy, about their enemies. The diviners then burned, heated, and cracked the bones to find the answer.

Why heating and cracking? What is the possible significance of heating things up until they crack? In a way, ever since we explored the technique of burning in Chapters 5 and 8, we have been "burning and heating" things to "crack" and divine the way forward. "Cracking through" consensus reality has always been used by shamans everywhere. Some use drugs to go into altered states, to "crack up" and to help individuals and governments find the way. Some ancient diviners would even cut themselves and bleed onto the bone. What is the significance of this bleeding? Perhaps they bled onto the bone to "pour" themselves totally into the divination procedures, with all their emotions. Burning and bleeding created altered states that opened them to dreaming.

Cracking was later replaced in China by the *I Ching*, a divination method of counting yarrow stalks and spinning coins. Why? Perhaps because cracking ox bones is more work. You have to kill an animal, take out its scapula bone, start a fire, and crack the bone in the fire. Also, bone cracking is earthy, whereas coins are more "civilized." You don't have to clean up afterwards, you don't have to start a fire, there is less dirt and blood!

But the ancient bone-cracking method has an important psychological aspect for us today. Intense "cracking" procedures are able to crack through our consensus reality rigidity.

I am going to recommend a modern version of this ancient practice. The analogous BIGWAY procedure I recommend retains the various zigzag directions of the crack and shows the BIGWAY we need to go.

Zigzag is basic to cracking. Psychologically, and organizationally, we know that in principle, all the viewpoints and directions inside of you and in our groups are needed as part of nature's diversity! Bone-cracking divination simply says, "Use all the directions, all the zigzags in the crack; all your paths and energies are needed in order to flow." Democracies need to integrate all their people, and appreciate, at least in part, *all* directions. Leaders and facilitators who can appreciate all ways create atmospheres for new things to happen and space for everyone to work together.

As the ancient diviners did not leave messages (that I could find) about how to interpret their cracks, I will guess at their meaning. The beginning directions in the crack are like your "u" and "X," and the final direction of the crack shows the basic overall direction, or what I call the "*BIGWAY*."

Psychologically, we know that who you are is not just your everyday mind but your processmind as well. You are the "X" stuff you hate, and you are the "u" stuff that you love as well. You are everything you think of. You are a bunch of zigzags in life. Organizations are the same. They need all their paths, at least to some small extent. We all need to know the BIGWAY to elder organizations, to show them the way and even how to appreciate the "u" and the "X" paths.[58]

The BIGWAY is the end of the crack. It reminds me of the processmind view of how and where the universe is trying to move you. The BIGWAY is like the spin of the pen, or the spinning of your body. This BIGWAY final direction is easy to find. Just spin a pen and use the direction it is pointing as a way to detach and commune with and not only fight other views. The BIGWAY is a "vector," which is a direction with a magnitude or power.

How do we crack today? Cracking, like spinning around in circles, is a way to find phase 4 and the direction that the universe suggests that we go. This is a phase 4 vector experience to help us access the BIGWAY direction, a kind of "spiritual direction." To find the final direction giving us an answer, we can spin a pen to crack through our ordinary intentions. When we get into this BIGWAY attitude, we will be able to commune with all the other cracks—with all the other directions for ourselves, our groups, or our governments.

Now, instead of cracking bones to see the zigzag of the "u" and "X," we shall be feeling those directions and then using "cracking"—or throwing the pen—to find the BIGWAY. We shall "burn" and intensely feel the directions on earth corresponding to our feeling of where our "u" and "X" are headed. This creates a "zigzag." Then we shall add to that zigzag by burning to find the BIGWAY. From this BIGWAY's view, we will see that the "u" and "X" paths are all temporarily important in getting to the final answer to our questions.

Demonstration: A BIGWAY for the U.S. Government

I will illustrate the BIGWAY technique by sharing my inner-work practice with you. You will find the exercise at the end of the chapter so you can try it yourself.

I have been wondering what the BIGWAY is for the United States. I am sometimes asked to give opinions about governments, so I think a lot about governments, and the U.S. is one possible example. I did this inner work in the midst of the 2016 election conflicts between President Obama, Republican Donald Trump, and Democrat Hilary Clinton.

First, I need to find the directions of my "u" and "X," and then burn and spin the pen for the BIGWAY. Next, I'll draw the u+X zigzag ways, and BIGWAY directions on paper.

So, first I walk my "u," my favorite direction for the U.S., which is democratic. Then, I find and walk the X, which for me is Donald Trump or the "X" direction. Finally, I spin a pen and find the processmind direction, the BIGWAY, and use it to understand, to commune with the other paths.

So, first I walk the direction of my primary process about the United States, which feels more like the democrats, and for me, this direction feels like it goes north. I take some steps toward the north and feel this vector.

That is one of my zigzags, it goes north which for me, means a democratically ideal position.

My "X" direction feels like Donald Trump, and when I feel and walk his direction, I notice it is headed towards the east from Portland, Oregon. The "X" way goes east, towards New York City, where Trump is from. That east direction is, for me, right wing, Donald Trump. He says, "My way is the only way!"

The "u" north direction, the democrats are (at least in my mind), more open to the people. But the "X" east direction says, "No! *I* know what to do, shut up and follow me! Let's be great and powerful again! We gotta be great!" He is too racist and sexist for me, yet somehow, at the essence, he is part of my BIGWAY.

Now, I seek the BIGWAY. It is also a vector, something that has both the feeling of magnitude and the feeling of a direction. I could follow an ancient shamanistic practice to find the Tao or universe by throwing coins, but instead I simply throw the pen in the air and see how the universe moves it. This is similar to letting your body be moved by the universe, but even simpler.

The "u" and the "X" as vectors are two parts of the "crack." They both belong to the consensus reality description of a given situation. But the BIGWAY, the processmind level, involves *throwing the pen in the air, and letting the field show the way*, and using that as my main direction.

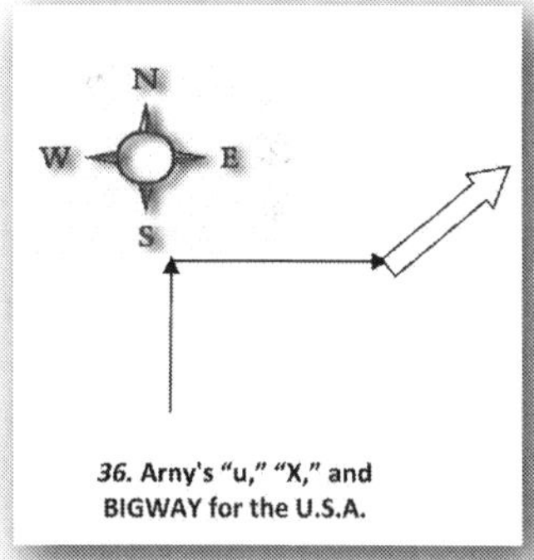

36. Arny's "u," "X," and BIGWAY for the U.S.A.

To find that BIGWAY, I am going to "crack up." So, I let myself dance and move in an emotional, spontaneous way as I "crack up" and then throw a pen to find the BIGWAY direction. The pen points to the northeast, which I understand as the universe pointing towards Montreal for my BIGWAY. As I walk in that direction towards Montreal, I begin to think, "*Hmmm*, what is the name of that new Canadian leader? Justin Trudeau! I like that he stands for all the First Nations peoples in his country."

For me, that NE Montreal pen direction is associated with a very open heart, open mind. This was very touching, and made me almost cry. I felt my little "u" go north, and the "X" direction for Trump felt like it went east, towards NYC, and NYC is, "Develop your muscles or shut up!" I love NYC, but I don't love Trump that much.

The BIGWAY, a way of "the universe," is towards Montreal. It will help me understand and commune with the other paths. To learn how to do that, I walk along that BIGWAY and feel its significance, and use that to teach me how to get along with, and to "elder" the "u" and the "X." As I walk the BIGWAY northeast towards Montreal, I feel love for all the First Nations peoples—we need to take care of our people, of all people. I feel open-hearted.

Now with this BIGWAY feeling in mind, I walk the "u" and the "X" again, to elder them. The direction of the BIGWAY reminds me to feel for the "u," as in "Let's be democratic and be open to all people." Then I walk towards the "X" direction with the BIGWAY feeling in mind and sense Trump saying, "My way must be the only way! My way wins!" And, I realize that I can value that "X." How? I do see the importance of communing with Trump and appreciating the need to take a strong stand for what I believe in. While in the BIGWAY, I can commune with the "X's" energy. It is hard and deep and normally impossible—you have to be "cracked" to do it!

The BIGWAY practice teaches you how to at least *tolerate* other paths. What happened to me in my inner work was new and real for me. We need "all people and all hearts," and sometimes we need to take a "firm stand" about things as well. Openness to all people and taking a strong stand are part of the BIGWAY that is open to the earth, to the spirit of all people. The BIGWAY helps me elder the other paths and "cracks."

To practice this BIGWAY inner work, remember to ask yourself what is your preferred "u," and which earth direction seems to you to fit that direction most. Do the same with "X." But for the processmind, you must burn, you must get excited and throw a pen! That direction will help you commune and "elder" these other states of mind. This can relieve the tensions between the "u" and "X," at least temporarily.

Demonstration: Amy's BIGWAY Inner Work on an Organization

For another example of the BIGWAY practice, here is Amy's inner work, exploring the BIGWAY that can include both academic thinking and dreaming.

Amy: I'll show how I worked on the common recurring tensions here at our own organization, the Process Work Institute of Portland. Everyone has their solutions for PWI, and I want to find mine.

When I worked on PWI last night, I wanted to find the BIGWAY for the recurring community tension, present even many years ago in Zurich. That tension creator is an "X." That "X" energy is always trying to do things linearly, academically. My little "u" is my dreaming side. The u + X are often in conflict, both inside and outside of me. My everyday "u" energy sort of flows; for me it went towards Mexico. I loved being there; the culture was very warmhearted and community-oriented to me.

Then, the linear academic "X" energy was a chopping energy: "Get things together, be clear! Get things to work in consensus reality!" And for me, this direction went towards the Midwest where I grew up. It is more linear, more conservative.

Then I "cracked up" and burned, spun the pen, and it went south. That direction made me feel like going towards Bali! I have been studying some of the creative things from there. I love their masks and that they act things out in a community, really expressing stuff.

The Bali direction was the BIGWAY, and when I walked there I could appreciate the other vectors too. While still feeling "Bali," my little "u" path felt really good, and I even wanted to express my little "u's" dreaming more. When I walked the "X" to the

Midwest with the BIGWAY in mind, I started walking very intensely. Somehow, I even began to enjoy that intense academic "X"!! I felt like a soldier. I really liked it. (Amy marches with legs really high.) That Bali BIGWAY even made the academic "X" fun! The BIGWAY makes every way possible. It was fun and even creative.

Then I got an insight. The BIGWAY processmind direction was encouraging me to feel that everything was dreaming. I realized that I had been cutting off parts of myself as if those parts were not dreaming. I needed the attitude that everything that is, is part of the dreaming, and I needed to be creative with life and with the Process Work Institute. I could not separate the "u" and "X" anymore. It helped me a lot.

Amy's example shows how the BIGWAY can help include even those zigzags that are a little complicated, and make them more creative and useful.

You might be wondering if you have to associate the directions you find with an actual location, like Montreal for me, and Bali for Amy. For this practice, throw the pen and wherever the pen goes, ask yourself what you feel or associate with that particular direction on earth. Why does that particular direction draw you and your pen?? The answer may be irrational or it may be reasonable. It can be a location on earth, or your sunflower, or a vacation spot, etc. The feeling of the BIGWAY is the point.

Now try finding the BIGWAY for yourself with the following exercise. It is a walking meditation that you can do on your own. This practice is intended to make it easier to elder troublesome energies inside of you and in the world. When you practice this BIGWAY technique, you are seeking the elder in you who can understand *the whole* of the organization, to help all its parts evolve.

Exercise: Pyromantic Bone CRACKING for the BIGWAY (for Yourself, Organization, or Government)

1. Note a group, business, or government problem. Note your "u" direction with that problem, the direction with which you normally identify. Feel, move, and then sketch that "u" direction. Then, note the worst "X" personal or group energy in that problem. Now, feel and move and then sketch the direction of that "X."
2. Then fire up your breath and emotions, heat up the problem until you "CRACK" and feel altered; then (carefully) *throw the pen in the air + map its (processmind's BIGWAY) direction.* Begin to walk in that direction and ask yourself, what possible power and reason might have called you in this direction? What draws you there? Sense the meaning of this BIGWAY direction.
3. Now, while identifying with and feeling this BIGWAY, keep this feeling in mind to elder and understand the "u" and "X." With the BIGWAY in mind, *walk the "u" and "X" parts of the BIGWAY.* Notice how the BIGWAY communes with, and may even appreciate, aspects of the "u" and "X." Record your insights.

I have used this BIGWAY approach with leaders who had heard that they would be shot by some hidden terrorist. In a government, "X" people who are against you, even threatening you, may relax because of the nonlocality of your processmind BIGWAY eldering experience.

Recall how your "u" often feels tense with that "X" energy. If your normal "u" sometimes seems self-negative, it is probably because it is having a "secret inner affair" with that "X"! The "X" probably says for example, "I cannot stand your stupid face," and the little "u" often says, "OK, how about some sex tonight?" Then "u" wakes up in the morning and says, "What the hell did I do?"

To break up that secret inner "affair", use your processmind BIGWAY to understand the "u" and appreciate aspects of "X." Have a more compassionate attitude towards all of yourself. It is easy to say, but only your own BIGWAY body experience can teach you this.

Things to Remember from Chapter 28

1. Shamanize; that is, "burn and crack," then throw the pen in the air to find the BIGWAY direction, so you can elder and commune with system parts you like and don't like.
2. The BIGWAY is a deep (phase 4) experience to elder conflicting directions.
3. Note and walk the u + X zigzag road with the BIGWAY in mind to get along with u + X. Record insights and how to put all of this into practice.

CONCLUSION:

5-Minute Solutions to World Tension

• • •

It is shocking to recall that in the 20th century *100 million people died* in war. In the year 2015, 40 million people were displaced from their homes because of conflict. In part, these deaths and problems were due to our lack of training in effective conflict resolution methods. Therefore, in this conclusion, I streamline and highlight two 5-minute practices from the last chapters to help you work with the worst conflict moments in order to have the chance to create solutions and sustainable relationships. But first let me review.

Forums

Since the 1980s, I have stressed multilevel, partially detached facilitation skills that can wrestle with, but also appreciate, all sides. My 1980s deep democracy work with individual and large organizational tensions first appeared in writing in 1992 in *The Leader as Martial Artist.*[59] In this present book, I stress new forms of conflict work: processes that recognize and develop approaches to the different levels of consciousness and phases of relationships.

This present book emphasizes relationship process awareness for all conflicts we experience inside ourselves and in the world. Awareness in conflict work creates sustainable relationships, and is as important (or even more so) than the state of peace. In this work, I updated the concept and practice of deep democracy.

DEEP DEMOCRACY has evolved to include not only
LEVELS OF CONSCIOUSNESS,
but in this book, also

- **SYSTEM PHASES**: phase 1, phase 2, phase 3, and phase 4 for all community processes
- **"721" FORUMS**: 360 reality + 360 role switching + 1 spontaneous motion
- **"COMMUNING"**: feeling into the "other" nonlocally
- **"BIGWAY"**: a shamanistic "direction finder" to elder various conflict directions

Always notice "mainstreaming," which is the tendency to force yourself to look, act, and behave like the mainstream of the area and world in which you live. Bring up and burn mainstreaming tensions as soon as possible.

Practice working rapidly on conflicts when possible. If I could give you one message, it might be this: Facilitators, leaders, and all of us need to notice and work on tensions earlier. To support such an active interest in conflict, I now provide in this "conclusion" not just uplifting remarks, but two simplified brief and powerful practices from the final two chapters. If needed in your work and life, you can then always turn quickly to this conclusion for support in working on tensions as rapidly as possible.

Of course, depending upon the individuals and communities, conflict processes often require more time to resolve. But with inner work and practice, we can all help to intervene in conflict processes, so that times of high tension can be reduced, and solutions identified and implemented quickly and easily. Please practice the following methods for your personal psychology as well as for business, government, and international issues.

Remember to notice phases, forums, and levels, and adjust your attitude and work to a given situation. Recall that phases, for example, contain all methods; there will always be relaxation moments, strong activist viewpoints, dreamlike role switching, and openness to the dreamworld. Then try the following two central 5-minute practices: "Communing" and the "BIGWAY." I have "streamlined" them from foregoing chapters for simplicity.

Communing and the BIGWAY can create rapid de-escalation in just about all tense situations. De-escalation can then be followed by possible solutions of all kinds.

Communing (Chapter 24) and the BIGWAY (Chapter 28) can be done in minutes, so no one (including me) can complain that resolving the potentially violent phases of conflict takes too much time!

The central feeling for these methods, the central "metaskill" is generosity. Remember the eldership of Nelson Mandela, Gandhi, Martin Luther King, and others to recall "generosity."

Understand your struggles, be generous with yourself and the world, and try these two following abbreviated "solution processes" as first steps to better relationships.

I. Nonlocal Communing (In 5 Minutes)

COMMUNING is an experience of feeling into, and noticing how you are like the other—the person or people you want to help or the troublesome "X" person or group. Communing is a theory and a skill you can learn, and also what Amy calls a *metaskill*, a feeling skill.

In consensus reality, we are separate, different, and more or less independent. But in our fantasy and dream world, we sense the energy and presence of the "other." Communing brings this dreamlike sense into your awareness, so the other is not just "different" or "foreign," but also a presence, an energy, and a direction that you know and share.

1. Communing is possibly a nonlocal phenomenon found throughout the universe. In psychology, we can say, "You and I are connected emotionally, and are therefore part of *one system*. What you do changes me, and vice versa."
2. In many ways, there is no distance between us; we are very close.
3. As I mentioned in Chapters 3, 5, and 25, Einstein first doubted nonlocality in physics, saying that it sounded like "spooky" action at a distance. If he were here today, I imagine him saying, "Nonlocal communing in psychology is a key to solving world problems."
4. Recall that community feeling, such as the South African Zulu sense, "I am, because you are," implies that nonlocality is not just a modern invention, but also an ancient community idea.

5-MINUTE COMMUNING Practice. To reduce and resolve conflict, practice before meeting the "X." Alone or with a partner,

A. Choose a conflict and ask yourself, or your partner, to play the "X," the person with whom you have conflict.
B. Identify and appreciate the real-world differences between you. Imagine defending yourself or getting encouragement to defend your viewpoint.
C. Now "commune"; feel-dream into the other until you can be her, him (or them), until you understand the other's feelings as feelings you recognize in yourself. Sense how you are "X."
D. Remembering this "communing" experience, commune-icate with "X" (or your partner, playing "X"), sharing your similarity and understanding of where feelings come from.
E. Finally, ask "X" to give you feedback about your ability to "commune-icate."

With practice, this 5-minute process can reduce conflict. If this process takes more than 5 minutes, repeat the exercise until you can do it more easily, and more quickly.

II. The Bigway (In 5 Minutes)

Recall from the last chapter how the BIGWAY helps create a sense of community and elder personal or public conflict situations. With practice you may (at least temporarily) appreciate and not only condemn those you are in conflict with. Perhaps you will even like the world better.

1. Recall that the BIGWAY was derived from ancient Chinese bone-cracking divination methods. Their spontaneous unpredictable *crack*, or "path," was the key to finding the "way" in ancient times.
2. This bone-cracking method preceded and apparently evolved into the divination procedures known today, such as the *I Ching: Book of Changes.*

5-MINUTE BIGWAY Practice. The BIGWAY practice can be simplified and done alone, with, or for others. How?

A. Identify your normal everyday feeling and call it "u." Identify feelings belonging to the "X" person (or group) with whom (which) the "u" is in conflict.
B. Focus on and feel the "u." Let your body move in the direction around you or someplace on earth that you associate with that "u" feeling. Draw an arrow on paper for this direction. Then do the same for the "X" direction and draw the "X" arrow, starting from the end of the "u" arrow.
C. Concentrate, meditate on the need for a solution, a bridge between all views. Get "heated up" and "crack" through your everyday state of mind and throw a pen wildly in the air (don't hurt yourself or others). Let your body and the space around you move your pen to show the BIGWAY direction, that is the pen's final direction.
D. Notice, walk, and feel that BIGWAY direction and sense your associations to that BIGWAY path. Meditate for a few minutes to sense what might draw you (and your pen) in that direction. Notice the direction or the thing in that direction within your room, or in

the city or world, that draws you the most in the pen's direction. Think, feel, sense, and note meanings and the significance of that direction or thing that might draw you there.

E. Finally, with the feelings of the BIGWAY significance in mind, walk the *"u" and then the "X" paths again to feel how the they are potential aspects of the BIGWAY.* By remembering and even becoming the *BIGWAY—that is, the thing that draws you in that direction—* you may be able to sense how that "way" can best help you with that "u" and "X" relationship. Use the "eldership" of the BIGWAY to influence your next steps, whatever they are.
   - Use your COMMUNING and/or the BIGWAY to relate to your own conflicting parts and to the world's problems. Thanks for being a leader, an elder for our planet.

The Second Training

"Communing" and the "BIGWAY" are in part, non-cognitive, second training process experiences. They go together with all your first training skills and knowledge.

Remember your first training relationship methods, such as signal awareness, ghost roles, and the amazing diversity of people. (See Chapter 1 for more on the first training). Learn and develop more such first training methods to help communities in all states of consciousness.

Second training includes not just first training methods, but also non-cognitive, mediumistic approaches such as communing and BIGWAY eldering. With practice, these approaches can work with groups in all phases and states of consciousness, from quietness to violence, with spiritual communities and terrorist organizations.

So, remember your second training feelings of appreciating all the parts, phases, and directions in human nature. Fight, stand strongly for your side, then commune to feel, "I am, because you are." "Elder" all of us to know that the BIGWAY is the powerful elder in you who understands that *we are all* somehow seeking a home on this earth.

Finally, stay in touch with *your* teacher, *your* own experience of the way space moves you. Developing such second training experiences creates more appreciation, compassion, and understanding for yourself and others. You will tire less from working on your internal tensions and on external world problems.

In time, all conflict practices will be updated to fit the people and issues involved. But the nonlocal communing sense of, "I am, because you are,"[60] and the BIGWAY sense that you can elder nature's peoples and directions, will probably always be important. Why? Because communing and the BIGWAY allow us to work with *any* personal, organizational, or political tension.

In conclusion, dear reader, please consider that ***you are the facilitator, the leader we need.*** Be the new kind of leader, valuing the full life given to you—by sensing peace, and also conflict, its phases, and its solutions. Thank you for helping yourself and making our little planet a better home for all.

BIBLIOGRAPHY

Audergon, Arlene. *The War Hotel: Psychological Dynamics in Violent Conflict.* London N1 2UN: Whurr, 2005.

Brailler, Jeff. *Who Was Albert Einstein?* New York: Grosset & Dunlap, 2002.

Castaneda, Carlos. *Journey to Ixtlan: The Lessons of Don Juan.* New York: Simon & Schuster, 1972.

Goodbread, Joe. *Befriending Conflict.* Portland, OR: Harmonic Processes, 2010.

Harrison, David. "Complementarity and the Copenhagen Interpretation of Quantum Mechanics." *UPSCALE*, Dept. of Physics, University of Toronto, 2002.

Lao Tzu. *Tao Te Ching: The Book of Meaning and Life.* Richard Wilhelm, translator; translated into English by H. G. Ostwald. London & New York: Viking-Penguin-Arkana, 1985.

---1972. *Tao Te Ching: The Book of Meaning and Life.* Gia-Fu Feng and Jane English, translators. New York: Vintage Books.

Mandela, Nelson. *Long Walk to Freedom: The Autobiography of Nelson Mandela.* Boston, New York, London: Back Bay Books, Little, Brown, 1995.

Mindell, Amy. 2016. "*Worldwork, a Light Hearted Approach in 40 Lessons.*" A video film series available at https://amy-mindell.squarespace.com/configphase /|/worldwork-animated-film/

---2008. "Bringing Deep Democracy to Life: An Awareness Paradigm for Deepening Political Dialogue, Personal Relationships, and Community Interactions." *Psychotherapy and Politics International*, Volume 6, Issue 3, pp. 212–225.

---2007. "Worldwork and the Politics of Dreaming." http://www.aamindell.net/worldwork-applications/?rq=worldwork%20and%20the%20politics%20of

---1996. "Discovering the World in the Individual, World Channel in Psychotherapy." *Journal of Humanistic Psychology*, Volume 36, No. 3,

Summer, pp. 67–84. Available at http://www.ahpweb.org/pub/journal/menu.html

---1995. *Metaskills: The Spiritual Art of Therapy.* Portland, OR: Lao Tse Press.

Mindell, Arnold. *Dance of the Ancient One.* Portland, OR: Deep Democracy Exchange, 2013.

---2010. *Processmind: A User's Guide to Connecting with the Mind of God.* Wheaton, IL: Quest Books.

---2007. *Earth-Based Psychology: Path Awareness from the Teachings of Don Juan, Richard Feynman, and Lao Tse.* Portland, OR: Lao Tse Press.

---2004. *Quantum Mind and Healing: How to Listen and Respond to Your Body's Symptoms.* Charlottesville, VA: Hampton Roads.

---2002. *The Deep Democracy of Open Forums: How to Transform Organizations into Communities.* Charlottesville, VA: Hampton Roads.

---2002. *The Dreammaker's Apprentice: Using Heightened States of Consciousness to Interpret Dreams.* Charlottesville, VA: Hampton Roads.

---2000. *Dreaming While Awake: Techniques for 24-Hour Lucid Dreaming.* Charlottesville, VA: Hampton Roads.

---2000. *Quantum Mind: The Edge between Physics and Psychology.* Portland, OR: Lao Tse Press.

---1995. *Sitting in the Fire: Large Group Transformation Using Conflict and Diversity.* Portland, OR: Lao Tse Press.

---1993. *The Shaman's Body: A New Shamanism for Health, Relationships and Community.* San Francisco: Harper Collins.

---1992. *Leader as Martial Artist: An Introduction to Deep Democracy.* San Francisco: Harper Collins. (Republished in 2014 by the Deep Democracy Exchange)

---1992. With Amy Mindell. *Riding the Horse Backwards: Process Work in Theory and Practice.* New York: Penguin. (Republished in 2000 by Lao Tse Press)

---1989. *Coma: Key to Awakening, Working with the Dreambody Near Death.* Boulder, CO: Shambhala. (Republished in 2009 by Lao Tse Press)

---1989. *The Year One: Global Process Work with Planetary Myths and Structures.* London & New York: Viking-Penguin-Arkana.

---1988. *Working on Yourself Alone: Inner Dreambody Work.* New York: Viking-Penguin-Arkana. (Republished in 2000 by Lao Tse Press)

---1988. *City Shadows: Psychological Interventions in Psychiatry.* London & New York: Viking-Penguin-Arkana.

---1987. *The Dreambody in Relationships.* New York: Viking-Penguin-Arkana. (Republished in 2000 by Lao Tse Press)

---1986. *Working with the Dreaming Body.* New York: Viking-Penguin-Arkana. (Republished in 2000 by Lao Tse Press)

---1985. *River's Way: The Process Science of the Dreambody.* London & New York: Viking-Penguin-Arkana.

---1982. *Dreambody: The Body's Role in Revealing the Self.* Boston: Sigo Press. (Republished in 1986 by Viking-Penguin-Arkana; republished in 2000 by Lao Tse Press)

Reiss, Gary. *Changing Ourselves, Changing the World.* Tempe, AZ: New Falcon, 2000.

Richardson, Alan. Process-oriented psychology. In E. Neukrug (Ed.), *The SAGE Encyclopedia of Theory in Counseling and Psychotherapy* (pp. 805–807). Thousand Oaks, CA: Sage, 2015.

Suzuki, Shunryu. *Zen Mind, Beginner's Mind.* New York: Weatherhill, 1976.

Taylor, Edwin and John Wheeler. *Space–Time Physics.* New York: W. H. Freeman, 1992.

END NOTES

1 *Long Walk to Freedom* is an autobiographical work written by South African President Nelson Mandela, published in 1995 by Little Brown.

2 https://en.wikipedia.org/wiki/List_of_wars_by_death_toll

3 See the bibliography for my earlier books about conflict and deep democracy such as my *Deep Democracy of Open Forums,* etc.

4 Richardson, A. (2015). Process-oriented psychology. In E. Neukrug (Ed.), *The SAGE encyclopedia of theory in counseling and psychotherapy* (pp. 805-807). Thousand Oaks,, CA: Sage.

5 *The Deep Democracy of Open Forums* is a simple introduction to deep democracy.

6 Quoted in interview by G.S. Viereck, October 26,1929. Reprinted in *Glimpses of the Great,* 1930 and seen in Jess Brallier's, *Who Was Albert Einstein*, Grosset and Dunlap, NY, 2002, p. 96. Thanks to Amy Mindell for pointing this quote out to me. Another such quote from Einstein in "Interview by George Sylvester Viereck" in *The Saturday Evening Post*, Vol. 202 (26 October 1929), p. 117, "I believe in intuition and inspiration. Imagination is more important than knowledge. For knowledge is limited, whereas imagination embraces the entire world, stimulating progress, giving birth to evolution."

7 Thanks to David Clarke, Arlene and Jean Claude Audergon, http://www.processwork-audergon.com/

8 https://www.rt.com/uk/273226-camden-anti-gentrification-protest/

9 www.solarsystem.nasa.gov/galleries/phases-of-the-moon

10 See for example my books https://amy-mindell.squarespace.com/configphase /|/books/

11 https://en.wikipedia.org/wiki/Nataraja

12 *Processmind, A User's Guide to Connecting with the Mind of God*, Quest Books, 2010, p.2

13 https://en.wikipedia.org/wiki/Nataraja

14 Ibid. I am especially interested in that statue since dancing Shiva was not there when I lectured at CERN in 1976 on synchronicity, together

with my Jungian teacher at that time, M.L. von Franz. (Synchronicity was Jung's term for inner experience that spontaneously connects to outer events. Jung researched synchronicity in part with the Nobel prize winner, physicist Wolfgang Pauli.)

15 See for example my book, *The Deep Democracy of Open Forums.* Hampton Roads, 2002.

16 *Processmind: A User's Guide to Connecting with the Mind of God,* 2010.

17 See Amy Mindell's book, *Metaskills, The Spiritual Art of Therapy.* New Falcon, 2001.

18 https://en.wikipedia.org/wiki/Nonviolent_Communication

19 https://en.wikipedia.org/w/index.php?title=Open_Space_Technology&redirect=no

20 Wikipedia about "Black Box": "In cybernetics a black box was described by Norbert Wiener as an unknown system that was to be identified using the techniques of system identification.[5] He saw the first step in self-organization as being to be able to copy the output behavior of a black box." (*Cybernetics: Or the Control and Communication in the Animal and the Machine,* by Norbert Wiener, page xi, MIT Press, 1961, ISBN 0-262-73009-X)

21 https://en.wikipedia.org/wiki/Human_brain

22 https://en.wikipedia.org/wiki/Mushin_%28mental_state%29

23 https://en.wikipedia.org/wiki/White_box_%28software_engineering%29

24 My books, *The Deep Democracy of Open Forums* and *Sitting in the Fire* are good basic texts on worldwork.

25 http://www.aamindell.net/worldwork-animated-film/

26 See my book, *The Shaman's Body* for more about the warrior and her or his ally.

27 https://www.youtube.com/watch?v=3l4nVByCL44

28 In my book, *Coma, Key to Awakening,* I tell about a man who was dying, and how two women on each side of his bed, held each other as in his childhood dream.

29 *Working on Yourself Alone, Inner Dream Bodywork*, Rutledge and Kegan Paul, London, later by the Lao Tse Press, Portland.

30 https://en.wikipedia.org/wiki/Guanyin

31 Ibid.

32 http://www.sobonfu.com/

33 p.3

34 http://www.feynmanlectures.caltech.edu/III_01.html

35 http://www.physicsoftheuniverse.com/topics_quantum_probability.html

36 I can't use more recent conflict examples for political reasons.

37 Example of inner work. For those who need an example of how to integrate your deepest art in practice with a critic of your world task, in what follows, Amy worked with me to demonstrate all this.

--Amy: Can you re-feel and sense again that deepest art dance that you were working on before? . . . And as you are doing it, let it define the same task or maybe another world task that may be coming up?

--Arny: [moves more] . . . a sound "Whooosh!" Something says, "go down, come up and bring us together," whooooosh! ! ! Help us come together. . . Bring us together."

--Amy: What phase would you say you are in with that task? Phase 1, cruising enjoying it, phase 2 in conflict with it, phase 3 flowing with the different parts of it? Phase 4 just detached?

--Arny: Right now I am flowing with it a little bit, then when I think about certain sections of the world we will go to work in a couple of weeks, I get nervous especially about some of the terrorist interactions and groups that I talk with.

--Amy: Can you act out an "X" energy that is associated with or against that task in yourself?

--Arny: The "X" says, "We want you, and then will get rid of you. You are OK, but then maybe we have to kill you! . . . We will use you for the moment, but ha ha, watch your health!!" . . . I am in good health in the moment, still health issues come in. The "X" wanted to kill me as a child, and says now "Grrrrrrr! Ha!" "Grrrrr!" "You will die before you can do anything!" Something like that.

--Amy: (Amy plays Arny's "X":) "You will die before you can do any of these things!"

Now, just remember your deepest art dance if you can, and its recurring motions as you were just doing. Add sounds to it, and maybe you can associate feelings and sounds to an earth spot, an earth quality it reminds you of.

--Arny: Yes, I see the sea goes down and then splashes up, "WOOF!"

--Amy: Now, recall the task and see what happens next.

--Arny: The sea implies, "Go out and do these many things with sometimes impossible people, and bring us together"…. Hmmmm, I got it.

--Amy: Imagine you are doing that task and remember the "X" energy and just imagine how your deepest art deals with that "X"?

--Arny: My art-dance implies, "let go, die out so to speak, then woof and arise to help everyone."

--Amy: OK, now I am going to play the "X" for you, and then use your deepest art-dance to see how it deals with me.

--Amy as the "X": "Forget your hopes! You are done! You are going to die! That is it! Stop doing all of this!"

--Arny: (Also playing that same "X" against himself) "Yes, yes, kill him, *smash him!! Now,* I must say, thank you, dear critic!"

--Amy: (Playing the critic) No thanks! You are finished! We want to get rid of you! We don't want you!

--Arny: I am working with you dear monsters, in part because I need you to push me inside . . . that is what I love about you monstrous people! Thank you so much I just love being with you for that reason!

--Amy (still as the "X"): What do you mean? What are you talking about?

--Arny: I am with you dear "X," absolutely. I am with you when you are against me because *if I am too much out there you have to knock me back* inside myself. Inside out, . . . not outside out! . . . Not just outer focus but rather *inside-then outside world!*. . . In a way, *there is no "X," the "X" belongs to me*, it is no longer a split off "X" since it is part of my process. The bear from my childhood dream, drives me inside, and out! !! Inside out in a cycle . . . . Wow, thank you for helping me use my deepest art in conflict to make something good out of that work which sometimes looks dangerous. In a way, we need that "X"! (While working a few weeks later in Colombia, I could use this work in connection with terrorists)

38 Amy has written a great introductory article on 721 on our website. https://amy-mindell.square space.com/skills-and-metaskills/

39 http://www.deepdemocracyinstitute.org/

40 https://hbr.org/2011/10/the-fatal-flaw-with-360-survey

41 https://en.wikipedia.org/wiki/The_Interpretation_of_Dreams

42 *Quantum Mind*, p. 556

43 See my books, *Working with the Dreaming Body*, *Dreambody*, and *Dreaming While Awake.*

44 For more in-depth discussion of the links between physics and psychology, please see my book, *Quantum Mind.* For general background on field theory in physics, try Heisenberg himself, and Fred Allen Wolf or Amit Goswami on integrating quantum physics with transpersonal experience.

45 http://www.technologyreview.com/view/537676/quantum-life-spreads-entanglement-across-generations/

46 https://en.wikipedia.org/wiki/Gravitational_wave

47 Harrison, David. (2002). "Complementarity and the Copenhagen Interpretation of Quantum Mechanics." UPSCALE. Dept. of Physics, University of Toronto.

48 https://commons.wikimedia.org/wiki/File:Whriling_dervishes,_Rumi_Fest_2007.jpg

49 No one can see these waves, since they are mathematical descriptions of elementary particles. The originator of the wave theory, Erwin Schrödinger, also said he thought quantum waves were real, but they have never been directly measurable.

50 See the discussion of UBUNTU in chapter 17.

51 *Tao Te Ching*, Lao Tzu, Chapter 20. See Gia-Fu Feng and Jane English translation.

52 1988, pp. 38–39.

53 http://www.un.org/en/globalissues/briefingpapers/efa/quotes.shtml

54 http://www.dalailama.com/news/post/905-quantum-physics---his-holiness-the-dalai-lama-participates-in-the-26th-mind--life-meeting-at-drepung---day-2

55 *Long Walk to Freedom*, 1994, p. 518.

56 https://en.wikipedia.org/wiki/Oracle_bone

57 Wikipedia, https://en.wikipedia.org/wiki/Oracle_bonephase /media/File:Shang_dynasty_inscribed_scapula.jpg

58 In my book *Earth-Based Psychology*, I used earth-based directions to express the "u" and "X." In that book, I "added" the u + X vectors to find the "Big U." This "Big U" is close to the psychological idea of integration, of bringing your parts together. The BIGWAY is a more spiritual direction; it does not come only from integrating or adding the other paths, but from the "field" in which we live. It is like the Tao's direction, like an Elder who appreciates other directions as also "natural." Both the idea of psychological integration in my earlier work and the present BIGWAY or spiritual direction are important at one time or another. I suggest using BIGWAY for world decisions.

59 *The Leader as Martial Artist: Deep Democracy Leadership in Conflict Resolution, Community Building and Organizational Transformation.* Deep Democracy Exchange, 2014.

60 Remember Nelson Mandela's use of this community idea from South Africa's Zulu peoples.

Index

• • •

Printed in Great Britain
by Amazon